Managing People at Work

Employment Relations in Globalizing India

Subesh Das

SAGE www.sagepublishing.com
Los Angeles | London | New Delhi | Singapore | Washington DC | Melbourne

First published in 2010 by

SAGE Publications India Pvt Ltd
B1/I-1 Mohan Cooperative Industrial Area
Mathura Road, New Delhi 110 044, India
www.sagepub.in

SAGE Publications Inc
2455 Teller Road
Thousand Oaks, California 91320, USA

SAGE Publications Ltd
1 Oliver's Yard, 55 City Road
London EC1Y 1SP, United Kingdom

SAGE Publications Asia-Pacific Pte Ltd
3 Church Street
#10-04 Samsung Hub
Singapore 049483

Published by Vivek Mehra for SAGE Publications India Pvt Ltd, typeset in 10.5/12.5 Garamond Antiqua by Impel Digital, Noida and printed at Sai Print-o-Pack, New Delhi.

Third Printing 2016

Library of Congress Cataloging-in-Publication Data

Das, Subesh
Managing people at work: employment relations in globalizing India/ by Subesh Dash.
p. cm.
Includes bibliographical references and index.
1. Personnel management—India. 2. Industrial relations—India.
I. Title.
HF5549.2.I4D35 658.300954—dc22 2010 2010032781

ISBN: 978-81-321-0510-7 (HB)

The SAGE Team: Rekha Natarajan, Anupam Choudhury, Nand Kumar Jha and Deepti Saxena

Contents

List of Tables

List of Figures

List of Boxes

List of Abbreviations

AFL-CIO	American Federation of Labor-Congress of Industrial Organizations
AITUC	All India Trade Union Congress
BCCI	Bengal Chamber of Commerce and Industries
BIFR	Board of Industrial and Financial Reconstruction
BMS	Bharatiya Mazdoor Sangh
BOC	British Oxygen Company
CII	Confederation of Indian Industry
CITU	Center of Indian Trade Union
CPI(M)	Communist Party of India (Marxist)
CSR	Customer Service Representative
DGB	Deutscher Gewerkschaftsbund
EFI	Employers' Federation of India
EU	European Union
FDI	Foreign Direct Investment
GATT	General Agreement on Tariffs and Trade
GDP	Gross Domestic Product
GIS	Geographical Information System
HMS	Hind Mazdoor Sangh
HR	Human Resource
HRD	Human Resource Development
HRM	Human Resource Management
ICT	Information and Communication Technology
IHRM	International Human Resource Management
ILO	International Labor Organization
IMF	International Monetary Fund
INTUC	Indian National Trade Union Congress
IOC	Indian Oxygen Company

IR	Industrial Relations
IT	Information Technology
ITC	Indian Tobacco Company
ITES	Information Technology-enabled Services
ITS	Information Technology Services
JIT	Just in Time
MCC	Mitsubishi Chemical Corporation
MCPI	Mitsubishi Chemical PTA India
MIS	Management Information System
MNC	Multinational Corporation
MNE	Multinational Enterprise
NAFTA	North American Free Trade Agreement
NASSCOM	National Association of Software and Services Companies
NIC	Newly Industrializing Country
NSS	National Sample Survey
OE	Organizational Effectiveness
QC	Quality Circle
SICA	Sick Industrial Companies Act
TPM	Total Productive Maintenance
TQC	Total Quality Control
TQM	Total Quality Management
TUC	Trade Union Congress
VRS	Voluntary Retirement Scheme

Preface

THIS BOOK PRESENTS changes in employment relations in India in the post-reform period. The term "Employment Relations" encompasses both Human Resource Management (HRM) and Industrial Relations (IR). Important issues in this include behaviors of workers and managers, their interactions, nature of work organizations, work practices, union representation, and their changes over time. The strength of this book lies in its comprehensive coverage of contemporary issues within the framework of rich theoretical argument.

Most studies on employment relations are on developed countries. They indicate existence of a finite set of dominant employment systems, where each system is identified by an interrelated set of inputs, processes, and outcomes. The recent changes indicate growing variations in employment relation practices within countries (divergences) and emerging commonalities in employment relation practices across countries (convergences). The "converging divergences" thesis in employment relations has been developed based on studies in the industrialized countries. This book examines validity of the thesis in Indian context and finds similar changes. Further, it examines the global factors that influence firms' employment relations. It examines how nature of industries, global factors, and unionization influence the emerging commonalities and variations. It identifies how some firms in India are adopting world-class manufacturing practices and associated modern HRM practices, while others are unable to do so.

The book has nine chapters. Chapter 1 presents the theoretical framework for the study and puts objectives and scopes of the study in the context of work already done. Chapter 2 identifies the changes in the global and national environment in terms of economic, technological, legal, social, and political contexts. Chapter 3 examines shifts in capital–labor power balance, which has a major influence on firms' employment relations. It presents an account of the structure and functions of trade unions and their changes over time. Chapter 4 shows existence of four dominant patterns of employment relations in Indian textile industry: the low-wage pattern, the HRM pattern, the joint-team-based pattern, and the conflict pattern. The findings in the textile industry are then supported with examples from other industries. The textile industry does not capture all issues on changes in employment relations. Chapter 5 tries to fill up the gap; it examines the rapid and fundamental changes in employment relations in capital-intensive firms. Information and communications technology (ICT) has rewritten the agenda for the industrial world and has evolved new ideas of employee management. Chapter 6 examines employment relations in IT-enabled service (ITES) firms. Global factors now have major influence on firms' operations and it is not uniform across firms. The influences are more in multinational corporations (MNCs) than in local firms. Chapter 7 examines the global–local issues in employment relations and finds their impact on the growing variations in employment relations in India. Majority of workers in India work in small firms where employers most often directly control all aspects of workers' work life. Chapter 8 examines changes in employment relations in small firms. Chapter 9, the concluding chapter, aggregates the findings of the preceding chapters. It concludes that there are growing variations in employment relations within India and at the same time growing similarities of the variations with those in other countries.

The book is appropriate for students, professionals, academicians, and researchers. The global convergence issues in the book will attract readers interested in international and comparative employment relations. The various case studies presented in the book tell readers about the contemporary practices in HRM and how they differ across firms and across industries. They tell us about the new practices in HRM and how some firms have been successful in restructuring their organizations in the competitive environment. They explain how some firms have been successful in improvement of productivity, quality, and labor flexibility, while others have not. They describe how some firms have introduced modern practices like teamwork, multi-skilling, *kaizen*, quality circle (QC), total quality management (TQM), and 5S for housekeeping. The book covers important issues in managing people at work like selection and recruitment compensation, performance appraisal, training and retraining, employee communication, managing contract labor, dealing with unions, etc., which every professional in personal management would like to know.

My long stay for more than seven years as Labor Commissioner and Labor Secretary in West Bengal helped me to understand the field practices and the gap between the field practices and academic theories. My study in the School of Industrial and Labor Relations, Cornell University, USA gave me the opportunity to learn advanced theoretical arguments on changes in employment relations with comparative and international perspectives. This book has been developed within the framework of the advanced theories in employment relations and with the ingredients of the field knowledge acquired during my assignments in the labor department. The book thus combines field practices in the real world of work with frontline theoretical argument in HRM and IR. I expect that the students and professionals in the field will find the book stimulating and rewarding.

Subesh Das

Acknowledgments

I HAVE GREATLY benefited for this work from my dissertation committee members, Professor Sarosh Kuruvilla, Professor Harry Katz, and Professor Thomas J. DiCiccio. Their support and guidance have been invaluable. A special appreciation is due to Professor Kuruvilla for his inspiration and mentorship. Completion of this project would not have been possible without the generous financial support of Cornell's School of Industrial and Labor Relations, Cornell's Mario Einaudi Center, and the American Institute of Indian Studies. I am also grateful to Government of West Bengal and Government of India for granting me study leave and granting me permission for the Ph.D. program.

I would also like to thank Labor Department officials in the Government of West Bengal and other states in India, who helped me in contacting several managers and trade union leaders. They helped me to choose different firms for the study, provided me with information on individual firms and industries, and helped me to contact key persons for my research. I would also like to convey my thanks to the senior managers and trade union leaders who spared their valuable time and provided important information in relation to their firms and their employees or members.

I would like to thank my wife Rupa and my son Kaustav for supporting me to concentrate on my work throughout the study. They accompanied me during my stay in Ithaca, put up with me through all the difficulties, and provided me with emotional support and encouragement to complete the work.

Finally, I dedicate this book to my mother, Smt. Mridula Das, who has always supported me in my endeavor, always given me the strength and encouragement to follow my dreams.

Chapter 1

Convergences and Divergences in Employment Relations

OVER THE LAST two decades, employer–employee relations, popularly known as employment relations, have changed dramatically. The changes indicate growing dissimilarities in employment practices across firms within countries and at the same time increasing similarities in employment practices across countries. The similarities and dissimilarities are best described in terms of differences in employment systems. Each employment system, in this approach, is identified by a set of interrelated components, such as organizational structures, rights of workers, unions, and managers, and the nature of work practices. The differences in employment systems arise because of differences in the components of the systems and their interrelationships. The changes in economic and technological environment over the last two decades have led to increased competition and have changed the behaviors of workers, managers, unions, and other stakeholders. Faster flow of information and knowledge has led firms to adopt practices that have been successful in other firms. All these changes are leading to changes in employment relations of firms. There are now increasing differences in employment relations across firms and firms now have more choices to design their employment relation policies. Along with the diverging forces in operation within countries, globalization is contributing a homogenizing effect on employment systems across countries. In India, the contexts of employment relations have changed dramatically after initiation of the structural adjustment program in 1991. This book examines the changing employment relations in India in the post-liberalization period. It includes major issues in managing people at work concerning all categories of workers and employees, trade unions, and associations, and their changes over time.

Global convergences and local divergences in employment relations are now important issues for management of people at work. Multinational corporations operating in different locations need to know how to manage their employees and other people at work located in different social and political environments. More particularly, they need to know whether to adopt globally uniform corporate employment relation policies or tailor such policies to suit the local environments of each operation. The knowledge of global influences on employment relations are not only important for MNCs, they are also important for local firms and particularly for firms linked to external markets. In the global context, the knowledge of changes in employment relations in India is particularly important. It is not only because much of the studies on the subject focus on developed economies, it is also because India's entry to the global market is relatively new and India provides a huge opportunity for manufacturing and marketing. The study is not only important for the human resource (HR) managers, it is also important for the unions, policy makers, and researchers. The study is anchored in the global convergence–divergence debate on changes in employment relations. It examines how the changing global and national contexts are changing employment relations in India.

Our discussion in the first chapter presents the framework for the study. It examines the work already done in the field, explains the concepts, and advances the arguments. The key term in the study is "employment relations." It encompasses both IR and HRM.[1] Industrial Relations focus on trade unions, collective bargaining, and reduction of conflict between capital and labor. It emerged as a distinct function in personnel management with growth of trade unions and increase in industrial conflicts. HRM developed as a subset of IR with the shift in focus from "management of conflict" to "commitment of employees to the organizations' goals." It emerged in the non-union sector, but then expanded its role in the union sector too. Now, HRM professionals and academic personnel see IR as a part of HRM rather than vice versa. The book deals with all aspects of employment relations and includes issues of both IR and HRM. The book uses a "systems approach" in which an employment relation system is seen as a set of interrelated elements (inputs, processes, and outcomes) and emphasizes interactions and connectedness of different elements. It examines similarities and differences in employment relations within and across industrial sectors, across Indian states, within and across union and non-union sectors, and within the informal sector. It examines how the variations in different sectors contribute to overall variations in employment relations. It identifies the factors that influence the changes and makes a distinction between the forces that trigger the changes and that mediate the change process. It captures the changes in employment relations over time and examines how global and local influences lead to the emergence of different employment systems.

Employment Relation Systems and Their Elements

Employment relation takes place between an employer and an employee whenever an employee works in exchange for payment of wages. The relationship may be one-to-one, one-to-many, or many-to-many. In this relationship, interactions take place between various parties as individuals and in groups and at different levels of organizations. There are three main groups or parties in employment relations—primary, secondary, and tertiary parties (Figure 1.1). Primary parties are the employers and employees. They are bound together by a network of formal and informal rules, agreements, and procedures, such as employment contracts, employee handbooks, and informal customs and practices. Secondary parties are management and trade unions, who work on behalf of the primary parties (Farnham 2000: 4).

Figure 1.1: Employment Relation Systems

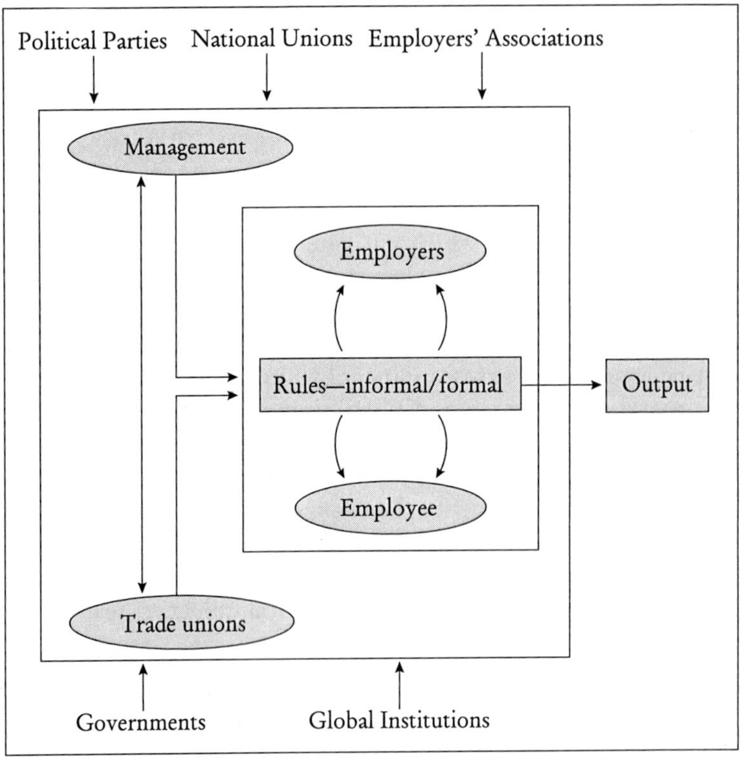

Source: Based on discussion on the "Parties in Employment Relations."

Interactions between primary and secondary parties result in employment relations practices. The tertiary parties are primarily agents of state, who attempt to mediate between different sets of primary and secondary parties, provide stable employment relations, and prescribe floors of employment standards (Farnham 2000: 4).[2] State policies influence distribution of power between the primary and the secondary parties, and hence their functions and decisions (Fox and Flanders 1969). National unions, employers' associations, and political parties, which influence formulation and implementation of public policies, also act as tertiary parties. In addition, some institutions and factors outside national boundaries like International Labor Organization (ILO) conventions and policies of MNCs also influence firms' employment relations.[3]

Interactions in organizations take complex forms. They include a variety of interrelationships between different groups and individuals: employers and employees, managers and workers, unions and managers, and among different workers. The parties in employment relation interact at different levels and between levels. In order to explain this complex details of the real world of work, literature in employment relations often explicitly or implicitly uses a system approach. In this approach, an employment relation system is seen as a collection of interrelated components that work together to accomplish the employment process. The "employment relation system" concept is variable in scope and can characterize an immediate workplace, an enterprise, an industrial sector, or a country as a whole (Dunlop 1958: 385). Most initial studies in the field assumed existence of "national industrial relation systems" and considered macro-institutional features as key dimensions of national systems. However, this approach, with assumed homogeneity within the national systems, failed to explain the continuing and persistent variations in employment systems across firms within countries (Katz and Darbishire 2000). Over time, it became clear that firm-level systems should be considered as basic units of analysis. The national system, in this approach, should be considered as a meta-system and within the systems there are the firm-level systems as sub-systems and additional mechanisms that control behavior and production of the sub-systems within the national systems. The additional control mechanisms are labor laws, national culture, and rules and practices developed at national levels.

Parties in employment relations interact and produce rules, processes, and outcomes that characterize firms' employment systems. Attributes of the parties are inputs for employment systems, but they do not describe the systems completely. A firm's employment system is described by its inputs such as quality of employees (attributes of the parties); processes such as organizational practices, teamwork, and wage bargaining, and outcomes, such as wages, benefits, and productivity. Interestingly, the components of employment systems (inputs, processes, and outcomes) are so related that if one knows some of them one can identify the whole system (Figure 1.2). Only inputs and processes, for example, can

Figure 1.2: Employment Relation Systems—Inputs and Outcomes

Environment: Contexts

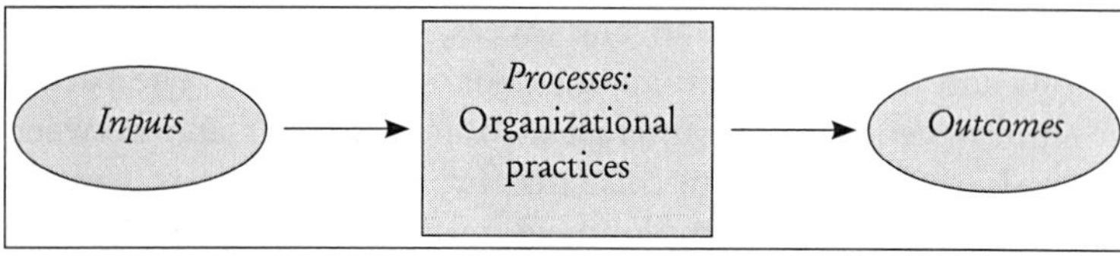

Source: Based on discussions on elements of employment relation systems.

identify a system and predict outcomes. As it is difficult to identify all possible components of an employment system, it is identified by a finite sub-set of inputs, processes, and outcomes.[4] Katz and Kochan (2000: 104) identify different dominant patterns of employment systems in the United States based on the differences in the various components of the employment systems. The components of employment systems are workplace rules, management style, complaint procedures, work organization, pay procedures, job security, and worker–manager relations. Identification of the different patterns certainly speaks about the existence of multiple systems.

Employment relations systems are dynamic entities with inner consistency between their parts. The systems continually interact with the environment, change, and adapt to develop congruence between people, process, structure, and external environment. A significant change in one of the elements displaces an old equilibrium and creates a new position (Cummings 1980: 76–77). Economic, technical, legal, social, political, and physical environments in which a firm operates influence its employment systems and set contexts in which the system functions. National culture is characterized by ideas, values, attitudes, and beliefs of individuals and groups. It influences the way people perceive the world and themselves in it, and hence influences firms' employment systems. In addition, several actors and institutions outside the systems also influence the systems' processes and outcomes. The contexts in which the systems function shape the behaviors of the parties, their relationships, and the way they interpret and understand their experiences (Farnham 2000: 158). The contexts change over time and may differ within countries. In India, for example, there are different labor laws for mining, factories, and plantations. Further, implementation of labor legislations varies across states. Chapter 2 presents the contexts of employment relations in India and their changes in the post-reform period.

Convergences and Divergences—The Debate

Convergences in employment relations within and across countries have been long debated in IR literature. The notion of IR emerged as a distinct sphere of socioeconomic activity with the argument that there exist distinct national industrial relation systems. In these systems, three groups of actors—workers and their organizations, managers and their organizations, and government agencies—interact and produce rules of workplaces as output. These key actors share an underlying consensus that defines and legitimizes their roles and produces an inner unity and consistency indicating convergence within national IR systems (Dunlop 1958). The convergence argument not only advanced a notion of homogeneity within national systems, but it also predicted global convergence of national systems. Based on a cross-national study of various countries, Kerr et al. (1964) concluded that while countries may differ in their industrialization processes because of diversity in policies of industrializing elites, over time the logic of industrialization would lead to convergence of IR practices within and across countries. This global convergence thesis was later rebutted by social scientists on the ground that there have always been wide and persistent variations in IR across countries. They argue that the variation in IR is in part due to national-specific institutional factors (Cole 1971; Dore 1973; Streeck 1984).

The convergence model with perceived homogeneity within the national systems and its emphasis on stability and shared consensus among the actors worked fairly well as long as the environment remained stable, but with increased competition it could not explain the dynamic aspects of industrial relations.[5] It failed to explain the persistent variation in employment relations within the countries. Over time, it became clear that there exist different patterns of IR systems at firm-level that are not determined solely by economic, technological, or other environmental forces. The strategic choices and values of union leaders, of workers, and more particularly of managers shape the systems, their process, and their outcomes (Kochan et al. 1986: 12–13). In the 1960s and 1970s, employment stabilization was a core feature of employment systems in industrialized countries. Increasingly competitive environment in the 1980s led to increasing variation in employment practices with increased variations in wages, work practices, and employment conditions. Locke (1992), based on his research in Italy, found wide variations in employment relations and predicted that the variations are likely to increase in the future. In a study on employment systems in seven industrialized countries, Katz and Darbishire (2000) found increasing variations in employment practices within the countries during the 1980s and 1990s, but growing similarities in the nature of the variation across countries.

Growing variations in employment systems within countries are seen in workplace practices and their outcomes. Some firms follow low-wage pattern with informal personnel policies and high job turnover, some firms focus on employment stabilization and job security, and some firms emphasize employees' individualized career development in place of job security. Firms differ by their employment security, by their contribution to employees' skill development, and by workers' participation in business decisions. Some firms have unions, some do not have, and some non-union firms have committees of workers promoted by management (Pil and MacDuffie 1999). In unionized plants, firms differ in involvement of union officials in resolving business issues. Some union firms have cooperative labor-management relations, whereas at other sites the relations are adversarial. The middle ground of traditional labor–management relations that included a bounded amount of conflict has become less common over time. In the non-union sector also, there is increasing variations in employment relations. Some non-union firms invest heavily in HR development and emphasize individualized communication and pay practices, whereas others do not (Katz and Darbishire

2000: 5). Firms also differ in adopting new work practices and in implementation of the practices. Some firms, for example, use team concept of work while others do not, and in some firms having teams, the team leaders are elected by the workers, while in others, they are selected by the management.

Firms differ in the way they control their employees and this leads to variations in employment systems across firms. Edwards (1979) identified three systems of employee control by looking at the historical evolution of firms. In the early days of industrialization, when firms were small and directly run by the entrepreneurs, the system of employee control was simple control. In this system, the employer sees everything, knows everything, and decides everything. There is no formal rule; the power and authority of employer constitutes the primary mechanism of employee control. As firms grew in size, simple control became more and more difficult and employers engaged foremen or supervisors and other officials to control their employees. This led to the emergence of hierarchical control, but this system also became unstable as arbitrary actions by supervisors and the officials resulted in a large number of conflicts. Over time, two systems of control, namely, technical control and bureaucratic control that are more formalized and more stable than an aggregate of simple controls developed (Box 1.1). In the contemporary methods of organizing work, there are examples of all the three types of employee control: simple control, technical control, and bureaucratic control.

Box 1.1: Technical Control and Bureaucratic Control

> In technical control, the physical structure or machinery directs the labor process, which is symbolized by the assembly line, where the pace of the line rather than direct authority of supervisors controls work. In bureaucratic control, employee control is through control of the social structure of the workplace that institutionalizes hierarchical power. In this system, firm laws and rules replace supervisor command over workers.

Source: Edwards (1979).

The divergence in employment relations within countries is not toward all possible forms of employment relation systems; it is toward a finite set of dominant patterns of employment relation systems. As discussed, the patterns are distinguished from one another by their elements and interrelationships of the elements. One feature that distinguishes different employment systems is the system of employee control. Another important parameter that varies across firms is the status of unionization—whether a unit is unionized or not. Katz and Kochan (2000) by considering the "control" and "unionization" aspects identify six dominant patterns of employment relation systems: conflict, New Deal, and participatory patterns for unionized firms; and paternalistic, bureaucratic, and HRM patterns for non-unionized firms. The identification of the six dominant patterns of employment systems is certainly an over-simplification of the real world of work and it is difficult to fit each firm in one of these patterns, but they certainly point to existence of different types of employment relation systems. In India, too, there exist some dominant patterns of employment relation systems; we try to identify them in this book.

Global Convergences and Local Divergences

Worldwide, there are now growing similarities in employment relations across countries. The similarities, however, differ from the expectation of a simple international convergence toward a single pattern of employment relations. It is toward a finite set of patterns. The similarities are seen in spite of the differences in national-specific institutional factors that influence employment systems and the historical differences in employment relations. Japan has enterprise unions, worker involvement in quality circles, seniority-based pay, and lifetime employment. Germany has a system of co-determination, sectoral collective bargaining, and work councils. In contrast, the United States and Britain have relatively voluntarist employment relations. In the past the argument was in favor of existence of national industrial relation systems. Over time, increased global and domestic competition have led to similar changes in structures and processes of employment systems across countries. In all countries, collective bargaining has shifted toward plant-level bargaining; and the locus of labor–management interactions has shifted downwards. There has been increasing individualization in employment conditions and emphasis on informal and direct communication with workers. On the basis of a study in seven industrialized countries, Katz and Darbishire (2000: 8) found broad commonalities in employment practices across countries and emergence of four patterns of employment systems: low wages, HRM, Japanese-oriented, and joint-team-based approach.

The global convergence in employment relations is not only seen in comparison of employment relations of individual countries, it is also seen in comparison of firms in the same industrial sectors across countries and in comparison of plants of MNCs in different countries. There are now growing similarities in employee control, work rationalization, and task and time flexibility in specific industries in different countries.[6] There are also growing similarities in employment relations in similar plants of the same MNC in different countries.[7] The similarities are partly due to management's imposition of standardized practices in both the plants. Introduction of common practices in some firms located in different countries has added to international convergence, but it has also increased within country divergences, as all firms in the recipient countries do not introduce such practices.

Global convergences in employment relations are to be seen in terms of the broad commonalities in employment systems across countries. Within the broad commonalities of employment relation patterns, there are some differences as one looks for details of the patterns in different countries (Katz and Darbishire 2000: 11). There are two important issues as we compare firms across countries. First, the classification of employment patterns are in broad terms and the exact definitions will vary from country to country. In other words, there may be some differences in the individual patterns across countries with their core elements remaining the same. In some joint-team-based systems, for example, unions and workers participate extensively in business decisions, while in others they have limited involvement. Further, firms in a country may adopt the innovative practices of firms in another country, but differences may appear in adoption of the practices and in their implementation.[8] Second, countries differ in the relative proportions of different workplace patterns and in the extent to which these patterns operate on a non-union basis.[9] For example, in the United States and the United Kingdom, low wage, HRM, and Japanese-oriented patterns operate mostly in non-union contexts, but it is not so in other developed countries (Katz and Darbishire 2000: 281).

The convergences and divergences in employment relations are not only seen in industrialized countries, it is also evident in the newly industrializing countries (NICs). In advanced industrialized countries, the increased pressures of globalization, privatization, and deregulation have affected behaviors of parties in employment relations and have changed firms' employment relation systems. There are similar pressures in NICs, but the contexts are somewhat different from those in industrializing countries. The differences are in part due to differences in time of introduction of neo-liberal policies by the NICs. Industrialized countries adopted the policies of deregulation, privatization, and liberalization in the 1970s or 1980s, whereas NICs introduced such policies only in late 1980s or early 1990s. Overall, the changes taking place in the NICs are similar to those in industrialized countries, but they are less robust and there are some time lags. Further, as NICs' entry to the global market is relatively recent, they still have some traditional patterns of employment systems. The changes in employment relations in Korea provide an interesting example of the international convergence. In Korea, the legal framework deliberately encouraged uncoordinated decentralization and the IR systems were never centralized or coordinated. The recent changes, however, indicate increasing pressure for coordination (Lee and Lee 2001). It is a change from a different direction, but it is making the Korean employment system similar to those in other countries. In India, the changes are similar to those in the industrialized countries in same sectors, and at the same time, existence of traditional practices and patterns in same other sectors.

Push and Pull of Globalization and Localization

Internationalization and globalization mean that economies and societies interact and lose some of their separate and distinct characters. The process involves intensified traffic of technologies, information, goods, and ideas that act together and put pressure for elimination of national differences. All countries are now simultaneously facing growing and similar influences on their employment systems. This is leading to convergence in employment relations across countries. One of the contributors to this convergence in employment practices across countries is the international diffusion of managerial and organizational techniques mediated by foreign direct investment (FDI). Indeed, if an employment practice improves productivity and efficiency of some firms, it spreads naturally via market forces to others and across national boundaries (Amante 1995: 645; Taira 1992). Development and spread of Japanese and American HR practices in workplaces all over the world illustrate the diffusion. The diffusion is faster in MNCs as it takes place through transfer of management practices from one unit to another. The diffusion process is constrained or facilitated by various factors, including global HRM strategies adopted by MNCs (Caligiuri and Stroh 1995). The existing practices of local firms, the legal framework, and the other local institutional factors also influence the diffusion process.

In the globalizing world, employment systems are intermingled between two forces: the "dynamic force of globalization" and the "conserving force localization" (Pot 2000: 80). There is debate whether globalization will eliminate the national differences in the end, but there is no doubt that national context still plays a crucial role in shaping firms' employment relations. This is more so for NIC where an increasing number of firms now produce for export markets or compete with importers in the domestic markets, but many firms are still relatively insulated from global competition. In the changing environment, while some firms adopt new and innovative practices, others continue with their traditional practices. Various factors, including firms' adaptability, influence the transfer of the practices from one unit to another.[10] Finally, as there are different models for adoption, firms adapt different practices depending on their adaptability and suitability. As a firm adopts a practice from another country, it contributes to international convergence in employment relations. If the practice is not common in the recipient country, it also adds to divergence in employment relations within the country.

The impacts of forces of globalization and forces of localization on employment practices differ across firms. The global influences are more in MNCs than in domestic firms. They also differ across MNCs depending on factors like ownership structure, export orientation, and local purchase of intermediate materials.[11] They differ depending on whether the units of MNCs in India are their international divisions, wholly owned subsidiaries, majority owned subsidiaries, or joint ventures with local partners (Figure 1.3).[12] Important factors include industry and country characteristics, structure of international operations, competitive strategy, intra-organizational networks, international entry mode, and organizational and industry life cycle (DeCieri and Dowling 1999; Schuler et al. 1993). An important management issue for MNCs is the extent to which their various operating units across the world are differentiated and, at the same time, integrated, controlled, and coordinated (Brewster 1999: 3). Firms' practices also differ by nationality of home countries. Japanese investments prefer joint ventures with local enterprises and send more expatriates from the home country, while American and European firms maintain sole ownership and send fewer expatriates from home. Another factor is the type of industry. Foreign firms in service industries have lower local ownerships and smaller shares of material, parts, and equipment locally purchased, but they are more likely to adopt local practices. In contrast, the export-oriented foreign firms in manufacturing are less sensitive to local culture (Tzeng and Uzzi 2000: 227–234). The tension between differentiation (local adaptation) and integration (internal consistency), otherwise termed "global vs. local dilemma," is not only important for MNCs, it is also important for local firms particularly for firms having higher "global content" like large shares of exports or firms using modern technology (Figure 1.3).

Figure 1.3: Global and Local Influences—Indian Firms and MNCs

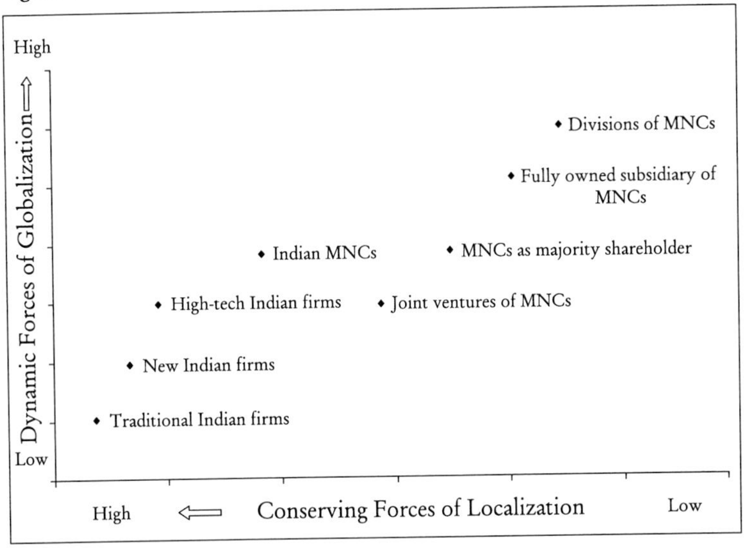

Source: Developed by author.

This book examines whether employment relations in firms in India are becoming similar to each other and whether the changes are similar to those found in other countries. Global diffusion of innovative employment practices plays an important role in the change process. This is particularly important for developing countries like India, as most innovative management practices in employee relations have developed in industrialized countries (for example, Japanese-oriented approach, HRM approach). Firms differ in adopting the innovative practices. Those closely linked to global markets with high export dependence (or competing with imported goods) act faster in adopting the new practices. By contrast, firms producing for local markets with no external competitors continue to remain more tied to their traditional employment relation practices. The net result of the changes is more variations in employment relations: some firms adopting practices similar to those in developed countries, while others continuing with their traditional practices. Overall, the changes in India are similar to those seen in other countries.

Indian Employment Systems of the Past

Employment practices that existed in the initial years of industrialization in India were no different from the employment practices in the United States or Britain at the turn of the 20th century. In this system, power was essentially devolved to foremen, who virtually had complete authority to hire, fire, and pay employees. Employment conditions under such arrangement appeared both arbitrary and uncertain, and varied across foremen and over time for the same foreman (Appelbaum and Batt 1994: 16). Pressures to increase production and reduce production uncertainties led employers to apply principles of scientific management in work organizations and adopt standard employment rules and procedures. In India too there had been similar changes for rationalizing and standardizing employment practices, where the state played an important role and trade unions added to the pressures. The state domination is in fact deeply rooted in India's colonial past. The British introduced the system to ensure uninterrupted industrial production, which was particularly important during the war years. It required capital and labor to resolve their differences through conciliation and adjudication. The system continued even after their exit, as planned economic development became the prime goal after independence and industrial conflict was seen as a dampener to that effort (Ramswamy 2000: 113).

In the first four decades of independent India, state intervention through political and institutional considerations in determination of wages and working conditions gained dominance. Industrial wage boards and tripartite industry-wide agreements became the ideal norms. The Bureau of Public Enterprises set wages in public sector enterprises (Bhattacherjee 2001: 249). In the private sector, there were cases of enterprise-level bargaining but over time the structure of bargaining became mostly centralized, usually at national, state, or regional levels. The period shows two distinct phases. The first phase represents the initial years of state-driven industrialization. The paradigm that dominated this phase was a paternalistic labor relations system, which was premised on the belief that state "knew more about the workers." In this phase, the state overdetermined labor relations outcomes and few strategic choices were open to either unions or employers. Over time, however, fractionalization became prominent within the union movement. The growth of leftist unions reflected alternative voices and employers often found it easier to deal with local unions than central unions (Bhattacherjee 2000: 3760). This led to the emergence of a new phase dominated by multiple unions. The system that emerged represented the employment relations system just before economic liberalization (Rudolph and Rudolph 1987).

Characteristics of employment system that existed in India in the pre-liberalization period and before 1990s were similar to those found in industrialized countries before their dramatic changes in the 1970s and 1980s. The models of internal labor markets best describe the system. In this arrangement, managers make all the important decisions and non-managers implement the decisions. Firms hire unskilled and inexperienced workers for entry-level work and training is mostly on the job. Most often, workers start with simple unskilled jobs, such as helpers, and over time they acquire skills for higher paid jobs. Promotion is most often seniority based and merit rarely influences the decisions. In the system, both managers and workers enjoy high level of job security. Workers' wages vary according to job title and seniority with almost no linkages to individual performance. The organizational structure is hierarchical with multiple levels in hierarchy between production workers and chief executive officers, and separate hierarchy for each function. Principles of scientific management determine the structure of work organization with clear job descriptions for each job and workers have no autonomy or variety in their jobs. There are different explanations for development of the internal systems—some argue that management introduced the system and institutionalized management control as it was efficient; others argue that it developed because of bargaining between capital and labor.[13] In India, there is support for both the explanations, but most importantly, the state and labor legislation played the most important role in the emergence of the system. The internal system is still common in many firms in India, but they have started to disintegrate in many of these firms with the changes in the factors that led to the emergence of the systems.

How the System Began to Change

The institutional framework for industrial policy making in India was created in the 1950s, with emphasis on heavy industry, public ownership, import substitution, and protection for both capital and labor. A license from the central government was required to start or substantially expand any industrial activity. This protected business from both domestic and foreign competition. The policies did not change much in the first four decades of independence. In fact, the changes during the period further reinforced the policies of protection and increased role of the state. The public sector expanded its activities even in areas not originally reserved for the sector through nationalization or fresh investments[14] (Joshi and Little 1998: 173; Mookherjee 1995: 5). The over-restrictive and self-defeating nature of the regulatory frame work began to be evident in the 1970s. It became clear that the public sector enterprises failed to produce the desired results and that the state over-regulated the private sector that restricted its growth. The policies started to change in the 1980s, when the pendulum swung toward increasing involvement of the private sector and a gradual retreat of the state from direct industrial production. There were many mild measures of deregulation throughout the 1980s following the announcement of 1982 as the "Productivity Year". The Sick Industrial Companies Act (SICA) 1985 was enacted with the objective to rehabilitate or wind-up/liquidate sick industries. In 1988, the government announced its intention not to nationalize sick industries, to close down unviable public sector enterprises, and to open up areas that were reserved for the public sector. Initially, the changes were slow, but finally there were dramatic changes with the initiation of the World Bank–International Monetary Fund (IMF) advocated structural adjustment program in 1991. The program initiated the process to free industry from bureaucratic control and increase both domestic and international competition. It included a whole range of policy measures that continued in the subsequent union budgets.[15] The most important of the changes were the removal of import restrictions, reduction of import duties, and withdrawal of industrial licensing.

Policy changes initiated in the mid-1980s that accelerated in the 1990s represent a gradual retreat of the state not only from the economic arena, but also from the IR arena. This led to changes in the contexts of employment relations, which is presented in Chapter 2. The changes in the contexts have led to changes in behavior of employers, unions, and workers; and most importantly they have changed the strategic decision making of the state governments (Bhattacherjee 2000; Kuruvilla 1996). The changes in employment relations appear dramatic because they represent a sharp contrast to the practices that developed during the first three decades of planned industrialization. In the pre-liberalization period, the national government played a determining and strategic role in industrial development and IR practices. The withdrawal of industrial licensing created new opportunities for the state governments. They started to adopt industry-friendly policies and actively lobby and compete for both national and international capital investments. As a result, union influence declined and management authority increased. The balance of power shifted in favor of employers and labor's tie with political parties weakened (Kuruvilla 1996). Chapter 3 presents how changing contexts have led to a decline in union power, increase in income inequality, and increasing variation in employment conditions.

Employment practices that developed and existed in the pre-liberalization period were never uniform across the entire economy, but they were both relatively stable over time and consistent across large sections of industry. They included tripartite centralized bargaining between well defined employer groups, large trade union federations, and government agencies. The legal framework of various labor laws reinforced government involvement in regulation of employment relations and created a state-controlled national IR system.[16] Maintenance and reproduction of the national system was considered not only viable and necessary but also fair and efficient (Bhattacherjee 2000: 3578). There were some differences in labor–management relations across individual firms, but those were considered to be due to differences in stages of development along the vertical trajectory leading to a system characterized by tripartite centralized bargaining. The expectation was that over time, all firms would come under industry-wide agreements. However, this did not happen. On the contrary, the developments since the 1980s indicate a change in the opposite direction with increasing variations in employment practices across firms.

Pressures on employers to restructure their organization that led to changes in workplace practices came from divergent sources. Employers in the changing environment found that producing for a competitive market is not quite the same as under a command economy. New ideas about how to manage organizations in competitive markets that originated in industrialized countries added new dimensions to the changes. A key issue was reduction and adjustment of the workforce.[17] Employers demanded an exit policy, but successive governments could not come up with such unpopular policy. So, they adopted new strategies. Their main strategy has been to shrink core employment through voluntary retirement and expand the periphery through contracting out of non-core jobs.[18] The changes have led to reduction in job security and growth of the contingent workers. Organizations that emerged from this restructuring process are flatter and have very different employer–employee relations. Firms introduced concepts like performance-based pay, worker empowerment, TQM, autonomous workgroups, and decentralization of control over work. They introduced new management information and control systems and reduced managerial jobs. Over time, quality control, Quality Circles (QCs), and teams became common terms in employee management. The changes have dramatically altered the employment relations landscape in India. Firms, however, differed in adopting new strategies. Some firms with more ability and opportunity to restructure (multinationals and reputed Indian firms) changed drastically, while some firms continued with their traditional practices. The changes have led to increasing differences in employment relation practices across firms.

Issues, Inquiries, and Findings

This book is about recent trends in managing people at work. More specifically, it is about changes in employment relations in India in the post-reform period. It focuses on convergences and divergences in employment relations in India and compares them with those in industrialized countries. It examines the relevance of the global–local debate in employment relations in India. The framework for the study draws from past research in developed countries and a few studies in NICs. It tries to answer the following questions in the Indian context: (*a*) What are the emerging patterns of employment systems in India? (*b*) How do the various elements of employment systems fit in those patterns? (*c*) What evidence exists about within country divergences and global convergences in employment relations? (*d*) What critical variables contribute to the changes in employment systems? (*e*) How do the forces of globalization and localization influence firms' employment relations? In this study, we answer these questions based on case studies of firms in different industrial sectors. They include data from industry, company reports, and collective bargaining agreements; and interviews of managers, trade union leaders, and government officials.

Most studies on changes in employment relations are based on case studies of firms in some selected industries. For example, Katz and Darbishire (2000) draw their conclusions on worldwide convergences and divergences in employment relations, from their studies on the automobile and telecommunications industries. Their choices of the two industries are because of their importance in developed economies. In the Indian context, the natural choice is the textile industry because it has the largest number of workers in manufacturing and contributes the largest share in GDP and exports. Over time, the industry has gone through a major transformation in organizational structure and employment practices. Most large mills in the past (until 1960s and 1970s) were composite mills that organized spinning, weaving, and processing operations under the same roof. Most of them are now either closed or have restructured as spinning mills. Those still in operation have heavily invested in new technology. Overall, there have been significant changes in employment relations in the textile industry. The changes are not uniform across firms and there have been increasing variations in employment relations within the textile industry. Some mills still use the traditional approach, while some have introduced new innovative practices.[19] This diversity across firms makes the industry an ideal choice for the study. Chapter 4 examines different patterns of employment relations in the Indian textile industry.

Pressures for change in employment relations differ across firms; they originate from different sources; and firms differ in the way they confront these pressures. The Indian textile industry has witnessed slow changes over a long period of time. In contrast, some capital-intensive firms have seen dramatic changes over short periods. They introduced new technology, downsized their labor force, adopted the core-periphery model, and introduced union-substitution strategy. The best examples are some MNCs. Increase in limits on foreign equity participation and removal of restrictions on machine imports have helped firms to invest in advanced technology. The fund for new technology most often came from increases in shareholding of parent companies. In the 1990s, most firms in India downsized their employment, and it was most dramatic in capital-intensive firms that introduced new technology. New technology needs fewer workers, but technology alone cannot explain the extent of the downsizing. Along with new technology, management introduced the core-periphery model of work organization. The workers in the core are high-skill employees and receive high wages and have high job security. In contrast, the workers in the periphery work under contractors, do most unskilled jobs, receive low wages, and have no job security. Some firms adopted union-avoidance strategies like re-designation of employees as managers, so that they cannot form unions or receive protection under labor laws. Chapter 5 presents employment restructuring in some capital-intensive firms and explains how it differs from those in the textile industry.

Globalization has induced changes in existing firms and has introduced new types of firms in the Indian economy. The most important of the new industrial sector is the information technology (IT) software and services industry. Breakthroughs in telecommunication and IT and global outsourcing of IT services have helped in the growth of the sector. The core area in the industry is software development, but IT-enabled service is the fastest-growing sub-sector in terms of employment generation. ITES sector firms engage large number of employees and majority of them are not software professionals or persons with specialized IT skills. Their employees are more similar to non-professional employees in banks or financial institutions. The labor-intensive nature of the sub-sector and its new arrival in India makes it an interesting subject for this study. As in most service sector firms, employees in these firms also deal directly with customers, but often their customers live outside national boundaries (most often in the United States). Chapter 6 presents a study of employment relations in ITES firms in India and compares them with the practices in similar firms in other countries and in other types of firms in India. The work organization of these firms mirrors practices followed in the advanced countries (similar to findings of Rasiah 1988, in Malaysia), but there are some differences because of cultural differences and global time gaps. The findings indicate that employment relations in this sector differ from those in the textile industry and also from those in other service sector firms.

Globalization has increased involvement of MNCs in the Indian economy. This is apparent in the dramatic growth of FDI in the last decade.[20] As investments by MNCs have come with new managerial practices, they have increased global influence on Indian firms and have increased complexity in employment relations. The recent trends indicate that, unlike in earlier times, global forces have the upper hand over local forces (Tzeng and Uzzi 2000: 234). Adoption of global policies in HRM differs across MNCs depending on various factors, including their country of origin and their global strategy in employee management. Chapter 7 presents employment relation practices of Japanese multinationals in India and examines whether they adopt typical Japanese practices or alter them to suit the local environment. The findings indicate that depending on various internal and external factors, MNCs differ in adoption of global or local practices.

Ninety percent of all workers in India work in small firms and about half of them are wage-employed. In small firms, employee control is informal, unstructured, and unsophisticated. In Edwards, (1979) term, employee control in small firms is simple control, where employers' personal power and authority constitute the primary mechanism of employee control. In most small firms, traditionally, employers control all aspects of workers' work life with practically no restriction on employers' absolute authority (except some minimum social norms). However, increasingly, employers of small firms are facing external influences that limit their absolute authority. Sometimes these are legal restrictions under labor laws, sometimes these are imposed by trade unions, sometimes these are self-imposed by groups of employers, and in small contract firms the principal employers impose the restrictions. The net result of all these is increasing variations in employment relations in small firms as some firms operate without any restrictions and others face restrictions. Chapter 8 identifies different patterns of employment relations in small firms and their changes over time.

Changes in economic, technological, social, and political contexts over the last two decades have led to changes in employment relations in all types of firms in India. They have changed the behaviors of people at work the contexts and their changes differ across firms. Some firms are closely linked to global markets, while others produce for local markets and operate in a relatively insulated environment. Some firms have performed well, while others have remained sick for long periods.[21] The relationship between capital and labor is cooperative in majority of firms, but in some firms the relationship is adversarial. Some firms have experienced small changes over long periods of time, while some others have seen dramatic changes over short periods of time. Some firms have adopted innovative practices, while others are continuing with traditional practices. The study includes different types of firms—firms in textile industry, capital-intensive firms, ITES firms, Japanese multinationals, and firms in small scale sector. Overall, the changes collectively show growing dissimilarities in employment relations across firms in India. At the same time, the changes in India are similar to those seen in other countries. Following is a capsule summary of specific findings of the study that underlie its broad conclusions:

1. The Indian textile industry shows the coexistence of four dominant patterns of employment relation systems: the low-wage pattern, the HRM pattern, the joint-team-based approach, and the conflict pattern (Box 1.2). In the past, employment relation practices were broadly uniform across textile firms with centralized tripartite wage agreements and bounded amount of conflicts between capital and labor. Over time, the four patterns have emerged. This indicates increased variations in employment relation practices across textile firms.
2. The four patterns are not only common in the textile industry; they are also common in other industries including

Box 1.2: Dominant Patterns of Employment Relation Systems

Low-wage Pattern: The main characteristics of the pattern are relatively low wages and fringe benefits, informal personnel policies, and substantial discretion to operating managers in matters of leave, discipline, and payment of wages. Employment is often temporary with limited employee commitment, limited promotional opportunities, absence of seniority-based pay, and high labor turnover. The pattern is common in small firms and some labor intensive firms.

Conflict Pattern: In this pattern labor and management are engaged in continuous struggle over their basic rights. Because of high costs of conflicts, the pattern is often unstable. However, in some firms labor conflict is perennial and continues for long periods with frequent strikes or lockouts. In India, this pattern of employment relation is seen in jute mills and steel rolling mills in union setting.

Joint Team-based Pattern: This pattern indicates cooperative relation between labor and management. There is more involvement of workers and unions in business decisions in matters like productivity, quality, flexibility, and productivity linked wages. In India, this pattern is seen mostly in firms that recognize single union and maintains good relations with workers and unions.

HRM Pattern: This pattern relies heavily on formal personnel policies. However, the nature of the policies differs from those seen in traditional firms. The pattern typically involves knowledge or skill based pay, elaborate employee communication and complaint procedure, and team form of work organizations. Some MNCs and capital intensive high technology firms exhibit this pattern.

Source: Indian patterns based on Katz and Darbishire 2000: 21–27.

labor-intensive industries. The patterns resemble the four dominant patterns in developed countries with some small differences as one looks into details of the patterns. The proportions of the different patterns in India also differ from those in developed countries.

3. IT-enabled service sector exhibits only one dominant pattern of employment relations: the HRM pattern. This is in contrast to the four patterns in the textile industry. The variation in employment relations in the industry is, therefore, much less than those seen in other industrial sectors. Further, the HRM pattern in the IT-enabled sector is different from the popular HRM model. The differences are in terms of limited

career opportunity and strong reliance on IT for supervision and control. This explains differences in employment relation practices across industrial sectors.

4. An important source of differences in employment relations across firms in India is related to unions: the status of unionization, types of unions, and management's strategy toward unions. Differences in India in terms of unions are much more than those found in developed countries. There exist different types of unions: internal unions, external unions, independent unions, and affiliated unions.[22] Over time, union power has declined and preference for union type has shifted from affiliated external unions to non-affiliated internal unions.
5 Many firms have changed their employment systems in the post-reform period. The changes are not uniform across firms. Labor-intensive firms exhibit small changes in their employment relations, but capital-intensive firms in the engineering, chemical, and pharmaceutical industries indicate dramatic and fast changes. The changes are particularly prominent in MNCs, which have introduced new technology and downsized their workforce. Most firms have adopted the core-periphery model of work organization and have contracted out their unskilled and non-core jobs.
6. Global influences are now important factors in firms' operations. The influences are more for MNCs producing for export markets than for local firms producing for local markets. Firms differ in their perceived need and ability to adopt global or local practices. Several internal and external factors that link firms to the global or local economy influence the adaptation process. These factors include external or local ownership, share of exports and imports, extent of internal and external competition, and firms' location in global commodity chains. Differences in these factors lead to differences in employment relations across firms. Firms with higher global linkages like higher foreign ownership or exports are more likely to adopt modern practices than firms with low global linkages.
7. The majority of workers in India work in small firms. Most small firms' employment systems represent simple control, where employers directly control all aspects of workers' work life without any external influences. However, increasingly,

small firms are facing external influences that restrict employers' absolute authority. The restrictions are of different types and vary across firms and across industries. As some firms face such restrictions while others do not, there are increasing variations in firms' employment relations in the small scale sector.

Changes in global and national contexts have led to some widespread changes in firms' employment relation systems in India. They include a shift to lean production, downsizing of employment, contracting out of jobs, emphasis on labor flexibility, linking wages to skill and productivity, increasing variation in wages, focus on training, and introduction of innovative employment practices. Employment relation systems in India are becoming similar to those seen in other countries with some small differences in exact patterns of the systems and their relative proportions. The findings are to be viewed in relation to the strength and weakness of evidence on which the conclusions are based. The study is based on case studies of a sample of firms. The sample may not be an ideal one, but it certainly captures important issues in employment relations. The study also tracks firms in industries covered in other studies (for example, Mathur 1991 and Hiers and Kuruvilla 2000) to ensure some degree of comparability. I believe that the analysis presented here gives a reasonably clear picture of changes in employment relations in India in the post-reform period.

Notes

1. The term employment relations is increasingly used in the literature to reflect the growing interconnectedness of labor-management relations, IR, and HRM. It includes aspects of both IR and HRM (Bamber and Lansbury 1998; Katz and Darbishire 2000; Kochan and Russel 1997; Locke et al. 1995; Strauss 2001).
2. The state plays a number of roles: as employer and primary party, as an actor in the labor market in determining wages and employment conditions, as regulator of industrial conflict, and as a lawmaker and law enforcer (Farnham 2000: 326).
3. National governments are now increasingly constrained by international organizations, such as the IMF, the WTO, and MNCs. For example, the ratified ILO conventions/recommendations appear as international rules.

Further, some MNCs have codes of conduct for their suppliers in developing countries (for example, codes of conduct by Nike and Adidas for suppliers in China).

4. In a more generalized form, one can identify a system by its components: elements, attributes, and their relationships. The elements make up the system, the attributes are characteristics of the elements, and their relationships describe how the elements and their attributes are related.
5. The term industrial relations is used here in place of employment relations, as most of the earlier studies used the term industrial relations.
6. Bae (2000) found such similarities in telecommunication industries in Britain and Korea.
7. Covarrubias (2002) found similarities in employment relations of two auto plants of Ford Motor Company in Mexico and Brazil.
8. In a study of telecommunication service industries in Britain and Korea, Bae (2000) found similarities in work practices, but differences in adoption of the practices in the two countries. Covarrubias (2002) found similar work groups in two Ford plants in Mexico and Brazil, but differences in the work groups in terms of size, function, and group activities.
9. Globally, the low-wage pattern and the HRM pattern are seen in the non-union sector, but in India they also exist in the union sector.
10. Practices differ in their transferability. The practices that are mandated by local regulations or shaped by strong local norms and affect the rank and file are more likely to adhere to local practices. However, practices with diffuse and poorly defined local norms are less likely to conform to local norms (Rosenzweig and Nohria 1994).
11. In India, the relationship between foreign ownership of firms and their export orientation indicates a positive relationship. Majumdar and Chibber (1998) in a study of over one thousand firms in India found that firms with over 51 per cent of foreign ownership fared better in exports.
12. For example, 24/7 Customer.com is an international division, Hyundai is a fully owned subsidiary, BOC India is a majority owned subsidiary, GE-Godrej is a joint venture company.
13. The neoclassical approach argues that the internal system provides an economically efficient solution to management problems in complex environments (Willamson et al. 1975). The radical perspective explains that employers created the internal system to institutionalize their control over labor (Burawoy 1979; Edwards 1979; Marglin 1974). The institutional view claims that ongoing bargaining between the management and workers led to the development of the systems (Doeringer and Piore 1971: 13–40).
14. The motives underlying the expansion of public enterprise were many including development, employment, equity, self-reliance, and support to weaker section. The public enterprises were seen as an instrument of economic policy. The central government nationalized major banks,

insurance companies, coalmines, and some sick units during the 1960s and early 1970s. In addition, state governments also nationalized many sick units. By the end of the 1980s the public sector accounted for a quarter of GDP and almost half of all investments in the economy (Mookherjee 1995: 19).

15. The structural adjustment programs include policies on (*a*) trade, (*b*) resource mobilization, (*c*) efficient use of resources, and (*d*) institutional reforms. They include measures like removal of import quotas, cuts in tariffs, public-sector reforms, support to agriculture and industry, and changes in exchange rates, export incentives, taxes, and interest rates (Economic Surveys, Government of India).
16. The two important pieces of labor legislation that play major roles in shaping Indian IR: The Indian Trade Union Act, 1926 deals with registration of trade unions and their legal authority. The Industrial Disputes Act, 1947 deals with conciliation, arbitration, and adjudication.
17. In India, the employment security laws are among the most stringent in the world; any reduction in workforce requires government permission, which is seldom given (Industrial Disputes Act 1947).
18. A survey of twenty-one manufacturing firms indicate a reduction of 43 percent of their labor force in twelve years although most of them expanded, enhanced their turnover, and increased their profits (Shrouti and Nandkumar 1994: 225–226). Employers started to adopt these strategies in the late 1970s, well before the economy opened up to global competition, but over time, the process accelerated.
19. Indian Rayon in West Bengal (a textile mill) has introduced innovative practices like *kaizen*, QCs, and total quality control (TQC) similar to those seen in the industrialized countries.
20. India is widely regarded as an underperformer when it comes to attracting FDI, particularly in comparison with China and the rest of East Asia. However, there are major differences in the definition of FDI and the interpretation of FDI data in India. The adoption of international standards in computing FDI data would raise India's net FDI inflows from the often-noted USD 2–3 billion figure to USD 8 billion (Srivastava 2003).
21. India is unique in having a very large number of sick industrial units. They perform poorly, make persistent losses, fail in debt payments; but still remain in operation. In the industrialized countries, one hears about poor firm performance, but one rarely comes across the phrase "industrial sickness" in the way it is used in India (Anant and Goswami 1995: 249).
22. A union may have a proportion of external leaders with or without political leanings. The extent of their influence determines whether a union should be classified as an internal or external union. Internal unions generally do not have any outsider on their executive committee, but some internal unions co-opt an outsider as president or adviser (Mathur 1991: 6; Ramswamy 2000: 54–56).

Chapter 2

Changing Contexts of Employment Relations and Shifts in Capital–Labor Power Balance

EMPLOYER–EMPLOYEE RELATIONS are always changing. In other words, employment relation systems are dynamic systems. The systems continuously interact and balance with the environment and, over time, acquire qualitatively new properties that result in continuous evolution.[1] Changes in employment systems thus have to be studied in the context of changes in the environments in which the systems operate. The environment is always changing and there are many changes; but of them, most relevant for the study are those that influence functioning of firms' employment systems. Following the general systems theory, the employment system of a firm is a part of a national employment system, and similarly a national system is a part of the global employment system. In this approach, a firm's employment system is described by a set of elements, their attributes, and their relationship; and a change in any one of them changes a firm's employment system. Environmental factors that change firms' employment systems are contexts of employment relations. This chapter briefly describes changes in the global and national contexts of employment relations in India. The most important national contexts are economic, technological, legal, social, and political contexts. The contexts and their changes influence the way firms manage people at work (Figure 2.1).

Most often, changes in firms' employment systems occur in small steps, but sometimes they are more rapid and fundamental than in other periods. The change process in firms' employment relations may be explained in two steps. The first step is identification of pressures that induce firms to modify their existing employment relationship. The next step is search and selection of new models of employment relations. The change process can be triggered by changes in various external factors such as: competitive conditions, state regulations, technological conditions, power balance between capital and labor, professional beliefs of mangers, and patterns and values of actors in employment relations. These factors can independently initiate changes in firms' employment relations, but most often a number of factors work in combination. Several factors influence the selection of new models and their implementation. First, the historical path that has led to an existing employment relationship in a firm restricts the available options. Second, the new models of organizing employment relationships need to be in accordance with the prevailing values of the actors and the community. Third, when alternative models are available for adoption, the division of power between the actors in employment relations mediates their selection. Finally, it is management's strategic choice to choose a particular model of employment relation (Pot 2001: 40–41). In summary, various external factors or contexts influence the change processes and their outcomes, and hence influence firms' employment systems. The changes differ across firms depending on whether a firm's system is relatively open or closed in relation to the contexts.

Indian IR developed in an environment that protected both industry and labor from internal and external competition. The government policies that shaped the environment started to change in the mid-1980s. Finally, with the initiation of the World Bank–International Monetary Fund (IMF) advocated structural adjustment program in 1991, the Indian industrial landscape changed considerably in response to both domestic and international competition. The changes have altered the strategic decision making of local and state governments and have affected behaviors of employers, unions, and individual workers. In the pre-liberalization period, the national government played a determining and strategic role in control of industrial development. In the post-reform period, with the withdrawal of industrial licensing and other restrictions, each state has started to actively lobby and compete for both national and international capital investment. With the states adopting industry-friendly policies, the balance of power between capital and labor has shifted in favor of employers. This has weakened labor's ties with political parties (Bhattacherjee 2000; Kuruvilla 1996). This shift is evident in the decline of union power and increased employer dominance in the post-reform period. The next chapter presents changes in union density and union power over time and how union decline is linked to increase in income inequality and growing variations in employment relations.

Figure 2.1: Changes in Employment Relations with Changes in Contexts

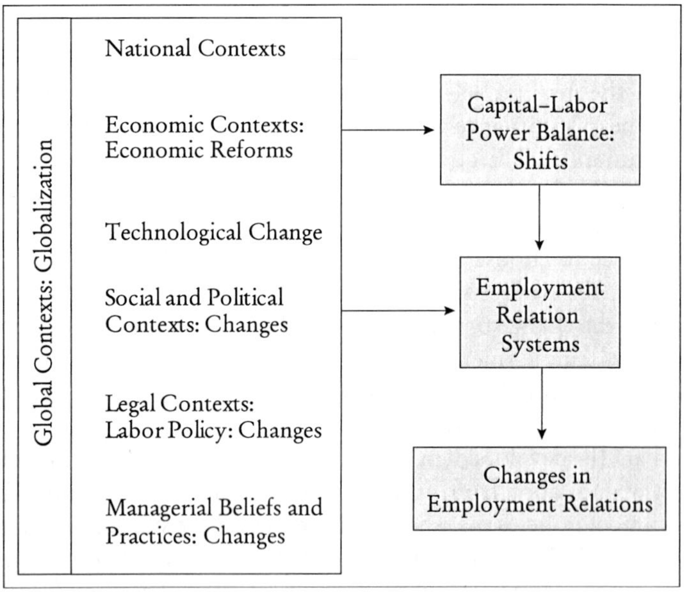

Source: Based on discussion on contents of employment relations.

Global Context: Globalization

The fundamental changes in the international economy captured under the label of economic globalization have changed the context of employment systems for firms all over the world. The World Development Report 1995 documents that the world economy is integrating and that working conditions of workers are changing all over the world. In the late 1970s, only a few developing countries, led by some in East Asia, opened their borders to flows of trade and investments. Now, most of the world's population lives in countries that are either integrated into world markets for goods and finance or rapidly becoming so. The joint working of the several forces has driven this process of globalization. Most important of them are the policies of liberalization and deregulation adopted by various governments. The advances in ICT, continuously falling transportation and communication costs, and diffusion of knowledge and technology have facilitated the process. In addition, worldwide production system by multinational firms and international efforts to reduce trade barriers (General Agreement on Tariffs and Trade, North American Free Trade Agreement, and European Union) has helped the integration process.

In the last three decades, governments of many countries have changed their development strategies and adopted policies that favor deregulation, privatization, and liberalization of trade and commerce. In developing countries, the changes have been initiated through adjustment programs advocated by the World Bank or the IMF. The programs have a number of policy measures and include: (*a*) withdrawal of import licenses, (*b*) reduction of import duties, (*c*) encouraging foreign investment, (*d*) increasing involvement of the private sector, and (*e*) abolition of industrial licensing. The removal of tariff barriers and reduction of import duties has made imported goods cheaper, and has created new opportunities for firms to sell their products in external markets. There has been increased international trade, especially export of manufacturing products from developing countries.[2] Further, given the opportunities and differences between developed and developing countries, there are indications of further increase in trade for developing countries.

Globalization is increasing the involvement of MNCs in national economies and has created new opportunities for local firms to export their products in global markets. The withdrawal of restrictions in foreign investments and low wages in developing countries have made developing countries attractive for investments by MNCs. Increased involvement of MNCs in developing countries is affecting firms and their employment systems in a number of ways. The easy availability of imported goods in developing countries, which is often of better quality or lower costs, is forcing domestic firms to become more competitive and match quality and price of imported goods. Further, with increased involvement of MNCs in domestic markets, the local firms now have to compete with these corporations that have better access to technology and financial resources. The removal of trade restrictions of other countries has created new export opportunities for local firms, but to avail this, they must be globally competitive. In brief, increased domestic and international competition has forced domestic firms to improve their product quality and reduce product costs by removing slack and inefficiencies. This has led to changes in work organizations' and firms' employment systems.

Global influences are different for product markets and for labor markets. Product markets have moved beyond national borders, but governance of labor markets is still primarily a national activity. Labor institutions and labor market regulations on employment, pay, working conditions, social security, and occupational health and safety are still determined at national level. There are, however, some global influences on labor markets. Emergence of transnational corporations as key global actors has a number of implications on the strengths of state and collective labor. As national governments are now trying to attract foreign investments, they are now facing corporate pressure to adopt labor regulations that promote competitiveness (Pot 2000: 50). The pressures of competition and demands for flexibility are now at a time when territorial nation states are increasingly losing their power to govern (Hobsbawm 1996: 424). Along with the changes, organized labor has seen decline in power. The differences in global influences on product markets and labor markets mean that suppliers to global markets now produce under different conditions. Global context is important for all countries, but it is more so for developing countries as their firms and workers have less ability to adjust to changes.

Economic Context: Economic Reforms

Government economic policies influence behaviors of people at work, conditions of work, employment security, and incidence of industrial conflicts. The policies have major implications for firms' employment relations. If the policy focuses on creating conditions for full employment, it strengthens unions' bargaining power, whereas if it focuses on containing price inflation, it strengthens employers' bargaining power (Farnham 2000: 104). Indian industrialization policy in the early years of independence emphasized heavy industry, public ownership, and import substitution. A license was required to start or expand any industrial activity engaging fifty or more workers. The protected environment led to the emergence of high cost and inflexible firms. The policy did not change much from independence to the mid-1980s, when the prejudices and the beliefs that led to these developments came to be widely questioned. Finally, the first budget in the 1990s marked changes in a new direction and it continued in successive budgets. The new policy aimed to move the economy away from import substitution to export promotion and increase domestic and external competition through delicensing, import liberalization, increases in foreign collaboration, changes in exchange rates, taxation, and export incentives (Joshi and Little 1998: 62, 171). The results have been impressive economic growth both in terms of growth in per capita income and GDP.

An important element in the structure of Indian industry is the division between public and private ownership. The Industrial Policy Resolution, 1956, classified industries into three categories. Seventeen key industries were reserved for the public sector. Twelve industries, such as those involved in production of intermediate goods and road transport were open to both public and private sectors. The remaining industries were left for private sector investments. However, all industries were subjected to licensing for production and investment. The policy prescribed limits for investments in the public sector, but in practice, the sector expanded into areas, such as consumer goods, tourism, and hotels, which were originally left for private sector investment. During the 1960s and early 1970s, major banks, insurance companies, and coalmines were nationalized with a view to ensure that the government gains the commanding heights of the economy. Further, many sick industries were nationalized to protect the interests of labor and investor (Joshi and Little 1998: 173; Mookherjee 1995: 5). It was only in the 1980s that the government departed from its policy that favored public sector. Enactment of the Sick Industrial Companies Act (SICA) in 1985 marked changes in a new direction. The new policy prescribed a greater role for private sector and withdrawal of some control and regulatory functions in the industry. Although the economic reforms program officially started in 1991, the shift toward private sector started in the mid-1980s.[3]

The Indian industrial environment that protected both capital and labor led to the emergence of a large number of sick industrial units. Poor performance of some firms in an economy is a natural phenomenon all over the world, including industrialized countries, but India is unique, as there are always large numbers of sick industrial units. Many units make persistent losses, but they continue to remain in operation even by defaulting in meeting their debt payment obligations. SICA aims to rehabilitate or close down sick units after taking views of both promoters and workers. Under the Act, many firms have been referred to the Board of Industrial and Financial Reconstruction (BIFR). Some firms have been able to restructure and recover from financial distress, while others have been recommended for liquidation. The BIFR and the liquidation proceedings take a long time and the processes are further delayed due to court cases. Often parties in dispute take advantage of legal loopholes to delay the proceedings[4] (Joshi and Little 1998). In India, there are still many sick units in operation, but unlike in the previous era, there is now a growing consensus that firms cannot sustain persistent losses and continue with their operations. In the past, sick units in the public sector survived with government support, but withdrawal of the support have led to closure of some units. In many units facing closures, unions and workers have agreed to various concessions like wage cuts or have accepted voluntary retirement. All these have changed the IR environment.

Influence of Technological Change

The influence of technology in shaping the relationship between workers and management has been long debated in employment relations literature. According to the technological deterministic view of social development, global diffusion of production technology will ultimately erase the cross-national differences in employment relations. "Social arrangements will be most uniform from one society to another when the societies are most closely tied to technology; they can be more diverse the farther removed they are from technology" (Kerr et al. 1964: 285). This technological deterministic view has been criticized on various grounds. The "social shaping" approach argues that technology does not develop along an implacable trajectory nor does it grow out of the self-contained logic of scientific or technical necessity; instead, it is shaped by social considerations. Whatever the debate, there is no doubt that technological changes induce changes in firms' employment relations. As firms adopt new technology, they create new options for managing their employees (Pot 2000: 57–59). Historically, new technology has always met with resistance as it threatens traditional occupations, and there are always some winners and losers (Farnham 2000: 146). As firms differ in use of new technology, they differ in their employment relations. This is particularly important in the Indian context, where both low-technology firms and high-technology firms coexist.[5]

The most important change in Indian firms in the post-reform period is increased investment in new technology. In the pre-reform era, import restrictions imposed severe constraints in technology upgradation. The economic reforms program has removed many of the restrictions. The decentralization of power to state governments and further decentralization in decision making at the state level (for example, the one window approach) has led to speedier decision making and reduction in friction between business and government. Relaxation in the limits on foreign participation in Indian firms has made foreign funds available for technology upgradation and made equity a viable financing option. Current account convertibility has removed restrictions on availing foreign currency, has made foreign travel easier, and has facilitated hiring of foreign consultants and international branding efforts. Entry of multinationals has increased competition and forced Indian companies to benchmark themselves against global firms. The policy changes have led to technology upgradation of many firms. An excellent example of this is the changes in Indian Oxygen. In the 1980s, British Oxygen Company (BOC) had only 39 percent controlling interest in Indian Oxygen and had very little interest in the company. Technologically, Indian Oxygen was twenty years behind its British parent. As things started to change in the early 1990s, BOC increased its stake to 55 percent and made fresh investments to introduce best available technology (*Business India*, 1993: 74). Its shareholding has been subsequently increased to 90 percent and Indian Oxygen has been renamed as BOC India. The policy changes have also helped in emergence of new high-tech firms like IT firms.

In the emerging competitive environment, manufacturers in India are increasingly turning to new technology. Along with changes in technology, firms are also adopting new approaches in managing their employees. Old ideas about how to manage an organization and its people at work are withering away and new ideas that emphasize technology upgradation and knowledge management are emerging. Increasing use of IT has led to an explosion of information and knowledge that organizations need for effective management. Firms differ in use of IT and its use as one of their core activities. Most firms still use personal computers in standalone mode and cover only a small part of personnel management activities, but some firms use IT-based integrated management system, starting with gate control, to payment of wages and rewards, to annual evaluation of employees.[6] In MNCs, IT has facilitated integration and coordination among production facilities in different countries and different locations. In India, most modern firms today use IT and some use IT for their core activities. This is not only changing workplaces in India, it is also changing the social, cultural, and political arrangements in society. The changes have a major influence on firms' employment relations.

Social and Political Contexts

Social and political contexts are important factors in shaping and influencing firms' employment systems. Changes in population structure, social structure and attitudes, women's roles, culture, and politics have direct influence on firms' employment systems. Many of the social changes are linked to changes in economic systems, technology, or labor laws, but they themselves are also variables in the total equation of change.[7] Economic reform programs in India have introduced many changes in the economic environment, but there have not been major changes in the social contexts. As in the past, the social structure has remained complex with distinct boundaries between different classes, castes, religions, and other social groups. In this structure, class has always remained linked to occupation and income: working class associated with manual or unskilled labor, middle class with white-collar work or professional jobs, and upper class with wealthy business people and industrialists. A social division cutting across all classes in India is the gender division: labor force participation of females is much lower than that of men, and they have a lower position in labor markets.[8] Over time, women's participation has increased in some sectors, but large differences still persist in most sectors.

The most important social indicators popularly used to compare the status of populations and workers across countries and within countries are inequality, poverty, literacy, and unemployment rate. These indicators together give us a picture about societies in which firms operate and their workforce. Poverty and inequality give indications about living conditions of the workers and their families. They also have significant influence in shaping firms' employment relations. The changes of the two indicators are different in the post-reform period compared to the pre-reform period. Some early studies indicate a decline in poverty after the mid-1970s, but there is no such steady trend in the initial years of economic reforms of 1990s[9] (Datt 1999; Gupta 1995; Sen 1996). In the subsequent period of the post-reform era, there has been decline in poverty, but the decline is slower than that in the pre-reform period. On inequality, the changes indicate significant increase in inequality in the initial years of the post-reform era and no decline in inequality in the subsequent years of post-reform era (Dev and Ravi 2007). Increase in inequality is also evident at the micro level in individual firms. There has been an increase in the wage gap between managers and workers and among blue-collar workers.[10]

Firms' ability to adopt new practices and increase productivity depend on the characteristics of individual workers and collective abilities of the workers.[11] In India, the existence of a large number of poor and illiterate workers is the main reason for low productivity. Literacy is not only an individual and social issue, it is a business and economic issue as well. If a sizable proportion of workers are significantly limited in literacy skills, they limit the country's ability for productivity growth. At firm level, illiterate workers and workers with poor literacy skills are unable to acquire new skills or adopt new practices that may enhance firms' performance. Illiteracy of workers results in low productivity and inflexibility in accepting new workplace practices.[12]

Large-scale unemployment is a serious problem in developing countries. The unemployment rate indicates the status of the supply side of labor markets, and thus is an important determinant of employment relationships. In India, the unemployment rate increased in the first one and half decade of economic reforms.[13] High unemployment is not unusual even in industrialized countries, but its implications are more severe in India. The unemployed are mostly from poor families and unlike industrialized countries they are not covered under any social security scheme. Income from employment is the only source of income for poor families.

Cultures of people who work in firms have a major influence on firms' employment relations. National culture consists of ideas, values, attitudes, and beliefs that influence the way people perceive the world and themselves in it. It fashions workers' behavior and the way they relate to each other. Given the multiethnic character of the Indian population and the large number of people in poverty, political leaders always have to make compromises on issues pertaining to sharing of power and income. The competition for power among communities, castes, and language groups has always been an important factor in many decisions. It has even taken an institutional form through the formation of associations based on caste or language. These divisions have been reflected in decisions of trade union leaders and politicians. At the national and state levels, one can find consensus between different groups on major issues, but the heterogeneous character of the country becomes prominent as one faces ground reality. Over the years, the differences between the groups have declined, but not eliminated.

Political contexts have strong influence on firms' employment relations. Political parties play important roles in formulation and implementation of labor policy. They not only influence firms' employment relations through general legislations and specific legislations for labor, they also influence balance of power between capital and labor. The political parties in power determine the roles played by the governments in dealing with labor conflicts and in resolution of conflicts. In Indian context, the most important influence of political parties on firms' employment relations is through their links to trade unions. Indian labor movement is essentially an outcrop of politics. Most trade unions are affiliated to some political party or the other, and they are founded and nurtured by the political leaders. In the post-reform era, the link between political parties and trade unions has weakened and this has reduced political parties' influence on firms' employment relations. The political parties in power have also shown similar responses to the reform program. Since 1991, there have been changes in political parties in power in the central government, but there has been no major change in the economic reform agenda.

Legal Contexts: Labor Policy

Governments, with their economic and legal policy preferences, determine whether firms' employee relations should operate in a corporatist or a liberal context.[14] Labor policy is a key contextual factor that directly influences firms' employment relations. Labor policy means legislation or government action calculated to affect labor markets for the purpose of attaining specific objectives of social and economic policy. It includes government policies on the relationship between employers and workers, protection of workers' rights, wages and conditions of work, social security, labor welfare, employment generation, and job security. The policies are implemented by enacting labor laws or through implementation of programs and projects for workers' welfare. In India, there is no single document that exclusively spells out labor policy, but its elements are found in a scattered way in the plan documents and labor legislations. In India, "labor" is an item included in the concurrent list of the constitution. It provides for labor legislation by both the central and state governments with certain matters reserved for the central government.[15] There are numerous labor laws, some applicable to all categories of workers, while others cover workers in specific sectors. The policy objectives are products of interaction of policy makers that emerge through a process of bargaining. Several individuals, trade unions, political parties, and employers' organizations play important roles in formulation and implementation of labor policies. The nature of interventions and corresponding provisions in major labor laws are indicated in Table 2.1. The central government has enacted most important labor laws; but for majority of the laws, their implementation is with the state governments.

Table 2.1: Government Intervention: Major Labor Laws[16]

Intervention	*Provision in India*	*Act and Rules*
Protection of workers' rights.	Workers can form unions; unions can negotiate wages and conditions of work.	Trade Union Act 1926; Industrial Dispute Act 1947.
Protection of the vulnerable.	Regulation and prohibition of child labour; equal wage and equal employment opportunity for women; maternity benefit.	Child Labour Act 1986; Equal Remuneration Act 1976; Maternity Benefit Act 1961.

(*Table 2.1 contd*)

(*Table 2.1 contd*)

Intervention	*Provision in India*	*Act and Rules*
Establishment of minimum compensation for work.	Workers to be paid minimum wage, and minimum non-wage benefits like medical, housing, etc.	Minimum Wage Act 1948; Plantation Labour Act 1951 (provides for medical and housing benefits).
Assurance of decent working conditions.	Minimum occupational and safety health standards, maximum hours of work.	Factories Act 1948.
Provisions for income security.	Social security: Workers get payment during sickness, disability, or old age.	Provident Fund Act 1952; Employees State Insurance Act 1948; Payment of Gratuity Act 1972; Workmen Compensation Act 1923.
Provisions for job security.	Limited right not to be dismissed; compensation when retrenched.	Industrial Dispute Act 1948.

Source: Malik 2006; World Bank 1996.

In India, there have been major changes in economic and industrialization policies since 1991 and there have been talks about changes in labor laws, but there has not been any major change in labor laws. There had been several attempts to amend the Industrial Dispute Act 1947 and the Trade Union Act 1926, but those could not succeed because of strong opposition by trade unions and political parties. Even the Rajiv Gandhi government (1985–1989), which had around four-fifth seats in the parliament, did not make any major change in labor laws. Although there has not been any major change in labor laws since the initiation of the economic reform program, there is evidence of changes in implementation of labor laws. In the past, neither the central government nor the state governments granted permission for layoff or closure under the Industrial Disputes Act 1948, but the central government and some state governments have now started to grant such permissions.[17] The Act provides for penal action for closure of any unit without permission, but in the recent past there has not been any penal action for violation of the provisions. Some state governments have restricted labor inspections. In Uttar Pradesh, for example, the state government has restricted labor inspection without prior approval of district magistrates. Further, the central and state governments have become more active in helping firms to adjust their workforce through voluntary retirement.[18] In summary, the labor laws have not changed, but there have been material differences in their implementation.

Changes in Managerial Beliefs and Practices

Management generally initiates changes in firms' employment practices to improve a firm's performance. Internal disturbances may sometimes trigger the changes, but most often changes in the external environment prompt management to initiate the changes. Managers introduce the changes based on their knowledge and experience. As new practices become successful in some firms, they are adopted by other firms. The rationalized myths in the form of new ideas about how to manage people at work that proliferate among professional managers constitute a powerful force to initiate the changes. Isomorphic pressures on professional managers play an important role in diffusion of management practices across firms. Consulting firms, academic institutions, business publications, professional associations, and quality contests reinforce the isomorphic pressures for adoption of similar practices (Pot 2000: 60). As new practices or models gain consensus among managers, they replace old ideas about the ideal model of efficient organizations.[19] Increased communication facilities, spread of knowledge through Internet, and experience of individuals in MNCs have helped dispersion and adoption of the new practices. Most new ideas have emerged in developed countries. Indian firms are now increasingly introducing these ideas. The terms such as TQM, benchmarking, customer focus, empowerment, de-layering, teamwork, and learning organization are now standard notions in the vocabulary of many professional managers in India.

Changes in the post-reform period indicate a "paradigm shift" in beliefs and practices of human resource managers. These changes contrast distinctly from those that existed until the mid-1980s and before. Examples of such changes include changes in areas of skills (from single function to multifunction), work organization (from detailed division of functions to integration of tasks), functional integration (from specialization to generalization), employee control (from bureaucratic to flexible), and work culture (from mechanistic to organic) (Mamkoottam 2000: 232). An important issue in the changes process is increase in labor flexibility. This is reflected in the proceedings of employers' associations in different forums and collective bargaining agreements.[20] In a stable environment, a firm's competitive strategy was about taking out a position, and manufacturing a strategy focussed on getting better at things necessary to defend that position. In the environment of intense competition, shorter product cycles, increased product diversity, and fast-changing customer choice, firms are now adopting strategies that emphasize flexibility. It includes acquiring the capability to scan the environment, evaluate markets and competitors, and quickly accomplish reconfiguration and transformation (Wright and Snell 1998). In India, since the early 1990s, there has been increased emphasis on both numerical and functional flexibility, and for this, changes have been introduced at different levels of organizations. At the individual level, the emphasis is on enhancing individual worker's ability to change through training and skill improvement programs. At the shop floor level, it is on introduction of teamwork that enhances functional flexibility. At the plant level, the focus is on numerical flexibility. And at the strategic level, firms try to gain flexibility through contracting out of jobs (Das 2004). With many firms adopting labor flexibility measures, it is now part of managers' beliefs and practices.

Over time, there has been a change in the attitudes of managers toward workers and trade unions. Managers have come to realize that reduction of excess manpower alone will not bring the required level of competitiveness. Along with technological and structural changes, the relationship with the employees needs to be changed. Workers should not be seen as liabilities; they should be seen as key resources that are to be carefully nurtured and constantly developed. Healthy work culture can be created only through proactive employment relation policies with preventive measures for reduction of conflicts at workplaces. The emphasis is now on getting workers committed toward larger corporate goals and organizations' missions. Personnel management is no more seen as merely concerned with procedural matters of recruitment and salary administration and industrial relations is no more seen merely as a fire fighting system. They are now considered an integral part of a holistic employment relation strategy evolved at the highest levels of management. The thrust now is to attract, retain, and develop human resources on a continuous basis to maintain organizational competitiveness. There is now increased emphasis on the creation of a new work culture that values quality, costs, and customer satisfaction. Decentralized decision making, teamwork, and improved communication are now on the agenda of top managers. Organizations are making focussed efforts to understand their workers and their needs, and are increasing attention on training and skill retention. There is more attention on communication with employees and their unions (Mamkoottam 2000: 248). The changes in managers' beliefs and practices have a major influence on firms' employment relations, but these are to be seen in the context of the shifts in the capital–labor power balance.

Shifts in Capital–Labor Power Balance

Management generally takes initiative to change firms' employment practices. The capital–labor power balance mediates the change process and thus influences firms' employment relations. This follows from radical analysis of firms. In a firm's work setting, the parties in employment relations vie for control of the workplace to get a greater share of the created value. On some occasions, management has the upper hand in employee control, and in other times, workers' collective power plays the most important role in shaping a firm's employment relations. The two situations represent two extreme positions in the spectrum of capital–labor power balance and most often the locus of the balance is in between the two. The declines in union membership and union density in developed countries indicate shifts in the capital–labor power balance away from labor. In India, the union density decline is not as strong as in developed countries, but there is clear indication of a shift in the capital–labor power balance away from labor.

In India, the decline of unions is evident in the changes in union membership. It is also evident in the growth of non-union firms, changes in the nature of union membership and union structure, growth of internal unions, and changes in management strategies toward unions. In India, most national or state labor unions are affiliated with some political party, and at the plant level, unions can function both as independent unions or affiliated unions. An important structural classification across unions in India is between internal unions (no external leaders as office bearer) and external unions (at least one office bearer is an external leader). In the past, there were only a few internal unions, but recent changes indicate management's preference for internal unions, with even some firms shifting from external unions to internal unions.[21] Shifts in capital–labor power balance are also evident in the growing proportion of non-union firms. In the formal sector, increasingly, new firms are adopting strategies to remain non-union.[22] Most new high-tech service sector firms in India, such as the software firms do not have any union (for example, Wipro). Employees in such units are not very keen to form unions, but there is no doubt that management's union-avoidance strategy has played a critical role in keeping the firms non-union (Hiers and Kuruvilla 2000).

A shift in the capital–labor power balance is also evident in employer behavior toward unions and workers. Employers are now more aggressive in dealing with them. In various locations, they are adopting practices that help them to avoid unionization or curtail union power. In some firms, for example, employers have promoted workers to administrative and supervisory ranks so as to take them outside the purview of the Industrial Disputes Act 1947 (Venkataratnam 1993). There is now increasing demands by management for concessions in collective bargaining agreements and an ascendancy of management rights in collective bargaining contracts. There is now more emphasis on labor flexibility. A study of 300 collective bargaining agreements in the private sector shows that one out of two agreements now includes provisions for greater numerical flexibility and closer cooperation in labor-management relations (Venkataratnam 1997). Overall, key management strategy has shifted away from "maintaining labor peace" toward "enhancement of firm-level competitiveness."

There has also been a shift in government influence: the government–labor coalition has been replaced by a government–business coalition. In the past, the link between unions and political parties (each major political party has its trade union arm) provided the labor movement with a considerable voice. With the state's enthusiastic support for economic liberalization and labor's opposition, the recent changes indicate a weakening of government–labor coalition (Kuruvilla and Hiers 2000). Some even argue that employers now feel that the government is on their side, and this has brought about what many call "employer militancy" (Venkataratnam 1997). In the post-reform environment, employers' practices clearly show more aggression than before and at the same time labor unions exhibit less militancy and more cooperation. Closure of many non-viable units, continuing threats of closure in many units, privatization of public sector units, and large-scale voluntary retirements have contributed to a decline in unions. There have been attempts to increase labor flexibility through changes in labor laws. The attempts failed because of strong opposition by unions, but it clearly shows an attempt to increase labor flexibility. There has not been any major change in labor laws, but there are clear indications of decline in union power and shift in capital–labor power balance away from labor.[23]

Summary

Employer–employee relations in labor markets and workplaces do not take place in a vacuum. The relationships between buyers and sellers of labor services are affected by a variety of economic, legal, and political factors. Changes in global, national, and local contexts influence firms' employment relations. An important determinant of the relationships is the demand for labor relative to supply. It depends on the firm's external labor market and its internal labor market, but more particularly on the buoyancy, or not, of its product markets. The determinants of a firm's employer–employee relations are complex and no one can provide an exhaustive list of the factors that influence them. This chapter has presented some of the important contextual factors that have direct and significant influence on firms' employment relations. The various contexts in employment relations are interrelated as changes in any one of them induce changes in others. It is not possible to describe any of the factors in isolation of the others; however, to have systematic discussions, we have presented them under the headings of global, economic, technological, legal, and social contexts. Globalization has swept away the traditional boundaries built on politico-cultural barriers. It has created a global marketplace and has changed national contexts of employment relations.

Changes in global and national contexts have led to dramatic changes in firms' employment relations. In industrialized countries, the changes started in the 1970s and early 1980s, while in India the changes started in the second half of the 1980s and accelerated in the 1990s. There have been shifts in the capital–labor power balance with a decline in union power. Evidence in industrialized countries indicates that union declines in most cases have coincided with increases in income inequality and divergences in employment relations (Katz and Darbishire 2000). In India, too, there are similar changes, but after a gap of a decade and the changes are not as strong as seen in the industrialized countries. This is not unexpected as India introduced the liberal policies long after those were introduced in industrialized countries. Further, in India, a large numbers of workers are self-employed or work in the informal sector and they have not seen any major changes in employer–employee relations. In India, the changes in union density and income inequality are not as dramatic as in industrialized countries. However, the heterogeneity across Indian firms indicates that the variations in firms' employment relations may be more than those found in developed countries and they are increasing.

This chapter identifies a set of interrelated contextual factors that influence firms' employment systems. These contextual factors change over time and induce changes in firms' employment systems. However, firms differ in the way the external forces influence their employment relations and the way the changes are mediated both inside and outside the firms. In other words, even if two firms are subjected to the same external changes, their reactions to the changes may differ. They may follow different change trajectories, adopt different practices, and produce different outcomes. The way the change process is mediated depends on the characteristics of individual firms and their links to the external world. Their ability to change also differs depending on roles played by internal and external actors, and on the nature of existing policies, rules, and employment practices. The need for change and types of changes needed vary across firms and from situation to situation. Some organizations need to change more frequently than others; some need small changes involving few workers, while others involve large numbers of workers. In some situations the changes are known sufficiently in advance, while in other situations firms do not get enough time to change. The period over which the changes are required and implemented also vary from situation to situation. Sometimes changes are permanent in nature, while at other times there are temporary shifts in working arrangements. In brief, firms differ in their need and ability to change, and the way they react in the change process.

Notes

1. Hyman (1975) describes the employment relationship between the parties as a continuous and shifting relationship, and points to fluidity of the "process of control of work relations."
2. The contribution of the Indian manufacturing sector to Indian exports increased from 59 percent in 1980 and 71 percent in 1990 to 77 percent in 2000–2001. Furthermore, Indian manufacturing exports, which was a little over 5 percent of the value of output of the sector in 1990, has already achieved close to 10 percent.
3. The changes in ratio of public to private consumption in GDP show increased role of the private sector since the mid-1980s (Das 1998).
4. Some firms even get themselves registered under BIFR to get legal protection against old dues.
5. For example, some detergent firms producing for high-income consumers use modern technology (unilever), while others producing for low-income consumers use low technology (local firms).
6. Mitsubishi Corporation, Torrent, Reliance, and Ingersoll Rand use the integrated system.
7. In India, for example, job security is not only a legal issue; it also has deep support from the social and political front. It is argued that what workers have got after a long wait should not be taken away.

8. The labor force participation rate (LFPR) was about 56 percent of rural males and 29 percent for rural females. The corresponding proportions in the urban areas were 58 percent and 15 percent, respectively (National Sample Survey Office, 2010, Report No. 531, "Employment and Unemployment Situation in India, 2007–2008).
9. The poverty measures increased in 1992, but then decreased in 1993–1994, increased in 1995, again decreased in 1996, and then increased in both the 1997 and 1998 surveys.
10. This is evident in a number of firms in West Bengal. There are now more differences in wages between skilled and unskilled workers.
11. Summarizing research from a number of studies, British organizational psychologist Furnham (1992) wrote that a good worker produces about twice than the output of a poor worker.
12. The literacy rate was 65 percent in 2001 (Census of India 2001). Further, many of the literates only know how to read and write, which often is not enough for learning new skills.
13. The unemployment rates based on current daily status basis increased from 6.01 percent in 1993–1994 to 7.31 percent in 1999–2000 and to 8.28 percent in 2004–2005 (NCEUS 2009).
14. In a corporatist state, the economy is largely privately owned but the interests of capital, workers, and governments are integrated and mediated through centralized institutional mechanisms. In a liberal state, the economy is privately owned, but as far as possible the political and economic spheres are disassociated (Farnham 2000: 22).
15. The central IR machinery implements labor laws in industries for which the central government is the appropriate authority like railways, air-transport, mines, oil, and banks.
16. In India, there are numerous labor laws. Table 2.1 presents only some of the important labor legislations that have wide coverage.
17. For example, the Tamil Nadu government has permitted Dunlop to lay off its workers and the Uttar Pradesh government has allowed Paharpur Cooling Tower to close its unit.
18. The central government has given tax exemptions for voluntary retirement scheme (VRS) payments and introduced such schemes in many public sector undertakings. Most state governments have also introduced VRS in some state undertakings and have helped private sector firms to settle disputes on voluntary retirements.
19. The lean production model, for example, is one of the most influential new concepts that have guided modern management thinking about the organization of employment relationships.
20. In the last decade, labor flexibility has been a widely discussed subject in the conferences and meetings organized by the labor arms of Confederation of Indian Industry (CII), Bengal Chamber of Commerce and Industries (BCCI), and Employers' Federation of India (EFI).

21. Indian Telephone Industries and Indian Organic Chemicals Limited had external unions that became internal unions after a change in office holders (Mathur 1991: 91–129).
22. Employers are not always successful in remaining non-union. For example, DCM Toyota started as a non-union enterprise, but after some years they had to recognize a union (Mathur 1991: 61–90).
23. The budget of 2001–2002 proposed to increase labor market flexibility through amendment of the Industrial Disputes Act 1947 and the Contract Labor Act 1970. The proposed changes could not be implemented, but it certainly indicates a move for change in labor laws.

Chapter 3

Union Decline, Growing Inequality, and Divergences in Employment Relations

"Two most important significant socioeconomic events of our time are growing income inequality and decline of unions." This quotation is not from a book on growth of income inequality, nor it is from a book on union decline; it is the first line from a book on worldwide changes in employment relations by Katz and Darbishire (2000). In the 1980s and 1990s, the alarming reports of increases in income inequality in advanced industrial economies coincided with the reports on the sharp decline in union membership and union power. Several studies on relations between union density and wage inequality show that the declines in union density during that period accounts for a sizable portion of increases in wage inequality (Card 2001; DiNardo et al. 1996; Freeman 1993). Most studies that explain the relationship between the two indicators use aggregate data of the indicators. Katz and Darbishire (2000), however, take a different approach to explain the relationship. They use an institutional perspective to explain how union decline has increased income inequality. They argue that decline in union density and union power has led to increased variations in employment conditions across individuals and across firms and it has in turn led to increase in income inequality.

The influence of unions on wages and other conditions of work has been long debated in labor economics. The debate is on the extent and nature of influence, but there is no dispute over the fact that wherever unions exist, they influence wages and other conditions of work. Unions "alter nearly every measurable aspect of operation of work places and enterprises" (Freeman and Medoff 1984). They negotiate wages and fringe benefits for their members, and affect productivity, equality, and workers' involvement at workplaces. They also influence employment conditions of non-union workers through a spillover effect. Finally, unions as pressure groups contribute to passage of labor legislation for employment protection, workers' welfare, and occupational safety and health. In sum, unions affect many dimensions of employer–employee relations. Over the last three decades, increased economic pressures of globalization with privatization and deregulation have led to the decline of unions and changes in employment systems in all parts of the world. In the past, unionization ensured a high degree of standardization in employment conditions through collective agreements or otherwise. The expansion of non-union greenfield plants, non-union subsidiaries, subcontracting, outsourcing, and union derecognition has increased the share of the non-union sector. This has increased the variations in employment conditions across individuals, firms, and across industries. The changes are happening in all parts of the world, but there are some differences across countries as union influence varies across countries. This chapter presents a brief account of the structures and functions of trade unions in India, their changes over time, and how the changes have led to increasing variations in employment conditions.

Trade Unions in India: Structures and Functions

Trade unions exist in all parts of the world, but what a union is and what it does varies from country to country. Unions differ in their structure and functions, knowledge of which is essential in managing people at work. It helps managers and policy makers to understand the limitations and scope of unions and how they are linked to and influenced by external institutions. Looking at differences in membership structure, there are three types of unions: (*a*) crafts unions, which organize workers engaged in a single occupation, (*b*) industrial unions, which organize workers on the basis of an industry rather than craft, and (*c*) labor unions, which have all workers regardless of craft or industrial division as their members. The dominant organizational form of the Indian labor movement is the industrial union, such as unions in textile, jute, plantation, and engineering industries. There are only a few craft unions (for example, airline pilots associations, artists unions, and journalists unions). Industrial unions are typical in old industries, but most new firms have unions limited to a single firm or factory.

Based on geographical coverage, trade unions are classified as local unions, state federations, and national federations. In India, national-level and state-level labor unions generally operate as umbrella unions and varieties of unions are affiliated to them. Excepting a few, most of them are affiliated to political parties. Typically, plant-level unions form fundamental units of organization and it is to these units of organizations that the members belong in the first instance. Plant-level unions can be independent unions or affiliated to some political or non-political federation. Unions can be classified as internal unions or external unions based on the absence or presence of external leaders on their executive committees. Internal unions do not have any external leaders on their executive committees, while it is not so for external unions. Some firms have workers' committees that do not have the legal status of unions, but they perform nearly all functions of unions.[1] Most often, the plant-level unions being fundamental units of union organizations each of the unions have a constitution, an office, membership, and an identity under the Act signified by a registration number (Ramswamy 2000: 54). In old industries, however, typically industrial unions are the building blocks of the labor movement. In most newer industries, the legal existence of a union is at the plant level. As presented in Box 3.1, on the basis of differences in functions, trade unions are classified into different types: business unions, friendly unions, revolutionary unions and predatory unions (Hoxie 1920). In the

Box 3.1: Different Types of Unions by Functions

Business unions: They are essentially trade conscious, rather than class conscious. They express viewpoints and interests of workers in a craft or industry rather than those of the working class as a whole. Independent unions and craft unions are examples of business unions.

Friendly unions: They are characteristically idealistic in their viewpoint. They may be trade conscious, or broadly class conscious, and at times they even claim to think and act in the interest of the society as a whole. Essentially they are law abiding and conservative in their actions.

Revolutionary unions: They are extremely radical both in viewpoint and in action. They are distinctly class conscious rather than trade conscious. There are two distinct varieties: (*a*) socialist unions find their ultimate ideal in the socialistic state and ultimate means is in invoking class political action and (*b*) quasi anarchist unions consider agitation as legitimate means, rather than methods for immediate betterment.

Predatory unions: They are ruthless in pursuing their objectives by whatever means regardless of ethical and legal codes or effect upon those outside its own membership. Some of them always operate directly against the employers.

Source: Hoxie (1920).

Indian context, as in other countries, individual unions may not perfectly fit into any of the typical types, but there is no doubt that trade unions in India can be classified into different types in terms of their functions. One of the distinctive features of the Indian labor movement is the existence of large number of unions of self-employed workers. They are weak, but their characters and functions differ widely from the trade unions in the formal sector.

In India, the differences in the functions of unions are also seen in their affiliation to the state or national federations. The apex of the Indian labor movement comprises a number of central organizations that affiliate individual unions (Figure 3.1). There are a few non-political federations, but most union federations are explicitly political. The political parties control them and supply them with the upper crust of their leadership (Ramaswamy 2000). Every central trade union claims to have a unique ideology, though in practice it is not easy to discern much difference between them. The Indian National Trade Union Congress (INTUC) is inspired

Figure 3.1: Structure of Labor Unions and Their Affiliations

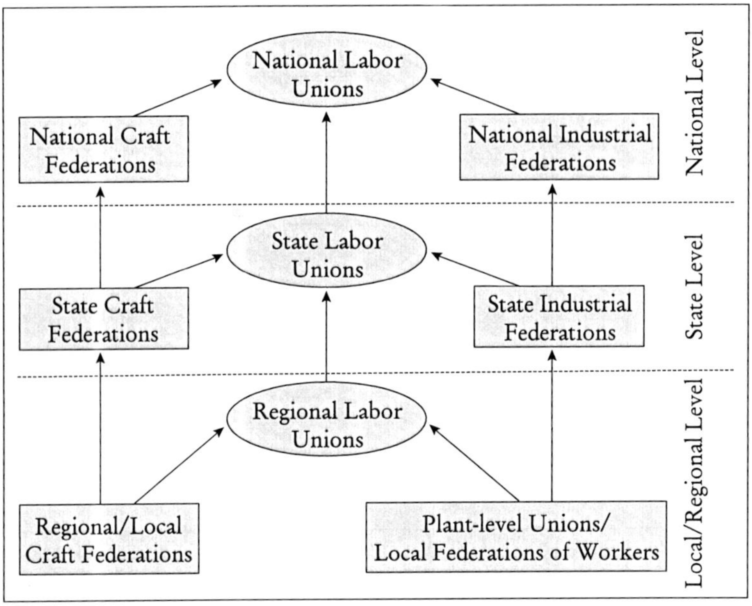

Source: Developed by author based on structure of unions.

by the Gandhian philosophy, with the principles of non-violence and emphasis on cooperation between employers and employees. The All India Trade Union Congress (AITUC) is the older of the two communist centers, but it is the Center of Indian Trade Union (CITU), which symbolizes radical Marxism in the Indian labor movement. The Hind Mazdoor Sabha (HMS) with its commitment to socialist ideology lies between the soft line of the INTUC and the radicalism of the communists. The Bharatiya Mazdoor Sangh (BMS) claims to be an independent and non-political union, but in practice it has close links to the Bharatiya Janata Party (BJP) (Ramaswamy 2000). The membership of major central trade unions in 1980, 1989, and 2002 is presented in Table 3.1. The central trade union organizations differ in their influence in different sectors and some of them put more efforts in organizing workers in the informal sector. Table 3.2 presents union membership of central trade unions in the formal and informal sectors.

Table 3.1: Membership of Central Trade Unions, 1980–2002 (Millions)[2]

Union/Year	*1980*	*1989*	*2002*
INTUC	3.51	2.69	3.95
BMS	1.88	3.12	6.22
HMS	1.84	1.48	3.34
UTUC (LS)	1.23	0.84	1.37
UTUC	0.61	0.58	0.61
NLO	0.41	0.14	0
TUCC	0.27	0.23	0.73
NFITU	0.53	0.53	0.60
AITUC	1.06	0.94	3.44
CITU	1.03	1.78	2.68
Others	–	–	1.94
Total	12.39	12.33	24.88

Source: Verification of Membership of Central Trade Unions, 2002 [Das (2008)].

Table 3.2: Membership of Central Trade Unions in Different Sectors (in '000)

		Unorganized Sector		
	Organized Sector	*Non-agriculture*	*Agriculture*	*Total*
BMS	2,842 (46)	2,037 (33)	1,336 (21)	6,216
INTUC	2,337 (59)	672 (17)	945 (24)	3,954
CITU	946 (35)	1,622 (61)	111 (4)	2,678
AITUC	894 (26)	1,078 (31)	1,470 (43)	3,442
HMS	1,816 (54)	866 (26)	656 (20)	3,338
UTUC (LS)	324 (24)	303 (22)	746 (54)	1,373
Others	712 (18)	789 (20)	2,381 (61)	3,883
Total	9,872 (40)	7,368 (30)	7,645 (31)	24,885

Source: Verification of Membership of Central Trade Unions, 2002.

Note: Figures in brackets are percent in total membership.

In India, the Trade Union Act 1926 recognizes workers' right to organize and engage in trade union activities and provides for registration of trade unions. Once a union is registered, it is formally considered as a union. The registration status is, therefore, a popular criterion for identification of unions, but it is not a necessary condition. In India, many workers' organizations are not registered under the Act, but they perform all functions of unions. An example of unregistered organizations is "Krishak Sabha," which is an organization of agricultural labors and small farmers affiliated to Communist Party of India (Marxist) [CPI(M)]. Another example is the government employees' organizations. They are not registered under the Act because of restrictions in their service rules.[3] Therefore, they are not unions under the Act, but on many occasions they have organized strikes and actively bargained with the government for benefits of their members. In the government sector, the railway workers, however, enjoy all trade union rights at par with the other industrial workers and can get their organizations registered under the Act.

Union Membership and Union Density

The two indicators frequently used to indicate union influence are union membership and union density (Korpi 1983; Shorter and Tilly 1974). Union membership gives a count of total number of union members in a firm, in an industrial sector, or in a country. Union density, which is the ratio of actual to potential members, is used to explain growth or decline of unions or to compare levels of unionization across industrial sectors or across countries. The knowledge of the two indicators is not only important for policy makers entrusted with the formulation of industrial and labor policies, it is also important for unions and managers to understand their bargaining positions. In recent times, low union density has become an important subject in discussions on linking trade with labor rights. It is sometimes argued that the low level of unionization in developing countries is leading to exploitation of workers, and hence there is need to strengthen labor rights.

In India, the estimates on union membership and union density as published in various documents indicate very low levels of unionization. The International Labor Organization (ILO) in its World Employment Report 1997–1998, documents trade union density in India to be 5.4 percent of salary and wage earners. Some researchers even compute union density as low as 2 percent of total labor force (Kuruvilla 1996; Venkataratnam 1997). All these indicate extremely low levels of unionization in India compared to other countries, but this is not the real picture. It is hard for union leaders, managers, and labor officials to believe that unions in India represent such a negligible percentage of workers. In fact, plant-level evidence in several studies of large firms indicates a very high level of union activity in the formal sector[4] (Table 3.3). The low estimates are because of inaccurate data on union membership published in the *Indian Labor Yearbook*. The published reports in the *Yearbook* do not include reports from all states in India. Further, the reports include only membership of unions submitting returns.[5] An assumption here is that the unions that do not submit their return do not exist, but this is hardly a valid assumption. In practice, majority of the registered unions in India do not submit their returns regularly. The inaccurate estimates have led to poor understanding of union strength in the country. In this chapter, an estimates include membership data of all the states with corrections for unions that have not submitted their returns. The results are far different from what is published in the *Indian Labor Yearbook*. The estimate for 2002, for example,

Table 3.3: Unionization in Large Firms

State	*Sector*	*Year*	*Union Density (%)*	*Source*
West Bengal	Tea Plantations	1991	96	Bhowmik (1992)
West Bengal	Jute	1990	100	Sen (1992)
West Bengal	Coal	1991	100	Sen (1992)
West Bengal	Engineering	1990	90	Sen (1992)
All India	Ports and Docks	1990	100	Vaidya and Arora (1992)
Andhra Pradesh	Automobiles	1990	71	Guptan (1992)
Andhra Pradesh	Engineering	1990	97	Guptan (1992)
Andhra Pradesh	Electronics	1990	71	Guptan (1992)
Uttar Pradesh	Glass Industry	1993	72	Raghuvanshi (1993)
Maharashtra	Chemicals and Pharmaceuticals	1991	80	Davala (1992)

shows the presence of 56.7 million union members in the country in place of 6.3 million reported in the *Indian Labor Yearbook*.[6]

Union density is defined as the ratio of union members to potential union members. There are some measurement issues in computation of union density. First, there is a dilemma about choice of potential members. The possible choices are: (*a*) wage and salaried workers, (*b*) workers in non-agricultural sector, (*c*) wage and salaried workers in non-agricultural sector, (*d*) workers in the formal sector, and (*e*) all workers. Depending on what aspect of IR one is interested in, one can choose from the different choices and compute union density. For example, if one is interested in union influence on government's policy, the most appropriate indicator is gross union density calculated as a percentage of union members to the total workforce. Similarly, if a manager is interested in knowing the probability of unionization in a unit, the most important is the union density measured as a percentage of formal-sector workers. Of the different choices, the most popular is the unionization among the wage-employed workers. It is most widely used as a comparative indicator for measuring impact of trade unions on firms and labor markets (Ebbinghaus et al. 2001; Freeman and Medoff 1984). Computation of union density needs to follow a standard procedure so that the estimates can be used to compare unionization across countries and over time. Unfortunately, the available estimates in India do not follow this standard approach. This chapter computes union membership after making necessary corrections for incomplete data and then follows the standard procedure followed in developed countries to compute union density. The results show union density as 31 percent of wage-employed workers in 2002, which is much higher than the estimates published by ILO and other studies referred to earlier.

Multiplicity of Unions and Small Size of Unions

Data on union membership and union density serves as a useful starting point for study of cross-national trends in unionization, but to understand IR practices and arrangements, one needs to consider issues and factors beyond unionization rates. The Indian Trade Unions Act 1926 stipulates that any group of seven workers or more can register itself as a trade union. It allows registration of multiple unions in a firm or industry. Further, it does not stipulate a means of determining which union is representative of workers, and thus any number of unions can claim to represent workers in a given workplace. As the Act does not have any legal provision for recognition of trade unions, it thereby creates an opportunity-structure for the coexistence of multiple unions in a single firm or industry.[7] It allows "union entrepreneurs" to form a union and deliver its services to workers for a price. Partly because of the liberal provisions in the Act on formation of unions, many workplaces in India have multiple unions and many of the unions are small.[8] The Act, by allowing the presence of multiple unions in a workplace, curtails the strength of unionized labor. Multiple unions within a workplace are not as powerful in their relations with management as a single union would be. This is partly because unions are often more interested in scoring against each other than against management due to their ties with the political parties. Fragmentation of unionized labor is often cited as the primary reason for the weak voice of organized labor in India (Rudolph and Rudolph 1987: 277).

In India, most trade unions have links to some political party or the other. Some unions are independent of political parties, but most unions are linked to union federations that are either wings of political parties or at least affiliated to political parties in some way or the other. The ties between union federations and different political parties have frequently resulted in polarization of union federations. This is partly because political parties often use union federations as weapons of political rivalry. This link of unions to political parties has prevented emergence of an apex organization that may represent a significant majority of unionized labor. Thus, whereas the American Federation of Labor-Congress of Industrial Organizations (AFL-CIO) in the US, the German Confederation of Trade Unions (Deutscher Gewerkschaftsbund) (DGB) in Germany, and the Trade Union Congress (TUC) in the UK are each empowered by a majority of union members in their countries, none of India's federations/confederations have been empowered in this way. However, the ties between unionized labor and political parties have not necessarily been all bad for the unionized labor. Union federations have used affiliated political parties and the governments that these parties have led for various kinds of protections (Kuruvilla and Hiers 1997). This dependency, however, has also made unions vulnerable to withdrawal of such protection.

Indian trade unions are small in comparison to unions in developed countries. The *Indian Labor Yearbook* reports the average size of unions for different years based on samples of unions submitting returns. The average size of unions was 790 during 1991–2000 and it varied from state to state.[9] In India, most unions are small and there are only few large unions. In West Bengal, for example, 80 percent of the unions in 1998 had less than 250 members. The size distribution of unions is somewhat similar to those seen in the UK in the 1950s and it is similar to the size distribution of firms (Hart and Brown 1957). This is not surprising because unions grow in the same way as firms: some expand more rapidly than others, some shrink and die, some swallow others, new ones are created, and big ones are formed by amalgamations. In most developed countries, the number of unions has fallen over time with increasing merger activity and growing concentration.[10] In India, however, there have not been similar changes. On the contrary, the fragmentation of political parties has led to further fragmentation of unions, and the fragments have become smaller over the years.

Unionization across Sectors and across States

Universally, there are wide variations in trade union activities across sectors and across employments. The differences are in terms of density, intensity, and strength of unions. In India, there are similar variations in unionization.[11] The levels of unionization are higher in manufacturing, transport, or public administration than in agriculture, trade, or financial services. Unionization is very high in mining, storage, and communication, and in some sectors it is almost total (Sheth 1993: 232). As in other countries, union density in India is higher in the public sector than in the private sector (Venkataratnam and Varma 1997). While most formal-sector firms have high levels of unionization, the majority of workers in the informal sector and agriculture are without any union power.

Table 3.4: Central Union Membership Density in Different Industrial Sectors

Industrial Sector	*Membership as % of Workers*	*Industrial Sector*	*Membership as % of Workers*
Agriculture	4.3	Iron and steel	28.2
Tea plantation	48.1	Textile	23.2
Mining and quarry	79.9	Electricity, gas, and power	54.5
Coal mining	100.0	Transport	30.6
Construction	17.0	Roadways	14.0
Manufacturing	15.4	Railways	100.0
Chemicals	9.2	Services	4.0
Sugar	32.8	Financial institution	8.6
All workers	8.0	Hotels and restaurants	3.3

Source: Verification of Membership of Central Trade Unions 2002, published in January 2008; NSSO Data on Wage-Employment 2003, 59th Round.

The more formalized a sector, the higher is its unionization rate. This is seen both in the data published in the *Indian Labor Yearbook* and in the results of Verification of Membership of Central Trade Union Organizations (Table 3.4). Unionization is higher in large firms than in small firms.[12] This is partly because the possibility of initiating and retaining collective bargaining is better in large firms. Unionization also varies among different types of workers. It is higher among blue-collar or factory workers than among white-collar workers or clerical staff.[13] It is higher among permanent workers than among contract or casual workers. Further, unionization for casual and contract workers also vary across industrial sectors depending on whether they work for the public sector or private sector.[14]

In India, there is considerable difference in trade union activity across states. The membership of Central Trade Union Organizations and their membership as a percentage of wage-employed workers in some major states are shown in Table 3.5. It clearly shows variations in trade union activity across states. In some states like West Bengal and Kerala, workers are more organized than in other parts of the country.[15] The differences are to be seen

Table 3.5: Membership of Central Trade Unions in Major States

State	*Wage-employed Workers ('000)*	*Trade Unions*							
		BMS	*INTUC*	*CITU*	*AITUC*	*HMS*	*Others*	*Total*	*Union Density (% of Wage-employed)*
Haryana	2,935	140	3	23	53	30	43	293	9.99
Karnataka	9,106	23	95	78	19	135	36	387	4.25
Assam	3,345	43	336	44	32	51	34	539	16.10
Punjab	3,685	265	83	9	183	53	0	593	16.08
Chhattisgarh	3,317	204	295	13	32	57	0	600	18.10
Gujarat	8,006	163	52	4	16	23	540	797	9.96
Rajasthan	8,200	448	25	26	180	237	2	917	11.18
MP	8,983	547	223	12	51	17	107	958	10.66
Uttar Pradesh	18,499	449	304	17	44	190	51	1,055	5.70
Kerala	3,873	152	71	659	217	134	60	1,293	33.38
Tamil Nadu	11,172	93	218	255	173	146	625	1,508	13.50
Maharashtra	16,340	526	448	39	100	410	2	1,526	9.34
Jharkhand	3,032	301	141	34	117	398	652	1,644	54.23
Orissa	4,509	462	315	29	143	729	17	1,696	37.61
Bihar	9,900	366	325	7	865	162	681	2,407	24.31
AP	13,656	1330	242	207	529	153	0	2,461	18.02
West Bengal	10,827	137	499	1127	576	251	2,311	4,901	45.27
All India	14,7191	6,216	3,954	2,678	3,405	3,338	5,256	24,848	16.88

Source: Verification of Membership of Central Trade Unions, 2002 [Das (2008)].

in conjunction with structural differences of unions across states. Structurally, unions in Gujarat, are mostly organized at the enterprise or unit level and not affiliated to any state or national federations (an exception is the textile industry), and the state has few apex unions.[16] In contrast, West Bengal has many trade union federations (jute, textile, engineering, and plantation), and most unions in the state are affiliated to state and national-level apex unions. In the informal sector, West Bengal has a higher level of unionization than in Gujarat.

Growth and Decline of Trade Unions

In developed countries, there has been progressive decline in union membership, union density, and union popularity in the last three decades. The decline is evident in the time series data of the two indicators for industrialized countries; they show that the decline started in the late 1960s and early 1970s. The growth and decline of trade unions in USA, UK, Germany, and Sweden are shown in Figure 3.2. In the NICs, union decline started in the 1980s and 1990s. In Mexico, labor unions made significant inroads in the 1970s, but with economic restructuring in the 1980s, they started to lose their power. In Korea and Taiwan, unions started to

Figure 3.2: Growth and Decline of Trade Unions 1950–2003

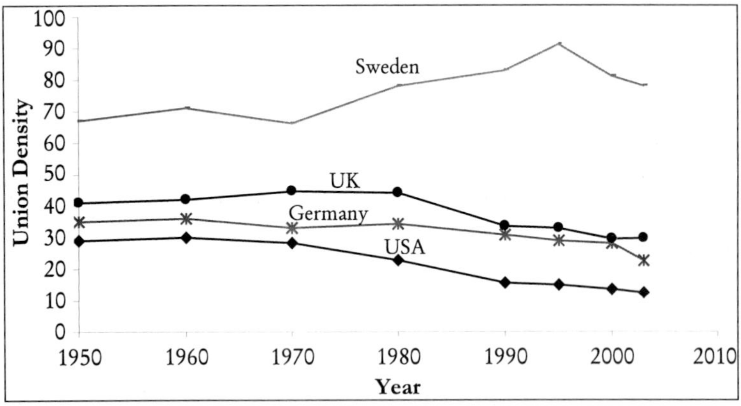

Source: Hirsch and Macpherson 2000; ILO 1993; Visser 2006.

grow in the 1980s and in the initial years of 1990s, but then they started to decline (ILO 1998). In India, the union membership and union density data do not show similar decline, but there are clear indications of decline in union power since the early 1990s (ILO 1997; Kuruvilla et al. 2002). The estimates of union membership and union density (measured as a percentage of union membership among wage-employed workers) and their changes over time are presented in Table 3.6. It shows that both union membership and union density have steadily increased over the years. In India, the absence of reliable union membership data does not allow us to evaluate changes in union membership and union density over the years with considerable accuracy. This chapter computes union membership by using primary data of number of registered unions and average size of unions.[17] In this method of computation, one may object that some of the registered unions may not exist. This is, however, somewhat compensated as some associations of workers perform all functions of unions, but do not get them registered as unions. Examples of this include associations of government employees, organizations of agricultural workers affiliated to CPI(M), and some workers' committees.

The changes in union membership and union density in India do not indicate decline of the two indicators similar to those seen in the developed countries. There are, however, enough indications of decline of union power in the post-reform years. The state-level data on registration of new unions indicate a decline in registration of new unions in the post-reform era. Further, most new unions are in the informal sector. There are indications that union membership has increased in the informal sector, but it has declined in the formal sector. The shift of unionization to the informal sector has a major implication, as unions in the informal sector are not as strong as the unions in the formal sector.[18] Another indication is that in the post-reform period, there has been growth of non-union firms, and increasingly firms are adopting union avoidance strategies to remain non-union. For example, some employers are promoting workers into administrative/supervisory ranks to take them outside the purview of the Industrial Disputes Act. The loss of job in the public sector through VRS and closures or privatization of inefficient and "sick" public

Table 3.6: Growth of Registered Trade Unions in India

				Unions Submitted Returns				
Year	*All Workers (mn)*	*Wage-employed (mn)*	*Number of Unions*	*Number*	*Membership (mn)*	*Average Size*	*Union Membership (mn)*	*Union Density*
1951	140.0	54.6	4,623	2,556	2.00	781	3.61	6.6
1961	160.2	63.6	11,614	7,087	3.98	561	6.52	10.2
1971	180.4	70.4	22,484	9,029	5.47	606	13.63	19.4
1976	210.2	85.1	29,350	9,778	6.09	666	20.20	23.7
1981	240.0	101.7	37,539	6,682	5.01	808	26.85	26.4
1986	279.0	124.6	45,830	11,365	7.37	720	34.01	27.3
1991	318.0	147.6	53,535	8,418	6.10	725	41.16	27.9
1996	360.6	164.2	58,988	7,242	5.60	773	46.92	28.6
2001	403.2	180.9	66,624	6,531	5.87	900	54.77	30.3

Source: Indian Labor Yearbook; see Das (2008) for detailed estimates.

Note: Union Density = Membership as percentage of wage-employed workers.
Indian Labor Yearbook is an annual publication of the Labor Bureau, Ministry of Labour, Government of India.

sector units has also contributed to decline in union membership and union density in the organized sector. All these have led to decline in union power.

The available data on union membership do not indicate decline of trade unions in India in the post-reform period, but the changes in the economic and social contexts give a clear picture of changes in union influence. In the pre-liberalization period, unions developed in an environment that protected both industry and labor and this led to progressive growth in union membership and union density. The new economic policy removed many of the protections and this has led to decline in union power. There has not been any major change in labor legislation, but economic liberalization has put pressure on the Indian IR institutions to change and has affected the behaviors of unions (Kuruvilla 1996). With the withdrawal of industrial licensing in the post-liberalization period, the states are now actively lobbying, and hence competing for both national and international capital investment and adopting industry-friendly policies. This has weakened labor's tie with the political parties and government support has shifted toward employers' side (Kuruvilla 1996). With the shift in the balance of power in favor of the employers, they are now more aggressive in dealing with the unions and workers. In various locations, they are adopting practices that help them to avoid unionization or curtail union power. In the post-reform era, the changes are leading to decline of union coverage and union power.

Union Decline, Growing Inequality, and Divergences in Employment Relations

In advanced industrialized countries, there have been progressive decline in union density and union power over the last three decades. Evidence shows that the decline in union density in the developed countries during the period accounts for a sizable portion of increase in income inequality. The relationship between earnings inequality and union density is a widely researched subject in labor economics. Unions reduce wage inequality within establishments, across establishments, and between blue-collar and white-collar workers. They not only influence wages in the union sector, they also indirectly influence wages in the non-union sector through intra-industry and inter-industry threat effects. Threats of unionization motivate firms to increase wages and introduce practices of union firms (Leicht et al. 1993). Further, union influence is not limited to wages or wage distribution, they also affect non-wage fringe benefits and other components of income, such as rent, dividends, social security, and employee welfare. Unionized firms generally allot more funds to deferred forms of compensation, such as pensions, insurance, and vacation pay.[19] All these have an equalizing effect on wages and non-wage benefits. As unions provide an equalizing force, decline of unions leads to increases in income and wage inequalities and variations in employment conditions.

The decline of unions and increases in income inequality in advanced industrialized countries accompanied growing variations in employment relation practices. In a study of automobile and telecommunication industries in seven industrialized countries, Katz and Darbishire (2000) explain the phenomenon of increase of income inequality with decline of unions by using an institutional approach. They argue that unionization ensures high degree of standardization in employment conditions and uniformity in treatment of employees through collective agreements or otherwise (like arbitration). As a result, there are lesser variations in employment conditions in union sector than in non-union sector. Decline of unions thus leads to increasing variations in employment systems and increase in earnings inequality. The growth of non-union sectors through expansion of non-union subsidiaries, outsourcing, opening of non-union greenfield plants, and union avoidance strategy has contributed to increased variations in employment relations. Inequality has increased both within union and non-union sectors, but the increases are more within the union sector.[20] Further, there has been a decline of union–non-union earnings inequality. This indicates that the union sector has become more similar to the non-union sector. In the union sector, union decline has led to decentralization of bargaining through disappearance or weakening of the strengths and coverage of centralized bargaining.[21] More and more issues are now decided at the firm level than at the industry level and increasingly wages are now linked to individual performance and skill. Use of contract labor has also increased overall wage variations as contract workers get lower wages than regular workers.

In India, the changes in wage inequality and union power in the post-reform period are similar to those seen in the industrialized countries in the 1980s and 1990s: unions have lost their power and influence and income inequality has increased. The decline in union power and increase in income inequality in India, however, are not as pronounced as in the developed countries. In India, there are many studies on changes in income inequality; they differ in their methods, but all show significant increases in inequality in the post-reform period (Datt 1999; Dev and Ravi 2007; Gupta 1995). In India, as unionization is mainly in the formal sector, the changes in wage inequality and union power are thus particularly important in the formal sector. There is no aggregate data available on distribution of wages for formal-sector workers, but the available piecemeal evidence shows growing wage inequality in the formal sector in the post-reform period. At the plant level, there has been increasing variation in wages with increasing wage gaps between managers and workers; and also among blue-collar workers. Increase in wage inequality in the formal sector is also evident in the fact that in overall changes in inequality in India, the increase is higher in urban sector, where majority of the formal sector workers live.[22] All these indicate that the decline of unions has been accompanied with increases in income and wage inequality. In industrialized countries, the decline of union and increase in income inequality has been accompanied with increased variations in employment relation practices. In India there have been similar changes in employment relation practices the post-reform era. In the subsequent chapters, we examine the changes in employment relation practices in different industrial sectors and compare them with those in the industrialized countries. The findings indicate that the changes in India in the post-reform era are similar to those seen in the developed countries.

Notes

1. Out of 185 units in Maharashtra surveyed by Davala (1992), 176 units (95 percent) had unions. The remaining units did not have any formal unions, but many of them had committees of workers.
2. Major Central Trade Unions are those having more than one million members. Others include Labour Progressive Federation (LPF) (0.61 million members), All India Central Council of Trade Unions (AICCTU)

(0.64 million members), and Self Employed Women's Association (SEWA) (0.69 million members).

3. The Trade Union Act does not restrict government employees to form unions, but the Civil Service (Conduct) Rules of the central government and the state governments restrict government employees to form trade unions.
4. Venkataratnam and Varma (1997) found unionization to be 90 percent in the public sector and 60 percent in the formal private sector.
5. In 2000, out of 65,286 registered unions in the country, only 7,224 unions submitted annual returns and reported their membership as 5.4 million (Government of India 2003: 125).
6. This is in parity with the rough estimate by Roy (1993: 2777) and also with the results of Verification of Membership of Central Trade Unions, 2002, Ministry of Labour, Government of India.
7. There are some state-level initiatives. Andhra Pradesh has a system of election for recognition of a single union in an organization, but few such elections are held. During 1995–1998, only 179 elections were held, while the state had about 10,000 registered unions (Labor Commissioner Office, Andhra Pradesh). The elections are under the "Code of Discipline in Industry" ratified at the sixteenth session of the Indian Labor Conference. In West Bengal, the state amendment of the Trade Unions Act 1926 provides for recognition of unions, but so far only few firms have had such elections (Government of West Bengal 2006).
8. Multiplicity of unions is more prominent in West Bengal. Most tea gardens have multiple unions; only 20 percent have single union (Bhowmik 1992: 28). All jute mills have multiple unions (Sen 1992: 47). In Maharashtra, out of 176 units studied by Davala (1992), 132 units had single union, and 39 had two competing unions.
9. In 1993, while the average size of unions in Gujarat was 950, it was 355 in Haryana. This variation across states is partly because the structure of the unions varies from state to state and partly because the states having larger firms have larger unions.
10. In the UK, unions with 100,000 or more members account for almost 90 percent of all TUC-affiliated trade union membership and the eight largest unions account for over 60 percent of total membership (Black et al. 1997; Buchanan 1992).
11. Of the total membership of central trade unions, the manufacturing group contributes the largest share (29 percent), followed by the transport, storage, and communication group (23 percent).
12. Unionization is 70 percent in mining (average firm size of 333), 15 percent in manufacturing (average firm size of 41), and 2.4 percent in shops and establishments (approximately 1.3 workers per firm) (Source: *Indian Labor Yearbook*). In Andhra Pradesh, Guptan (1992) found unionization to be 15 percent in small firms, 68 percent in medium firms, and 89 percent in large firms.

13. The interests of the clerical staff are different from those of blue-collar workers. In many units, the clerical staffs are not members of regular unions; they have separate unions (Davala 1992).
14. In West Bengal, Sen (1992: 161) found that in the engineering industry, unionization in the private sector was 87 percent for permanent workers and only 10 percent for casual and contract workers. In the public sector, it was 92 percent for permanent workers and 28 percent for casual and contract workers. In Andhra Pradesh, Guptan (1992) found unionization in large engineering firms to be almost total for permanent workers, but only 5 percent for casual workers and only 1 percent for contract workers. In Maharashtra, Davala (1992) found that only 12 percent of units had unions of contract workers.
15. Jharkhand and Orissa also have higher level of unionization, but these are mostly in agriculture.
16. Gujarat Engineering and General Kamadar Union, Gujarat Trade Union Council (Mookherjee 1996).
17. The average size of unions is based on a sample of unions. The number of registered unions includes reports of the previous years if there are no reports for a particular year.
18. In Karnataka, the increase in number of trade unions per annum was 8.5 percent during 1981–1985, but only 3.5 per cent during 1991–1995 (Patil 1998). In West Bengal, 2,661 new unions were registered during 1981–1985, but only 1,524 during 1991–1995. Fewer new unions were registered in 1995 than in 1985, but the share of informal sector unions was higher in 1995 (63 percent) than in 1985 (43 percent).
19. Wage contributes about 50–70 percent of the total income inequality, but other components of income are also equally important. Decomposition of income inequality into different components shows that pension has more equalizing effect than wage (Fei et al. 1978; Pyatt et al. 1980; Shorrocks 1982).
20. An analysis of the labor survey data in the US shows that the main reason for increases in earning inequality is the growth of the non-union sector. In the United States, growth of the non-union sector accounts for about 90 percent of the overall increase in wage inequality.
21. In the textile industry, the last industry-wide agreement in West Bengal was concluded in 1995. Now there are only firm-level agreements. In the engineering industry, many firms have come out of the industry-wide agreement and only a small part of their wages and other benefits are now decided on the basis of industry-wide agreement (for example, Alstom AEI, Alstom Paharpur).
22. The Gini Co-efficient of inequality increased from 28.55 in 1993–1994 to 30.45 in 2004–2005 for rural area and from 34.31 in 1993_94 to 37.51 in 2004–2005 for urban area (Dev and Ravi 2007).

Chapter 4

Divergences in Employment Systems in the Indian Textile Industry

Most studies on changes in employment relations in industrialized countries have especially focussed on automobile and telecommunications industries. This is because these two industries are important in industrialized countries, both in share of employment and share of total industrial production. In the United States, for example, the auto industry directly employs roughly 1 percent of the workforce, and auto-related industries engage another 1 percent. The telecommunications industry likewise is a major employer in most developed countries (Katz and Darbishire 2000: 3). While the two industries have substantial direct employment effects in developed countries, industrial structures of developing countries are somewhat different. The differences are in terms of share of various industries in employment and industrial production and their importance in the economies. In India, the automobile and telecommunications industries are fast growing, but they still represent only a small and negligible percentage in terms of both employment and industrial production. In contrast, the textile industry engages a large number of workers and contributes a large proportion of industrial output. In India, the textile and garment sector now employs about 35 million workers, contributes 14 percent of industrial output, 4 percent of GDP, and 17 percent of exports.[1] Apart from its importance in Indian economy, wide variations across textile firms in products, size, technology use, unionization, and management strategy make it an ideal sector for study of employment relations in India.

Textile Mills in India

India developed a modern textile industry in its early days of industrialization using indigenous cotton, cheap labor, access to British machinery, and a well-developed mercantile tradition. By 1950, it was among the leading nations in textile production, but then the industry receded steadily, both in share of world trade and its importance in industrialization process. This was because the policy regime in the pre-liberalization period relatively insulated the industry from world trade and investments. In India, the main source of growth for the industry was the domestic market, which was large but consumed low-quality products and grew slowly. The main sources of textile machinery in the early 1980s were the domestic producers, who had limited access to new technology. The industry was then largely characterized by poor capability and quality in terms of global standards. The policy changes in the late 1980s and early 1990s included two major changes. First, new policies encouraged export of textiles, import of textile machinery, and import of generic intermediaries. As a result, costs of resources of acquiring new capabilities came down from what they were in the protected market. Second, deregulation removed the barriers to expansion of mills and power looms. The changes started in 1985 with the new Textile Policy, which was then reiterated in the Textile (Control) Order of 1993. In spite of many difficulties and multiple phases of recession, the industry has shown considerable growth in production of yarn, fabric, and garments. The industry now plays a leading sector role in India with competitive advantages in availability of cotton, cheap labor, and accumulated knowledge in making textile products (Roy 1998: 2173).

The Indian textile and clothing industry is a large multi-sector industry in transition within the developing economy. In addition to natural fibers, such as cotton, silk, wool, and jute, the industry also uses a wide range of synthetic and man-made fibers. It covers a wide range of industrial production activities, which can be segregated into four distinct processes: spinning, weaving, processing, and garment making. Of these, garment making is not part of the mainstream textile mills. Most garment manufacturing is in the small-scale sector. In the past, most textile mills were composite mills that combined spinning, weaving, and textile processing operations in a single unit. Many of these mills have either closed down permanently or went through major restructuring. Few large mills now extend their activities beyond spinning and include weaving as a part of their production process. These mills that still operate as composite mills are mostly involved in specialized high-end products (example: Jayashree Textiles). Now spinning of both cotton and man-made fiber is mostly in large units, while fabric production and textile processing are mostly in the small sector.[2]

Textile firms in India differ widely in terms of their products, structure, and performance. This chapter presents case studies of a number of textile units that indicate the differences. While majority of old textile mills are now closed or sick, those that survived have restructured with heavy investments in new technology. In the textile industry, labor inflexibility is a major problem in the unionized setting. Only few firms have been able to acquire functional flexibility through multi-skilling and other programs, but numerical flexibility is still difficult to achieve because of legal restrictions. Even if a unit receives more orders, it has problems in accepting such orders, as additional workers if engaged cannot be retrenched.[3] The major part of production in the industry now comes from new units that are small in size and more flexible. The changes indicate disintegration of traditional production structure in the textile industry with separation spinning, weaving, and textile processing (Das and Panayiotopoulos 1996: L 58–59). New firms have come up in attractive locations that have competitive advantage, and this has led to closure of old units in other locations. In West Bengal, for example, there were nineteen textile mills in the private sector in 1980s; of them only five were in operation in 2003. The withdrawal of industrial licensing and discontinuation of freight equalization along with other reasons have made West Bengal unattractive for textile mills. This has led to the closure of many units. However, there are exceptions. Jayashree Textiles, which is a composite mill in an old location has emerged stronger over time and has increased its production, productivity, and profitability.

Textile mills differ in their structures and operations. Some are spinning mills, while others combine spinning, weaving, and textile processing. Some have less than ten workers, while others engage more than a thousand workers. Some produce for the low-cost domestic market, while others produce for high-quality export markets. Textile mills differ in the use of technology and skill. For example, in textile processing, the three sub-sectors, hand-processing units, independent power processing units, and facilities attached to composite mills, exhibit wide differences in use of technology and skill. In hand-processing units, most shop floor personnel do not have any scientific knowledge of dyes, chemicals, machines, and processes; their only knowledge is through their experience in work. The culture for quality and innovative work practices is almost absent here. Most independent power processing units use low or medium-level technology. Only a few that cater to higher segments in markets have state-of-the-art technology. In contrast, most processing units in composite mills use modern machines, qualified technical personnel, and in-house testing facilities, and have emphasis on quality (Government of India 2002: 30).

Use of modern technology is not uniform across different segments in the Indian textile and clothing sector. In the 1990s, firms in the spinning sector have seen massive investments in new technology and import of textile machinery.[4] With these changes, the Indian spinning sector has performed extremely well in the second half of the 1990s. Its world market share touched 30 percent in 1997. The level of technology used in the weaving sector is, however, low compared to those in other countries. In India, the power loom sector has less than 1 percent shuttleless looms. Textile firms differ in their business strategy: some follow a low-wage, low technology, and low-quality strategy, while others follow a high-quality, high-skill, and high-technology strategy. They also differ in terms of their supply chains.

The globally competitive countries have significantly consolidated their supply chain. In Indian textile industry, the supply chain has consolidated in some areas, but in most areas it is still fragmented.

Wide variations across textile units in terms of their products, size of units, technology use, management strategy, and other characteristics have led to increasing variation in employment relations across textile firms. This chapter identifies the dominant patterns of employment relations in the textile industry and examines how the shares of different patterns have changed over time. It also examines how the differences in firm characteristics and management strategies contribute to variations in firms' employment practices. As a large number of firms in the textile industry are small firms, we start our discussion with the stories of two small textile units in the next section. The subsequent sections present case studies of five medium and large firms. The firms in this study have been so chosen that they can capture the dominant patterns of employment relations in the Indian textile industry and their changes over time.

Bharti and Jyothi—Two Small Textile Units

Small firms dominate the Indian textile and garment sector. They are involved in different activities in the total production chain. The garment sub-sector traditionally has small firms, but increasingly, small firms are also emerging in other sub-sectors. In the past, composite mills combined all activities—spinning, weaving, and textile processing—under a single roof, but over time their structures have fragmented. Fabric production has shifted to the power loom sector, and textile processing is now mostly done in small processing units. Most spinning still takes place in large firms; however, small spinning units are also coming up in different locations. In the small scale sector, employee control is in general "simple control," and the employment system is "paternalistic system." Most employers in these small firms operate without any external influence in controlling their employees. However, small firms in clusters that cooperate with each other for common services are subjected to external influences. We present here employment practices in two small textile units.

Jyothi Weaving is a small unit, both in terms of number of machines and number of employees (ten employees). It is not registered under the Factories Act and it does not have any union. In this unit, the centrality of owner, his self-image, and informality is the main driving force in the firm's operations. The business is seen as his possession and he does as he wishes. His personality and attitudes have major influence in the process of organizing workers. He has close supervision on his workers, he sits in the workplace, sees all problems, and solves them immediately. The system emphasizes the importance of non-formal channels of management and interconnected relationships between the employers and the employed at an individual and person-to-person level. Family and friendship ties between the employers and the workers influence their decisions. The close individual relationships establish a form of organic solidarity within the firms. This solidarity, however, should not be always taken as harmony, as it is partly due to submission of workers to employers' authority. This system of management has great strength in achieving motivation and commitment, but at times, it is at the price of precariousness for the workers.

Procedural informality is a key characteristic of management in small firms. This is not only in terms of lack of existence of any written or formal procedure, it is also evident in the employer's actions. Labor relation here shows little evidence of pre-planning. As long as the workers are working, the employer does not see any problem in the relationship. The employer would initially do very little to offend an employee until he/she can bear it no longer. If a conflict develops, emotions become highly charged, and usually the employee is told to leave the firm. Management policy is not formulated in a self-conscious pattern; informal routine plays a large part in the day-to-day running of firms. The minimalist form of management is allied to employers' belief that they know what is best for their firm and everyone in it. This possessiveness together with self-evaluations stressing fairness, even-handedness, and reasonableness leads them to believe in their primacy over the labor process. On some occasions, the employer consults senior workers, but he makes all decisions. The firm uses informal methods of recruitment through personalized networks and relies on subjective assessments in selections. There is extensive use of family labor and part-time employment. This system of management minimizes the potential for collective action on behalf of workers and as a result, most small firms do not have any union (Vrijendra 1995: 713). In brief, employee control in small firms is simple control with employers exercising unlimited authority over their employees.

Bharti Knitwear is a small firm of ten employees, which is a part of the knitwear production cluster in Kolkata. It operates on a contract basis, knitting fabrics for traders who supply yarn and pay knitting charges. The cluster has a large number of small firms engaged in different operations that include production of hosiery cloth, hosiery garments, bleaching, dyeing, screen printing, and so on. In this cluster, an interesting aspect of the production system is the way various components of knitwear production fit together. The process begins with industry centers and knitwear companies that manufacture nothing, but put everything out for production in different small units. Yarn enters the complex from spinning mills; it goes to fabrication units for production of knitted fabric. The fabric is then sent out to various units, where it is cut, stitched, checked, ironed, and packed to produce the final garments. The units of production are connected through tasks or labor service contracts called "job-work." Finally, the garment goes either to the firm that is the final seller or to various market intermediaries. The traders are pseudo-manufacturers and have no direct stake in production. They are not responsible for statutory obligations, such as factory licenses, contribution to provident funds, Employee State Insurance (ESI), and gratuity, but they ultimately control the deployment of labor power.

Bharti Knitwear, being a unit in an industrial cluster, is subjected to cluster norms that restrict employers' absolute authority. In the cluster, the different activities are so integrated that a unit cannot be studied in isolation of other units. There are three forms of integration: horizontal (across the range of different operations), backward (integration into yarn spinning units), and forward (integration into marketing). The presence of employers' associations and trade unions reestablishes the close link between different firms. In West Bengal, the hosiery industry has four employers' associations representing different groups of employers: one for knitters, one for bleachers and dyers, one for tailors and cutters, and the other for traders or brand owners.[5] There are seven workers' unions, each affiliated to different political parties. Agreements between the employers' associations and workers' unions determine the wage rates, productivity norms, and other conditions of work.

In the cluster, the industry-wide agreement covers major issues on wages and other conditions of work, but there are some differences in its coverage and implementation of the agreement. There are often complaints about non-implementation of agreements in some parts of the cluster and there are continuous negotiations at different levels and for different parts of the industry. The unions put pressure for uniformity in wages across firms and across different operations, but the differences still exist. Workers in bleaching and dyeing have the highest wage rates followed by workers in the knitting section. The stitching and cutting workers get the lowest wages of all. Unions demand for uniform wages in all sections is mainly to ensure better wages in the cutting and stitching sections. The bargaining processes in different sections are interrelated. For example, the employers in the cutting and stitching sections cannot increase wages independently unless they receive higher rates from the brand owners or traders. The knitters' union not only bargains with knitters' associations, they also bargain with traders' associations. Other employers' associations are also involved in the negotiations, as increase in wages in one section influences distribution of wages in other sections. In the clusters, the state government also plays an important role in determination of wages and in shaping employment relations.[6] In the process, the employers in clustered firms are not absolutely independent in dealing with workers, they experience pressures for uniformity from external agencies—the government, the employers' associations, and the unions.

Aarvee Denim: A Non-union Textile Mill

Most new textile mills in the formal sector in India are spinning mills, and most new weaving and textile processing units are small firms. There are, however, some weaving mills in the formal sector. One such unit is Aarvee Denim, near Ahmedabad city, established in 1969. It uses modern technology including high-tech processing facilities. The unit exports about 60 percent of its production and the balance is sold in the upper segment of the domestic market. Of the 250 direct employees, 80 percent are workers, and 20 percent are managerial and supervisory staff. Employment relations in this weaving unit is typical of employment relation in medium-size non-union firms. About half of the blue-collar workers are unskilled, who were recruited from the open market and did not have any work experience. The skilled workers need to have work experience. The unit was modernized in 1996–1997 by introducing new looms, when it required workers with new skills. The existing workers were trained in new machines and some of them even received training in Germany from the suppliers. The skilled workers now receive regular training from the Indian agents of the European firm.

There is no union in Aarvee Denim. Management unilaterally decides about wages and other benefits based on market conditions and the firm's performance. The lowest category unskilled workers receive state-notified minimum wages, while at higher levels wages are fixed based on wages prevailing in similar firms. Every year, annual increments are decided based on the firm's financial performance. In recent years, they were around 3–6 percent. The wage rates are lower compared to those in large mills in the formal sector, but they are higher than the prevailing wages in power looms. Low level of wages leads to high employee turnover. There is no incentive scheme to link wages to productivity. According to management, workers can hardly control production as most machines are automatic, and thus there is no need to link wages to productivity. There are no casual workers, but there are contract workers in peripheral jobs, such as packaging, machine maintenance, housekeeping, loading-unloading, and security.

Management's authority in employee control is also seen in the informal system of grievance administration. There is no formal procedure for grievance resolution. In the event of any grievance, a worker takes it up with the supervisor, then with the departmental head, and finally with the general manager in charge of administration. Personnel administration does not have a big role in plant management. The manager in charge of administration looks after personnel department functions in addition to other duties. There is no problem in mobility of workers from one position to another. Overall, the relationship with workers is cooperative and the unit has never witnessed any major industrial dispute. It does not have any union and management strategy toward unionization is that of union avoidance.

Employee control in Aarvee Denim is no doubt hierarchical with substantial roles for supervisors at the shop floor. The senior managers closely supervise workers' performance and supervisors' activities. Every day they go on rounds and monitor floor-level activities, ensure that supervisors maintain good relationship with the workers and resolve floor-level conflicts in a way that reduces arbitrary actions. This has helped to minimize labor conflicts. Employee control is not formalized through collective agreements or detailed rules on expected employee behavior, but the rules followed are not arbitrary. Employee control is more structured than simple control in small firms and is closely linked to the physical structure of the labor process. It appears that machinery "directs and sets the labor process" and has strong influence on employee control and management decisions. The emphasis is more on high-performing machines than on high-performance workplace practices like teamwork and multi-skilling. In the plant, management has been able to match low wages with high technology, and both are integral parts of their competitive strategy.

Eastern Spinning and Vikram Spinners: The Conflict Pattern

Eastern Spinning Mill at Barasat, West Bengal, was established in 1966 by the Aditya Birla Group. In the early years of its operation, it produced cotton yarns for exports, but over time it shifted to production of synthetic yarn. It had a glorious past till the 1980s and was well known for its quality, productivity, and profitability. Unfortunately, it failed to remain so in the new competitive environment. Its employment relations in the past are best described as the traditional pattern with a "bounded amount of conflict" between capital and labor. It included detailed and formal contracts, where major wage issues were covered in the industry-wide agreements and other employment conditions were covered in the mill's standing order and local-level agreements with the plant-level unions. In the past, there were industrial conflicts, but those were within reasonable limits. Over time labor–management relations deteriorated and its employment relations shifted to the "conflict pattern."

In 1994, Vikram Spinners was set up as a sister concern of Eastern Spinning at a location close to the unit. It is located a region that had experience of industrialization for more than five decades. It was not in a "green-field" area. Its workers were familiar with trade unionism and labor militancy and the management was not a stranger to trade unionism, either. However, in the new unit, the management adopted a union-avoidance strategy and tried to keep workers out of union influence. The main objective was to lower labor costs, but they also believed that over time workers would come under union influence. Since its inception, the management tried to project it as a separate unit and introduce new norms for employee control, but its close proximity to Eastern Spinning made it difficult to do so. The workers and unions saw it as a part of Eastern Spinning and this had a major influence on the plant's employment relations. The unit started with low wages and a large number of casual workers. It was, therefore, a fertile ground for launching union activities. Over time, the three unions of Eastern Spinning affiliated to CITU, INTUC, and Trade Union Coordination Committee (TUCC) extended their activities in Vikram Spinners. The plant went through many difficult phases of labor conflicts. Management found workers and unions to be difficult, while workers and unions felt that the management was unfair. In sum, the employment relations in Vikram Spinners resembled the "conflict pattern" with labor and management engaged in continuous struggle over various issues.

Ownership of Vikram Spinners changed hand in 2001. The new management took steps to reduce overhead expenses, improve product mix, utilize idle machines, install new machines, and improve their relationship with workers. However, the unit continued to struggle. Along with competition from new units, non-cooperation of workers and unions contributed to its poor performance. According to the management, they made every effort to ensure full cooperation of workers and resolved many of the old grievances, while unions felt that they have received a bad deal. On several occasions, unions tried to put pressure through "gehrao" and other agitation programs in support of their demands, while many management requests agreed upon were not implemented. There were several incidents of go-slows, strikes, gehraos, and lockouts.[7] On each occasion, lockouts were withdrawn, there were agreements for improvement in discipline and increase in production and productivity, but it did not happen. The conflicts continued, but over time the management increased its dominance.[8]

Eastern Spinning and Vikram Spinners were two units under the same management, had same products, were located in the same area, and had the same unions representing workers in both the plants. However, there were some differences between the two plants as we look in more detail at their employer–employee relations. Production in the two units was almost the same, but Vikram Spinners employed only one-third of the workers employed by Eastern Spinning. Higher productivity in Vikram Spinners was mainly because of modern machines and the differences in the way workers were deployed, controlled, and managed.[9] Eastern Spinning had a large number of *badli* workers, but Vikram Spinners had no *badli* worker. The *badli* workers are semi-permanent workers, get at least twenty days' work in a month, receive same wages as permanent workers, and have more job security than casual workers. They are promoted from casual workers and they are promoted to permanent status over time. In Vikram Spinners, the employment structure was more simple and flexible than those in Eastern Spinning. This is evident in the standing orders and plant-level agreements. The standing order of Eastern Spinning has *badli* as an employee category; but it is not so in the standing order of Vikram Spinners. The standing order of Vikram Spinners is more stringent on discipline and employee behavior with specific clauses on punctuality, leave procedure, attendance, and prohibition of political activity inside factory premises, but it is not so in Eastern Spinning. In Vikram Spinners, adoption of bad working procedures and practices is considered as misconduct and has clauses on maintenance of machines, cleanliness, and flexibility in deployment. The standing order and agreements indicate differences in the employment practices in the two units, but in practice the differences are small. The employment relations in both the units resemble the conflict pattern of employment relations.

Reliance Textile: A Large Restructured Mill

Reliance Textile, a wholly owned subsidiary of Reliance Group, is located near Ahmedabad. It started as a small-line textile manufacturer in 1966 with four warp knitting machines and sixty-eight people and soon became well known in the textile industry. In 1975, the World Bank described it as an excellent unit even by developed country standards. Starting with the textile unit, the group pursued a strategy of backward vertical integration in polyester, plastics, petrochemicals, petroleum refinery, and oil and gas exploration and production. The group became India's largest private sector enterprise by extending its activities in different sectors. Employment in Reliance Textile increased from a small number in the beginning to about 10,000 workers in late 1990s. It was then a composite mill that combined spinning, weaving, and textile processing activities. Over time, it restructured the organization with offloading many of the activities outside the organization and relocation of some activities. Its employment declined to about one-third from its peak level by 2002. In India, the stories of many old textile mills are similar to that of Reliance Textile.

Like most large textile mills in India, Reliance Textile has unions. Its two unions represent two different groups of workers. The General Workers Union, affiliated to the National Labor Organization (an independent federation), represents all workers in textile processing; and the Mill Mazdoor Sabha, affiliated to HMS, represents all silk and artificial-silk division workers and workers in the weaving and spinning sections. There is no union of the staff members. The unions are recognized under the Bombay Industrial Relations Act, 1946. Once, a new union tried to come in, but it failed. Management has a clear policy on what issues to discuss with the unions. The issues that involve all workers (common interest issues like wages, VRS for manpower reduction, and so on) are discussed and settled with the plant-level unions.[10] However, on individual issues, management deals directly with the workers and unions have no objection to this. There is a joint management council for discussion of issues that need immediate attention. The employer–employee relationship in the unit is different from that in Vikram Spinners; there is certainly more cooperation than conflicts.

In Reliance Textile, besides the managerial staff, there are three categories of employees and workers working for the organization—the office staff, the blue-collar workers, and the contractor workers. There are no casual workers. The contract workers perform peripheral work, such as house keeping, security, and canteen work. The staff members appear to be more close to the managers than to the blue-collar workers. This is evident in the use of canteen facilities. The office employees, supervising staff, and managers, including the president and vice-president, take meals in the staff canteen, while the blue-collar workers have a separate canteen. The average wage is higher than the wages in local textile firms. Wages increase with seniority and are not linked to production or productivity excepting in the weaving section. There is detailed job classification. The rules governing employee relations are formal and include a well-developed grievance redressal system. The unit has not introduced concepts like teamwork, multi-skilling, or suggestion schemes and management does not consider them necessary. There is no problem in mobility of workers between different positions, including workers in lower positions. The relationship with the unions is cooperative. Employee control in Reliance Textile is certainly bureaucratic control with cooperative relationships between management and unions. It resembles the "Joint Team" based pattern of employment relations.

Jayashree Textiles: The HRM Pattern

Textile mills are labor-intensive and always employ large number of unskilled workers. The use of new and innovative management practices, such as teamwork, multi-skilling, QCs, employee communication, empowerment, and new HRM practices is generally uncommon in textile mills. However, few mills have adopted these innovative approaches in HRM. An example of this is Jayashree Textiles (Indian Rayon) established in 1949. It is a unit of Aditya Birla Group, which has sixty manufacturing units with twenty units located outside India. The unit not only managed to survive difficult times, it also continuously improved and changed its position through diversification. It started with production of flax or linen using imported raw material, but when there were problems of import, it diversified and started to produce cotton canvas. Over time, it included woolen products, woolen wear, synthetic linen, worsted wool combing, fire fighting hosepipes, and fabric for flax. All through it specialized in production of high-end products for export markets.[11] The unit is located in an old industrial area in West Bengal that houses large number of sick industrial units, but it stands up distinctly because of its emphasis on productivity and quality and its performance over the years.[12] It received ISO-9002 in 1994 and ISO-14000 in 1999. It is certainly one of the best-managed textile mills in India.

Jayashree Textiles is a large composite mill with 2,600 workers and 400 staff members. Of the workers, 1,700 are permanent and 900 work as *badli* workers. The *badli* workers get a minimum twenty days' work in a month, and have wages and working conditions similar to the permanent workers. Most unskilled workers in the unit started as casual workers, over time they were promoted as *badli* workers, and then as permanent workers. In 1994, the company changed its recruitment policy and stopped engagement of casual workers. The unit now does not have any casual workers, but it has 200 contract workers. Unlike many firms, the regular workers in the unit still do many of the non-core jobs, such as jobs in security and canteen. Management has plans to contract out some of these jobs, but they plan to do so after normal retirement of the existing employees. There have been many changes in the unit, but the changes have been slow and without any drastic reduction in employment or sudden replacement of direct workers by contract workers. The plant has three unions, two for the regular workers and one for the contract workers. Wage rates and other benefits are broadly determined at the industry level through tripartite agreement. However, workers of the unit also receive some additional payments and their gross wages are higher than the industry rates.

Jayashree Textiles is known for its modern management approach, worker commitment programs, and innovative workplace practices. The initiatives for introduction of high-performance workplace practices in the unit were driven by the corporate policy of the Aditya Birla Group. The group adopted "world-class manufacturing" practices as its corporate strategy and established a system of annual competition among its units for their implementation. These practices include: (*a*) defect-free production, (*b*) autonomous maintenance, (*c*) zero waste, (*d*) QCs, and (*e*) worker involvement (a worker should come to work with his hands, mind, and heart). Management at all levels are actively involved in this program and this has paid dividends in many areas. "*Kaizen*" has been particularly successful in Jayashree Textiles, and with suggestions from the workers they have been able to improve firm performance.[13] Emphasis on use of high-performance workplace practices is seen in different displays in the plant, which include guidelines for waste reduction (*Muda*), defect tags, and information on achievement of targets. The company has taken initiatives to create a multi-skilled workforce. About three-fourth of its workers are multi-skilled and it is now expected of all workers. There is no extra remuneration for multi-skill workers, but they get preference in promotion. The unit has also introduced Just-in-time (JIT) supply for machine maintenance, and this has influenced the way the maintenance workers work.

Jayashree Textiles has successfully introduced teamwork at different levels of the organization. Each employee is at least member of one high-performance team. These teams deal with issues relating to reduction of defects, implementation of *kaizen*, innovation of product or process, and monitoring of performance-improvement activities. The importance of teamwork is displayed in different display boards all over the factory. The displays in factory premises present identity of the teams, their functions, their team leaders, and team activities. There are functional teams at the shop floor, section, and department levels and there are cross-functional teams to increase coordination among

Box 4.1: Teams in Jayashree Textiles

Shop-floor teams: At the shop floor, workers doing related jobs form the lowest level teams, where generally the supervisors or senior-most employees act as team leaders.

Section-level teams: The leaders from the first level along with some senior management staff form teams in the second level (there are thirty such teams).

Department-level teams: The leaders from the second level and department/production heads form teams in the third level.

Cross-functional teams: In addition to the teams at the three levels, there are teams in the form of sub-committees at two levels to increase coordination among different functions.

Source: Developed based on field information/study.

different functions (Box 4.1). The teams meet at least twice in a month and there are meeting facilities in all the departments. Finally, a committee of senior officers presided over by the president regularly monitors the functioning of the committees/ teams. The teams and the committees have helped the firm to improve workers' involvement and sense of belonging in company programs.

Implementation of high-performance workplace practices in an organization needs extensive training of its workers. It is more so for firms that traditionally engaged large number of low-skilled workers. The trainings are not only for the new practices; they also aim to resolve conflicts, remove doubts, promote employee cooperation, and enhance employee commitment to company programs. Jayashree Textiles has strong emphasis on employee training. It has established an in-house training center and has drawn up an exhaustive plan for training. The plan provides for a minimum of six hours' training in a year for each and every employee and for most employees it is for longer duration. The company has also taken many initiatives to promote employee communication (Box 4.2). This extensive communication system has helped to build direct relationship with the employees and promote employee commitment. According to the management, the workers now prefer to meet managers and tell their problems rather than approaching their unions. This is a "union

Box 4.2: Employee Communication Initiatives in Jayashree Textiles

1. The president, who is the senior-most representative in the plant, addresses all the staff members once in every two months, when the staff members are encouraged to raise questions.
2. Every week, the president is available at a pre-notified time and place to directly hear from the workers.
3. Any worker irrespective of his rank can meet the vice-president, Human Resource Development (HRD), at any time of the day.
4. The divisional vice-president or production manager in charge along with the vice-president HRD periodically interacts with the workers in the division.
5. The in-house magazine keeps employees informed of different issues, which includes good performance by a worker or a group of workers.
6. Displays all over the factory display the principles of new workplace practices and the names of high performers.

Source: Developed based on field information/study.

substitution" strategy, where management is trying to take over some traditional functions of unions. Employment relations in Jayashree Textiles can be best described as the HRM pattern, which is characterized by formal policies in employee control, teamwork, skill/knowledge-based pay, and elaborate employee communication and employee training.

Employment Relation Systems in the Indian Textile Industry

Textile mills in India differ in their products, size, structures, operations, technology use, and skill of workers. We have presented case studies of two small textile units and five medium and large textile firms. Important issues of their employment relation practices are summarized in Table 4.1. Firms differ in use of regular and non-regular workers. They differ in their management strategies, employment regulations, and employment rules. They differ in their status of unionization and in their relations with unions and workers. They differ in terms of wages and benefits paid to the workers and the way the wages are bargained or fixed. Some firms

Table 4.1: Employment Relation Systems in Different Textile Units

Name of Unit	*Year of Establishment*[14]	*Employment Relations System*	*Number of Worker*	*Management Style, Employee Rules*	*Unions*	*Labour Relations*	*Wage Agreement (Wage Level)*
Vikram Spinning	1994	*Conflict Pattern*	Regular: 82 Casual: 194	Conflict management, formal rules	Three unions	Adversarial	Local agreement, (Low wage)
Eastern Spinning	1966	*Conflict Pattern*	Regular: 634 Casual: 112	Conflict management, formal rules	Three unions	Adversarial	Industry wide/local, (Medium wage)
Aarvee Denim, Weaving	1989	*Low-wage Pattern*	Regular: 200 Contractor: 40	Managerial discretion, semi-formal	No union	Informal and cooperative	No agreement, (Low wage)
Reliance Textile, Composite	1968	*Joint-team-based Pattern*	Regular: 2,240 Contractor: 600	Joint team based, formal rules	Two unions	Cooperative	Plant level, (Medium wage)
Jayashree Textiles, Composite	1949	*HRM Pattern*	Regular: 2,600 Contractor: 200	HRM pattern, innovative practices	Three unions	Cooperative	Industry wide/local, (High wage)
Jyothi Weaving Bengal	1990	*Paternalistic Pattern*	Regular and casual: 10	Simple control, informal rules	No union	Informal	No agreement, (Low wage)
Bharti Knitware	1980	*Coordinated Paternalistic Pattern*	Regular and casual: 10	Simple control coordinated	Local union	Informal	Industry wide (Low wage)

Source: Developed based on field information/study.

have highly detailed employee contracts that provide procedures and norms for governing the relationship between management, workers, and their unions. In others, such contracts cover only few aspects of the relationship. Firms differ in the way they involve their employees in decision making or emphasize employee motivation. In summary, firms differ in their employment relations.

Employment systems of the two small firms discussed are representatives of employment relations of small firms in India. Jyothi Weaving is a power loom unit producing cotton fabric, while Bharti Knitwear is a hosiery knitting unit in an industrial cluster. The differences in their employment relations are not because they operate in different sub-sectors in the textile industry, it is mainly because they differ in their linkages to other firms. Employee control in Jyothi Weaving is simple control and its employment relation system is "paternalistic system." In this employment system, the employers directly control all aspects of work and workers' work life. In Bharti Knitware too the employers directly supervise their employees, but cluster norms restrict their absolute authority. The employment system in Bharti Knitwear is best described as a "coordinated paternalistic system." In most small firms, employers do not face any external influences in managing their employees, but in some small firms they face external influences that restrict their absolute authority. The external influences are from different sources—labor laws and state rules, union agreements, and association norms. In clusters, these influences often work in combination and restrict employers' absolute authority. The two employment relation systems in small firms are briefly described next.

1. Paternalistic system: In this system, unadulterated interaction takes place between employers and employees with no formal rule to regulate employer behavior. In this system, the centrality of employer, his/her self-image, and informality are the main driving forces to shape firms' employment relations. The employer has close supervision of his/her workers; he/she sits in the workplace, and controls all aspects of production and relationship with the employees. The workers are always at the mercy of their employer in matters of pay and other employment conditions. The relationship with the employees

is at an individual and person-to-person level. In this system, recruitment is informal and based on subjective assessment. The close ties between employers and employees ensure stability and reduce the possibilities of conflict. If there is a conflict between an employer and his employees, the employee quits or is asked to leave.

2. Coordinated paternalistic system: In many ways, the system is similar to the paternalistic pattern, but employers' authority is no longer absolute. They still dominate in employee control, but their absolute authority is constrained by external influences that influence employment relations in small firms. The restrictions or constraints may be from different sources: government rules, trade union agreements, and association norms. The restrictions are more prominent in small firms in clusters. This coordinated paternalistic system has developed from the paternalistic system and in both the systems a set of minimal cultural norms regulates activities of owners and workers in the labor process, but in the coordinated pattern there are additional influences on firms' employment practices. It ensures similarities in employment practices across small firms.

Most small firms in India have the "paternalistic system" of employment relations; only few firms have the "coordinated paternalistic" system. Several factors may impose restrictions on employers' absolute authority, but the influences are stronger when the factors operate in combination. This happens when firms are part of industrial clusters. Examples of such clusters in India include the knitwear industry in Tiruppur (Chari 2000), the woolen hosiery industry in Ludhiana (Tewari 1998), and the hosiery industry in West Bengal.[15] These clusters are similar to the clusters of small firms in Third Italy described by Piore and Sable (1984) in *Industrial District Models of Flexible Specialization*. They consist of more or less equal small enterprises in an area bound in a complex web of competition and cooperation. In this arrangement, while small firms compete with each other, there is also cooperation between small firms and sharing of indirect costs like legal services, wage fixation, design, raw material procurement, and machinery maintenance.

Employment relations in large firms are more complex than those in small firms. They have more variations in their employment practices. One distinguishing feature that differentiates firms' employment relation system is employee control. In small firms, employee control is simple control. As firms grow in size, simple control becomes more and more difficult and firms need more formalized system of employee control. In large firms, employee control may be technical control (control of the physical process of production), or bureaucratic control (control of social structure of workplace), or a combination of the two. In the Indian textile industry, there are examples of both technical control and bureaucratic control.[16] In Aarvee Denim, technical control is more dominant than bureaucratic control. It has rules that guide employee behavior, but technical aspects dominate the production process. In Reliance Textile, employee control is more bureaucratic and less technical. One needs to remember that technical control and bureaucratic control represent two ideal types of employee control, and no firm exhibits the ideal models. One needs bureaucratic rules even to technologically link labor to production. The changes over time indicate that bureaucratic control, which involves company rules and procedures as the basis for control, has become more common and popular than technical control. Bureaucratic control has also changed over time; there is now increased emphasis on reduction of conflict and increase in employee commitment toward company objectives. This has transformed the bureaucratic system to HRM system.

The HRM pattern represents a type of bureaucratic control. It relies heavily on formal personnel policies, but these policies are different from those found in traditional bureaucratic patterns. It includes policies such as skill or knowledge-based pay and elaborate employee communication, which are absent in the traditional model of bureaucratic control. The objective here is to motivate every individual in an organization toward common objectives without making explicit distinctions between different groups in the organizational hierarchy. Initially, HRM developed in capital-intensive and high-technology firms, but over time it has been also introduced in other types of firms. Initially it developed in non-union setting, but over time it has also expanded in union setting.

The HRM pattern is more common in high-technology capital-intensive firms, but some of its components are also seen in labor-intensive firms. The employment practices in Jayashree Textiles represent an HRM pattern with world-class manufacturing practices, such as teamwork, QCs, and *kaizen*.

The foregoing discussions identify different employment systems in the Indian textile industry. The units chosen for the study are not random samples; these have been so chosen that they together can capture the dominant patterns of employment relations in the Indian textile industry. The different patterns of employment relations have been identified based on the criteria used by Katz and Kochan (2000: 104) for identification of different emerging workplace practices in developed countries. The criteria are the core elements or work practices, such as nature of work organization, managerial discretion, workers' autonomy, pay procedure, and roles played by unions. A key indicator for distinction between different employment patterns is the status of unionization. In the union sector, the distinction is also in terms of whether the relationship between capital and labor is adversarial or cooperative. Our study indicates existence of four dominant patterns of employment relation systems in India. The patterns are described next.

1. Low-wage pattern: In this pattern of employment relations system, wages and fringe benefits are low and personnel policies are informally administered. Often, there are no formal rules on issues like leaves and allowances; these are granted by the management on a case-to-case basis. There is substantial discretion to operating managers; the supervisors and other managers exercise high degree of discretion over discipline and pay policies. The employment conditions of employees in these firms generally vary relatively widely across workgroups, plants, and firms. Employment in a low-wage pattern firm is often temporary, part-time, or on contract basis. With limited commitment to employment continuity, limited opportunity for promotion, and absence of seniority-based pay; labor turnover is generally high in low-wage firms. The paternalistic pattern and the coordinated paternalistic pattern in the small-scale sector belong to the low-wage pattern.

2. Conflict pattern: In conflict pattern of employment relation labor and management are engaged in a series of struggles over their basic rights. It typically involves high incidence of strikes, work to rule, and lockouts. Such conflicts often impose high costs on the firms through lost output or low productivity and on employees through lost earnings. Because of high costs to both the parties, the conflict pattern tends to be unstable and in general it is seen as a transitory phase, but in the Indian context some sick firms continue to have conflict pattern for a substantially long period of time. The pattern is seen in union setting and is common in labor-intensive firms. All firms generally exhibit a mix of conflict and cooperation in their employment relations, and firms differ in the mix of the two and their strategies to resolve conflicts or promote cooperation.[17] In some firms, labor conflict is a transitory phase. In some others it is perennial; their employment relation system represents the conflict pattern. The best examples of the pattern are jute mills in West Bengal.
3. Joint-participation pattern: Pressured by the need to improve productivity, product quality, and production flexibility, employers and employees are now adopting joint-team-based approach. It involves more direct participation of workers and unions in business decisions and as a result there is less resistance to change. The pattern tries to create mechanisms through which workers are involved in solving production and personal problems. The pattern is very good in stabilizing labor–management relations. Some of that stability derives from the formal channels (grievance procedure) through which the problems are addressed. These procedures are attractive to employees because they provide due process, they are attractive to employers because adherence to the procedures ensures that production will not be interrupted by labor disputes. The pattern includes detailed job classifications and pay systems that rely heavily on formal rules, but includes contingent compensation system with wages linked to productivity.

4. HRM pattern: In order to increase flexibility and cost competitiveness, various firms started to adopt a new pattern of

> personnel policies—the HRM pattern. Like the traditional bureaucratic pattern, this pattern also relies on formal policies, but the nature of the policies differs from those traditionally found in non-union firms. The HRM pattern typically includes skill or knowledge-based pay, and elaborate communication and complaint procedure. Team form of organizations is also common in HRM-oriented firms, where the activities of teams are directly controlled by the management. The HRM firms are also known for the extensive measures they take in trying to induce employees to identify their interests with the long-term interest of the firm. The measures include publishing company newsletters, paying all employees on a salary basis, and nurturing strong corporate culture.

One needs to remember that the aforementioned description of the different patterns describe the patterns in broad terms. In practice, the employment relations system of a firm may not exactly fit to any of the patterns. There is always scope for some differences, but its major characteristics are expected to be close to one of the patterns of employment relations.

Changes in Employment Relations in the Textile Industry

Changes in employment relations in the Indian textile industry that began in the 1980s appear dramatic because they represented a sharp contrast to the practices that developed over the fifty years prior to the changes. In the past these practices were never uniform throughout the industry, but they were relatively stable over time. In the small-scale sector, the old system was simple control or paternalistic employment relations. The coordinated paternalistic system emerged with increasing external influences on employment systems of small firms. The external influences increased as small units appeared in clusters and coordinated their activities. In these clusters, employers' associations and trade unions play important roles in shaping firms' employment relations. The resulting networked arrangement in employment relations is relatively more complex than the simple paternalistic control. The share of this new pattern in the small-scale sector is still small, but it is increasing. Emergence and growth of this new pattern is a marked departure from the past practices and this has led to increased variation in employment relations in small firms.

Study of employment relations is more concerned with large firms. In the past, most textile mills in India were large; they existed in a protected environment and the state played a dominant role in shaping firms' employment systems. State intervention through political and institutional determination of wages and other working conditions of work became the norm. Few strategic choices were open to either unions or employers as the state overdetermined the labor relation outcomes. In the 1970s and 1980s, the employment relations system in the industry was characterized by tripartite centralized bargaining between well-defined employer groups, government agencies, and large national trade union federations. In majority of firms, industry-wide agreements were at the state and regional levels. In this system, employers' associations and trade union federations had significant roles in shaping firms' employment relations. This traditional system was not without problems, as labor and management were often engaged in serious struggles and multiplicity of unions further complicated the systems. However, the system has stable as both industry and labor were protected from external and domestic competition. This system is still seen in some parts of the textile industry, but it has started to disintegrate.[18]

Changes in workplaces began with pressures on employers to change. Changes in industrial policy, withdrawal of industrial licensing, and removal of freight equalization policies for raw cotton made some locations more favorable than others. The old mills are now either closed or have restructured with fresh investments in technology. New mills with new technology have come up in new locations. Increasingly, new firms adopted union-avoidance policies and some unionized firms adopted union-substitution policies. Over time, the changes have led to increased variations in labor relations across firms. In the past, the system included a bounded amount of conflict between capital and labor, and the main task of management was to balance the interests of employers and employees within acceptable limits and prevent unnecessary conflict. Representatives of this system still exist in many firms, but increasingly the system is showing its weakness with decline of tripartite bargaining. The transfer of production activities to the small-scale sector has also weakened the traditional structure. Some firms still have conflict pattern of employment relations, some firms have been able to establish cooperative relationship with the unions and workers, and some firms have been able to improve workers' commitment to organizations' goals and objectives. The changes have led to increased variations in employment relations across firms in the Indian textile industry.

Conclusions

Textile mills, whatever their sub-sector, size, ownership, or outputs, are always labor-intensive and employ a relatively larger proportion of blue-collar workers. In India, the textile industry has always represented a large proportion of formal-sector workers, and its employment relations have always directly or indirectly influenced employment relations in other industries.[19] This makes the textile industry an important sector for study of employment relation systems in India and their changes over time. This chapter identified the dominant employment relation patterns in the Indian textile industry and described how they have changed over time. The four dominant patterns in textile mills are the low-wage pattern, the joint-team-based pattern, the conflict pattern, and the HRM pattern. In the small-scale sector, the dominant pattern is the low-wage pattern and within this pattern, there two types of employment relation systems—the paternalistic pattern and the coordinated paternalistic pattern. The changes in employment relations over time indicate growing variation in employment relations in the post-reform era.

One important question is to what extent the findings can be generalized. In other words, to what extent the findings are valid for other industrial sectors. As discussed, a number of factors make the textile industry different from other industrial sectors, which raises the questions about generalization of the findings. First, textile industry is a labor-intensive industry and uses a relatively low level of technology than capital-intensive industries, such as engineering or chemicals. The levels of skill required in the textile industry are lower than those required in other manufacturing sectors like automobile, telecommunication, or electronics industry. With increased opportunities for investments in new technology in the post-reform era, firms in the engineering and chemical industries went through dramatic changes in use of new technology. In the textile industry, the changes have been slow and over a long period of time. In contract, some capital-intensive firms have seen fast and dramatic changes. The findings, therefore, may not apply to capital intensive firms that went through fast changes over small period of time. Second, textile industry is a manufacturing industry with large number of blue-collar workers and the findings may not apply to firms in the service sector that mainly engage white-collar workers. More particularly, the findings may not apply in the IT sector firms. Third, most textile firms are Indian firms and their employment relations may not capture the global–local issues in employment relations. More particularly, the textile industry may not capture employment relations in MNCs and the way their global policies influence their employment relations. The three chapters that follow examine employment relations and their changes in capital-intensive firms, in ITES firms, and in MNCs.

Notes

1. Ministry of Textile, Government of India, Annual Report 2007–2008.
2. Most large textile mills in the organized sector are spinning mills, and only 10 percent are composite mills. By the end of 2007, there were 1,744 large mills (other than Small Scale Industries [SSI] units). Only about 5 percent of total spun yarn production was in the small-scale sector, while only 3 percent of cloth production (weaving) was in the large mills. The average number of workers in spinning units was about 600; while the average number of workers in power looms was ten, and that in processing centers was twenty (Ministry of Textile, Annual Report 2007–2008).
3. Jayashree Textiles received some order from Russia and additional workers were engaged, but the unit had to continue with these excess workers for five years and finally absorbed them against regular vacancies.
4. India was the world's leading buyer (28 percent of global shipments) of spinning equipment during 1989–1998. Spindles purchased during this

period accounted for 33 percent of total installed capacity (Verme 2002: 25). Major investment was in new ring spinning machines. In 1996, of the total such machines purchased around the world, about 53 percent were by Indian firms (Chandra 1999). The weaving sector, however, has not seen such technology upgradation. Shuttle and shuttle less looms installed during 1989–1998 accounted for only 1.6 percent of the installed capacity.

5. The West Bengal Hosiery Association represents the traders or brand owners, the Bengal Hosiery Manufacturers' Association represents the knitters, the West Bengal Bleachers and Dyers Association represents the bleachers, and the Bengal Hosiery Tailors' Association represents the tailors.
6. The West Bengal government notified minimum wages for the hosiery industry in 1998. This prompted the unions and the employers associations to reach an agreement.
7. In 1975, there was a strike in the ring frame department followed by lockout for three months. In 1977, workers' agitation in the form of go-slow was followed by lockout for four months. There was again lockout in 1988 and many incidents of indiscipline in the intervening period.
8. In the 1980s, the charged workers were mostly taken back or paid monetary compensation for leaving the organization, but in 1996, a changed employee, who was an office bearer of the CITU union, was suspended and then dismissed. This shows more severe action by management against errant employees in 1990s than in 1980s.
9. Eastern Spinning had 746 workers (280 permanent, 354 *badlis*, and 112 casual workers), while Vikram Spinning had 276 workers (82 permanent and 194 casual workers).
10. It does not follow the industry-wide agreement for textile workers in Gujarat except that it pays 99 percent of dearness allowance (DA) specified in the industry-wide agreement.
11. The unit exports 65 percent of its products, which is exported to 50 countries. The group has similar plants in Indonesia, Thailand, the Philippines, Malaysia, Egypt, and Canada.
12. The company has attempted to create appropriate physical environment. As one enters the road leading to Jayashree Textiles, as well as inside the unit, one can see several banners on display emphasizing importance of productivity and quality.
13. The management has received many suggestions from the workers, and had implemented about 500 such suggestions by 2002. It has gained substantially from the suggestions. According to the management, it has saved about Rs 50 million per annum by implementing the suggestions.
14. Aarvee Denim and Reliance Textile are located in Gujarat; other plants are located in West Bengal.

15. In the clusters, there are strong employers' associations and trade unions that bargain wages, other benefits, and productivity.
16. An example of firm with technical control is Aarvee Denim. Other examples include the mini steel plants and jute mills in West Bengal. The best examples of bureaucratic control are unionized firms like Reliance Textile.
17. Most often, the "balance of interest" strategy and "commitment" strategy are used in combination, but the emphasis is always on one or the other approach. The two strategies are interrelated, as managers cannot get the commitment of workers unless they are able to reduce conflict. Similarly, if managers can get the commitment of workers, then it is much easier to balance the interests of the parties.
18. There are examples of industry-wide agreements in different parts of the country. An example of this is the collective agreements between the South India Mill Owners' Association and trade unions. The agreement in 1991 covered 200 textile units (Patil 1993: 431).
19. Some of the senior trade union leaders have started their trade union life in textile industry and the structure of industry-wide collective bargaining in India also first developed in the textile industry.

Chapter 5

Restructuring of Firms and Transformation of Employment Relation Systems

Economic reform measures in India over the last two decades have radically changed the context of employment relations. They have put competitive pressure on firms and their employment systems and have major influence on managing people at work. The pressures are from diverse sources; they are different on different firms; and firms differ in confronting these pressures. Most firms in India have seen changes in their employment systems in the post-reform period—for some the changes are small and for some they are significant. In the textile industry, there have been slow and incremental changes in employment relations over a long period of time. In contrast, the changes in employment relations of some capital-intensive firms have been dramatic, over short periods and often discontinuous and abrupt. Many firms in the engineering, chemical, and pharmaceutical industries, for example, have seen such fast and dramatic changes. They have heavily invested in new technology (often with imported machineries), downsized their workforce substantially, and adopted core-periphery model of work organizations. The changes are more spectacular in the subsidiaries of MNCs, where the funds for new technology often come from increases in the shareholdings of the parent companies. This chapter examines the rapid and fundamental changes in the employment practices in capital-intensive firms. The issues are examined by presenting the changes in BOC, India and they are supported with examples from other firms. The new employment systems in these firms are distinctly different from their old systems; they indicate "transformation," in their employment systems.[1]

Pressures for Change: Restructuring of British Oxygen

The Indian industrialization experience in the pre-reform period can be divided into three distinct phases. The first phase, which coincided with the first three Five Year Plans, was characterized by high rates of growth in industrial output. This growth came partly from large doses of public investment and partly from a significant degree of import substitution. The second phase, which lasted from mid-1960s until 1980, was characterized by significantly slower growth resulting from a slowdown in public investment, slower agricultural progress, problems of coordination in production of intermediate goods, and low productivity. The third phase, which lasted the decade of 1980s, in contrast witnessed a gradual recovery of industrial growth and increase in productivity. This growth phase was qualitatively dissimilar from the first phase, as attention shifted to consumer durables. A host of different factors contributed in this growth phase: improved labor utilization, easier access to imports, de-regulations, and increased attention to exports. This phase came to an abrupt end with the onset of the fiscal and balance of payments crisis, and introduction of new economic policies in 1991 (Mookherjee 1995: 28). The shifts toward liberalization started with piecemeal moves in the 1980s and were consolidated in a comprehensive wave of deregulation in the early 1990s. The liberalization program increased competitive pressures, demanded technology upgradation and organizational restructuring. All these led to major changes in firms' employment relations.

The changes in employment relations in India in the post-reform period have taken different forms in different firms. The changes were slow in some firms and rapid and dramatic in other firms. Many researchers have examined the changes in employment relations in the post-reform era (Kuruvilla and Hiers 1997; Mathur 1991; Ramswamy 2000); however, none of them have specifically focused on the rapid and dramatic changes leading to transformation in firms' employment systems. This chapter examines the various aspects of transformation of employment relations in BOC India and supplements the argument with examples from other firms. BOC began its operation in India as Indian Oxygen Company (IOC) in 1935 and has experienced many changes in the different phases of industrialization. In the pre-reform era, it received the comfort of dominant monopoly because of strict government control through industrial licensing. In the controlled environment, the market rigidities also restricted increase in its productivity and flexibility. Prior to the 1980s, the company managers were so content and confident with the status quo that they did not explore a larger role in business offered by some of India's fast-expanding industrial sectors. The situation started to change in the 1980s; IOC saw sharp decline in its fortunes. In the years leading to 1990, the company with more than 5,000 employees had a technology thirty years behind its parent British company.

The liberalization program increased competition in the Indian economy. The de-licensing of the gas industry in the mid-1980s led to establishment of more than 200 small units in the sector. There was also new competition from the international manufacturers of oxygen and industrial gases such as the US giant Praxair, the French giant L'Air Liquide, and AGA of Sweden (Banerjee 2001: 13). IOC burdened with obsolete technology and a bloated workforce, found it difficult to cope with the competition. In the five years leading to 1990, its net profit declined precipitously by over 90 percent (*Business India* 1993: 74). The changed scenario, however, created new opportunities for growth. In fact, IOC with the pre-existing international links was in a better position to avail the opportunities than other Indian firms, such as Hindustan Gas, Asiatic Oxygen, and Bombay Oxygen. The new environment made BOC interested in IOC. In the 1980s, the parent company had very little interest in IOC and, in fact, at one time it wanted to divest its 39 percent controlling interest and get out of the business.

Figure 5.1: BOC India: Sales Growth

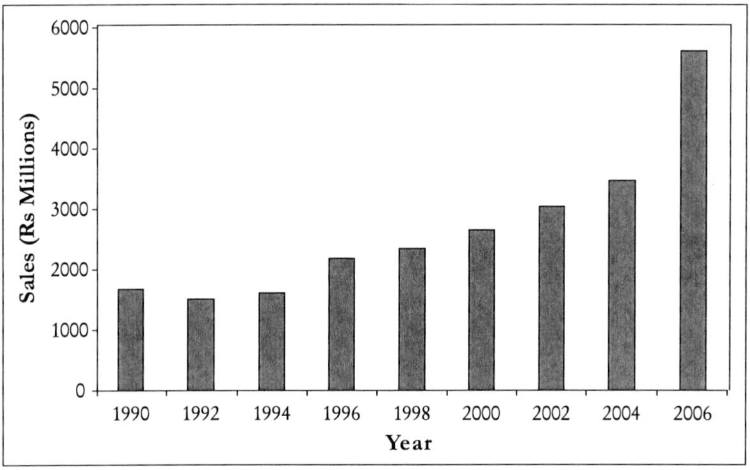

Source: Annual Reports of BOC India, 2000 and 2006. Available at www.boc-india.com

As things changed, BOC started to put all its might behind IOC; it increased its holdings to 55 percent by 1998, and took over full control of its operations. This changed IOC's status from a mere member of the BOC group to a part of the BOC group. The most important effect of this was fresh investments in new technology. This led to increase in production and sales (Figure 5.1).

In the 1970s and 1980s, there was hardly any technology transfer from the British company to its Indian subsidiary. IOC was saddled with two major problems: outdated technology and high employee costs. Because of the government's stringent rules, the parent company was unable to breathe in enough funds to resolve these problems. With the removal of restrictions in foreign investments, the BOC group increased its holdings in IOC and provided funds for technology upgrades and restructuring (*Business India* 1993: 74). They introduced the latest tonnage technology and replaced the old and outdated air separation plants for production of oxygen and other gasses and introduced new technology in other operations. The main components of the restructuring program were: (*a*) closure of unviable businesses, (*b*) divestment of non-core businesses, (*c*) improvement of productivity, (*d*) elimination of wasteful practices, (*e*) employment restructuring, and (*f*) reduction of the workforce. The restructuring was fast and dramatic with drastic reduction in employment and changes in employment structure. There have been similar changes in other capital-intensive firms in the engineering and chemical industries (for example, Texmaco, Alstom Power, Alstom AEI, and ICI Paints). The firms differ in their approaches, but at the strategic level they have many similarities; all of them had drastic reduction in employment, reduced union involvement, and introduced new employment practices. This story of employment restructuring is different from that of the textile mills that went through slow changes over a long period of time.

Closure, Divestment, Modernization, and Downsizing

Many capital intensive firms in India have undergone profound changes in firms' organizational structures in the post-reform period. Most organizational restructuring programs have been accompanied by large-scale reduction in employment through closure of unviable units, divestment of non-core business, and downsizing of firms. The organizations that made fresh capital investments, introduced new technology, and adopted new ideas about how to manage their people at work. The major aspects of employment downsizing and organizational restructuring in BOC India are discussed next.

Closure of Unviable Businesses

The Industrial Disputes Act 1947 requires that every employer employing 100 or more workers should get approval of the "appropriate government" (usually the state government) to close any of its establishment or retrench any of its employees. Legally, employers in principle may get such permission, but in practice this rarely happened in the past and even it is not common in the post-reform era. This is because the ruling political parties feel that granting such permission can be politically damaging and loss of electoral support from the working class (ILO-SAAT 1996; Venkataratnam 1994). As it is difficult to get permission to close an industrial unit, employers often use other approaches. Some employers declare lockouts (temporarily closing a place of employment) or temporary suspension of work in their establishments that continue for several years. This leads to virtual closure. This procedure, however, takes time and is not without problems. In most cases, unions raise industrial disputes and sometimes it is further complicated by legal battles in judicial forums.[2] Because of these difficulties in closing industrial establishments, VRS has become a popular option. BOC India closed many of its unviable units in the 1990s. Some they closed after obtaining necessary permission of the state governments, others they closed by declaring lockout, offering VRS, and indirectly forcing employees to leave.[3]

Divestment of Non-core Businesses

BOC in the 1980s had four business divisions: the gases division, the contracts division, the health care division, and the welding division. In the new competitive environment, BOC India decided to focus on its core business of industrial/medical gases and cryogenic engineering, and divest its other divisions. It realized that to remain market leader in welding business, it needed constant technology upgrades, but the scope was limited, as the BOC group, barring few exceptions, had divested its welding business worldwide by the end of the 1980s. In 1991, the company sold its welding business to Esab, which was a global market leader in welding consumables and equipment, and was already present in the Indian market. The company then sold its health care business following a decision of the BOC group to withdraw from the business.[4] The divestment of non-core business helped them to focus in the core business and to ensure commitment of its employees and workers toward excellence in core business. One of the problems was to persuade the 2,000-strong workforce in the factories and sales offices of the two divisions to accept change of ownership.

Modernization of Core Business

In the 1980s, technologically BOC India was thirty years behind its British parent, BOC, and technology upgrade was a major challenge for BOC India. The most important was the gas production plants. The old classical plants of around 12 tons capacity were technologically backdated with high power consumption and high employee costs. In 1985, the company took the first step to establish two plants using tonnage technology at Tarapur and Jamshedpur. It then added another 110 tons-per-day tonnage plant at Taloja in 1994, which was a state-of-the-art plant, the only one in India at that time. In 1998, the company commissioned a new 1,290 tons-per-day plant in Jamshedpur, which was then the largest oxygen plant in Asia. BOC's gas production capacity per day increased from 400 tons in the 1980s to 1,700 tons in 2003. The company also modernized its downstream cylinder bottling distribution business and introduced a customer-focussed quality improvement program (Banerjee 2001: 21). This bridged its technology gap of at least thirty years with the BOC group worldwide. The tonnage plants, equipped with sophisticated machines, control systems, and new compressors, now produce and supply gases, with lower power consumption and fewer employees (only three/four qualified engineers per shift). The new technology and the redesign of work process led to manifold increase in productivity.

Downsizing and Voluntary Retirement

In India, the restrictive provisions in the Industrial Disputes Act 1947 on layoffs and retrenchment, and the refusal of the government to grant permission under Sections 25(O) and 25(N) in almost all cases makes it almost impossible for employers to find a legal solution to the problem of excess staff. If the number of employees in a unit is below 100 no permission is needed, but there are other complications.[5] Legally, the employer's right to effect retrenchment cannot be challenged, but tribunals can examine whether the impugned retrenchment is justified or not. If it is not justified, then reinstatement with full back wages is the normal rule. Further, employers are also expected to follow the "last come, first go" principle and a departure from this principle is allowed only on valid and justifiable grounds (Section 25 G). Because of the legal complications, voluntary separation has become the most popular route for employment reduction. There is a cost associated with such schemes, but often the monetary cost is not that great in relation to the benefits (Amadeo et al. 1995). The union government has encouraged such schemes by giving income tax exemption and by introducing them in public sector undertakings. In theory, the schemes are voluntary in nature and it is up to the employees to accept or reject them, but in most occasions employers and unions try to influence employees' decisions. Employers, for example, often force their employees to apply for VRS by putting them under difficult situations like transfer to far away places. Similarly, unions often pursue their members to accept or reject such schemes.

The closure of unviable units, divestment of non-core businesses, large-scale technology upgrades, and plant-level downsizing have led to drastic reductions in employee strength in BOC India. The number of direct employees dropped from 5,600 in 1989 to only 630 in the year 2,000. The divestment of two non core business involved separation of nearly 2,000 employees (Figure 5.2). The manpower restructuring in BOC India involved a number of steps and negotiations at different levels and included issues such as:

Figure 5.2: BOC India: Decline in Number of Employees

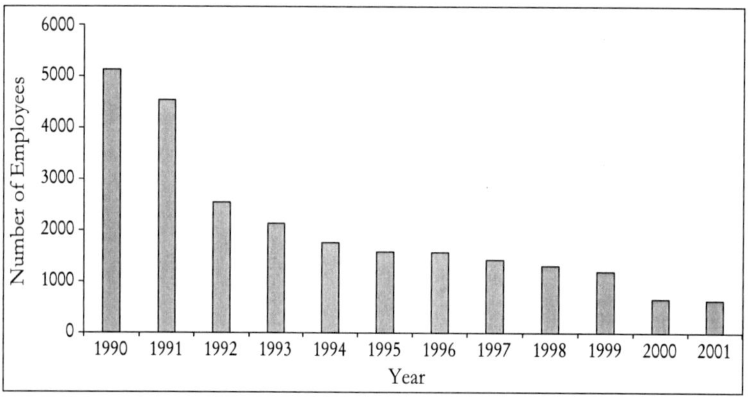

Source: Annual Reports of BOC India, 2000 and 2001. Available at www.boc-india.com.

(*a*) identification of units/departments with high employee costs, (*b*) fixing benchmarks for manpower and productivity, (*c*) exploring redeployment potential of employees by identifying their skills and experience, (*d*) freezing hiring at non-management/non-expert levels, and (*e*) identification of employees who could be voluntarily retired. VRS typically included payments on the basis of number of years worked or number of years of service left before superannuating subject to a maximum limit on the amount payable to each employee. The payments are in addition to normal benefits, such as pension, medical, provident fund, gratuity, and leave encashment. The scheme was modified several times and included special treatment in some units that required special attention.

Introduction of new technology, new machines, and new practices is always accompanied by changes in work practices, job descriptions, job allocation, and redeployment of the workforce. Employees often oppose the changes because they are apprehensive about likely effect of the changes on the employees. Disputes particularly arise on manning of new machines, production norms, effects on workers' earnings, and sharing of productivity gains. Delays in settlement of such disputes delay introduction of new technology. If settlements are reached before installation of new machines, it can reduce the delays, but for this, the parties need to know details about the modernization programs.[6] BOC India introduced new management practices in all its plants. In its tonnage plants, it adopted a new approach in employer–employee relations. These plants do not have any blue-collar workers in regular employment and none of the regular workers are union members.[7] Only a few qualified engineers operate the new machines and the contract workers do all blue-collar jobs. Majority of the old composite plants have been restructured as bottling plants. They have also modernized and downsized their employment, but they still have substantial numbers of blue-collar workers.

Changes in Organizational Structure

BOC India, started major changes in its organizational structure since the mid-1980s. With the divestment of the health care and welding divisions, it now has two divisions—the gases division and the contracts division. The contracts division, with its factory in Kolkata and technology support from the BOC group, specializes in cryogenic engineering and turnkey projects. It encompasses design, engineering, manufacturing, installation, testing, and commissioning in cryogenic engineering in various core sector industries.

More than 90 percent of the company's turnover is from the gases division.[8] It sells gases either in liquid form to large consumers or, more commonly compressed gases in cylinders to small consumers. The gases division has undergone major restructuring with the changes in the production process in the 1980s and 1990s. Prior to the major changes, its fourteen gas factories produced gases through air-separation technology and bottled them in captive bottling plants (Figure 5.3). It closed down six such units. Now, the gasses are produced in three tonnage plants at Taloja, Tarapur, and Jamshedpur, which are then supplied to bulk consumers or bottling plants through dedicated pipelines or tankers.[9] The smaller bottling units, known as compressor units, receive liquid gases from the tonnage plants, and compress them into cylinders in gas form for supply to small consumers. These units are located across the country and thus provide wide geographical coverage.[10] The manufacturing strategy has thus shifted from the earlier concept of production, bottling, and sale of bottled gases from the smaller units to turning the smaller units as receivers of liquid gases from the mother plants and bottling them for the consumers (Figure 5.4). In the decentralized structure, the compressing units also need fewer workers, but can still maintain faster delivery schedules.

Figure 5.3: BOC India Gases Division: Before Restructuring

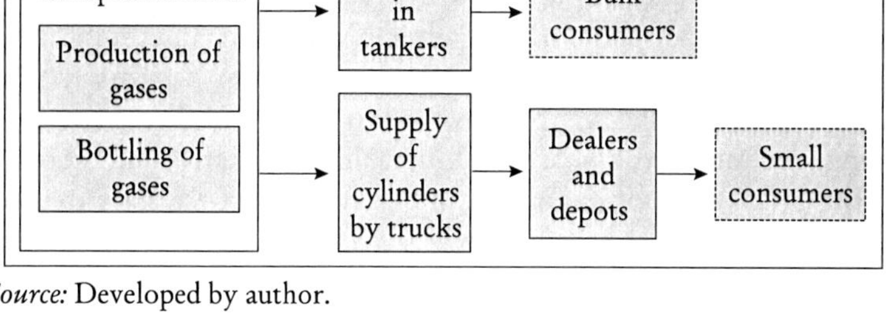

Source: Developed by author.

Figure 5.4: BOC India: Gas Production and Distribution—After Restructuring

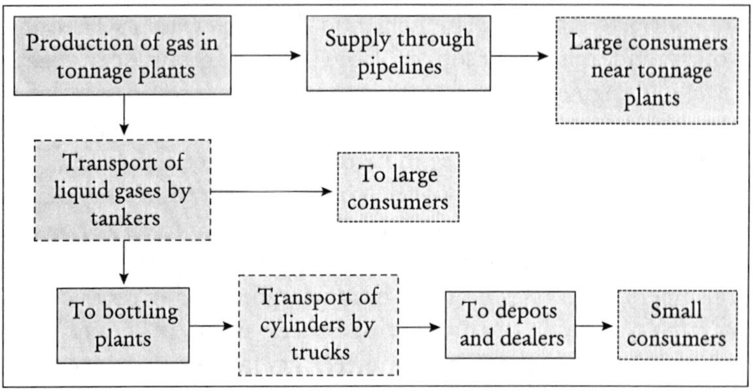

Source: Developed by author.

The main aspect of organizational restructuring in BOC India is the division of its operations into different segments with each segment performing specialized functions. In the decentralized structure with the separation of production, bottling, and gas distribution, the coordination of activities of different parts has become particularly important. In India, the distribution of gasses needs particular attention because of poor road infrastructure and unpredictable terrain. It needs adequate backup to meet any dislocation so that customers never dry up and supply is made within the stipulated time.[11] BOC India has introduced a management information system (MIS) that maintains computerized stock records, continuously analyzes customers' usage patterns, and determines the optimum moment to deliver further supplies. The changes in production structure have led to changes in structure of employment. The new tonnage plants need only few engineers and professionals. The Taloja plant, for example, produces 110 tons of gasses per day and has only sixteen permanent employees with two engineers per shift looking after production. In comparison, the Ghatkopar plant, produced 60 tons of gas per day with about 300 employees. The changes have led to decline in direct employment, decline in the share of blue-collar workers, and increase in the proportion of engineers and technicians.[12] Along with the changes, BOC India has also contracted out most of the unskilled and non-core jobs. There has been increase in contract workers, but even if we include them, there has been an overall decline in employment.

Contracting Out of Jobs

Introduction of new technology, with fragmentation of activities into production, bottling, and distribution, has been accompanied by strategies that involve large-scale reduction in regular employment and increased use of contract labor. BOC India now has more contract workers than regular workers. The contract workers now do most unskilled and non-core jobs. Increasing use of contract labor is not restricted in BOC India, it is now widespread in all industries and in all types of firms in India (Patel 1997). It is more common in activities like security, canteen maintenance, transport, and housekeeping. Most new firms have a higher percentage of contract workers than old firms and some firms even have more contract workers than regular workers (Table 5.1). Further, increasing use of contract labor is not an Indian phenomenon, there are examples from all over the world (ILO 1997). The contract workers get wages and benefits lower than the regular workers and have relatively inferior working conditions. Their wages are higher than the prevailing wages in the informal sector and they are expected to receive benefits under social security legislations on PF, ESI, and get overtime wages. However, these legislations are less effective for the contractor workers than for the regular workers. The wages and working conditions of contract workers vary from state to state. They are higher in locations and in firms having trade unions. The objectives of engagement of contractor workers are minimization of labor and overhead costs, and increase in labor flexibility. The lower cost and increased labor flexibility is because most contract firms are small and are outside the coverage of major labor legislation.[13]

There are two main types of contract labor: those engaged in labor contracts and those engaged in job contracts. In labor contract, contractors' only task is to supply labor to the user enterprises

Table 5.1: Firms and Their Contract Workers—Union/Non-union[14]

Name of Firm and Location	*Year of Establishment*	*Type of Firm*	*Number of Regular Employees*	*% of Executives in Employees*	*Contract Workers as % of Employees*	*Union Status of Contract Workers*	*Wage Determination*
Alstom AEI, Kolkata	1942	French MNC	550	29	15	Unionized	Union wage agreement
Indian Rayon, Rishra	1949	Indian MNC	2,100	19	10	Unionized	Union wage agreement
Alstom Power, Durgapur	1959	French MNC	560	28	17	Unionized	Union wage agreement
Hind Leaver Chemicals, Haldia	1979	Indian Firm	388	18	115	Unionized	Union wage agreement
BOC India (Restructured in 1990s)	1935	British MNC	637	51	69	Unionized	Union wage agreements
Mitsubishi Chemicals, Haldia	2000	Japanese MNC	313	34	120	Unionized	Union wage agreement
Haldia Petro-chemicals, Haldia	2000	Joint venture	1,050	66	40	Unionized	Union wage agreement
Ingersoll Rand, Ahmedabad	1965	US MNC	404	53	12	No Union	Minimum wages
Reliance Textile, Ahmedabad	1968	Indian Firm	3128	28	20	No Union	Minimum wages
Hitach Amtrex, Ahmedabad	1982	Joint venture	180	46	110	No Union	Minimum wages
Torrent, Ahmedabad	1991	Indian Firm	450	75	90	No Union	Minimum wages

Source: The data is based on the numbers reported during plant visits; some of the plants have been further restructured.

and in return get a percentage of wage costs as agency fees.[15] The second type is based on contract of services, such as loading–unloading (Egger 1997: 3). There are examples of both these types and sometimes the contracts are a combination of the two. Employment relations for contractor workers are different from those of regular workers. In India, the basic legal framework provides a system of dual control over contract labor by both the contractors and the principal employers. Unlike direct labor, which is on the payrolls of establishments, contract labor is neither on the payrolls of the principal employers nor paid directly. In payment of wages, there is no direct link between contract labor and principal employers, but the legal provisions require the principal employers to conform to certain aspects of the employment relationship between contractors and their workers. The extent of influence of the principal employers and the contractors on contract workers varies depending on the type of contract. In labor contracts, the principal employers have more control over labor relations for contract workers than in job contracts. In most labor contracts, the principal employer closely monitors the activities of contractor workers, provides training, and has final control over their shop-floor behavior. Most often floor-level managers see them as casual workers, as if they are part of the organization. There are some disadvantages of contracting out of jobs (Domberger 1998), but close supervision by the firms' managers can minimize some of the disadvantages. This has added new responsibilities for the HR managers.

A contractor in relation to an establishment means a person who undertakes to produce a given result for an establishment other than mere supply of goods or articles of manufacture.[16] In India, engagement of contract labor in perennial jobs is prohibited under the Contract Labor (Regulation and Abolition) Act 1970, but this provision has remained ineffective because of legal loopholes and lack of faith in its application. The Act provides for abolition of contract labor in perennial jobs, but does not provide for their absorption in the permanent rolls of the principal employers. This provision has been applied in some public sector units and some court orders favor their absorption, but it has remained ineffective in the private sector.[17] The liberal policies adopted by the governments with reduced involvement of the state and more reliance on markets have made contracting of jobs more attractive than in-house production (Domberger 1998: 9). Employers have demanded for removal of the restrictions on engagement of contract labor, but the attempts to remove the restrictions have failed.[18] The Act has not been amended, but there have been changes in the perceptions of policy makers and unions. They are now more tolerant about use of contract labor. Increased use of contract labor has added new dimensions in managing people at work. The segregation of contractor workers from regular employees means that the management can now have different approaches in managing the two groups of people at work. In the core the main task is now on getting the commitments of regular employees towards company objectives, and in the periphery the focus is on reduction of conflicts in managing contractor workers.

Changing Roles of Unions and Employees

BOC India, established in 1935, is not only one of the oldest industrial organizations in India, it also has a long history of unionization. In its Kolkata plant, a union was formed in 1948. Sri Jyoti Basu became its first president and he remained president throughout his tenure as Chief Minister of West Bengal for about two decades. Initially, the union was affiliated to the AITUC, but after its bifurcation it became affiliated to the CITU. At the time of restructuring, the Kolkata union was affiliated to the CITU and in other locations the unions were either independent or affiliated to the INTUC. The types of unions and their affiliations are still the same in most old locations, but their power and influence have declined and some new firms are now without any union. The decline of unions is not only because of a decline in employment, it is also because of drop in the proportion of blue-collar workers. Although there were multiple unions for brief periods in some plants, BOC India all through recognized only one union in a location.[19] In new units management adopted union-avoidance strategy. The new tonnage plants do not have any blue-collar worker in direct employment and they do not have any union.

The unionization of contract workers differs across locations (some have unions and some do not) and the unions of contract workers also differ in their relationship with the unions of regular workers.[20]

In BOC India, the presence of different unions in different locations has led to different wage agreements in different locations. There are, however, many similarities among these agreements, as unions in different locations have coordinated their activities. This has resulted in a form of pattern bargaining. Most often, the wage agreements signed with the CITU union in West Bengal have been followed and re-created in other locations with some minor modifications like changes in linkages of dearness allowance (DA) with the cost of living index. The coordination between the unions is also evident in the formation of a coordination committee with office bearers of the trade unions from different locations that bargain annual bonus. The active and passive coordination between the unions in different locations and adoption of union agreements in some non-union locations have led to similarities in working conditions in different plants.[21] The restructuring of BOC India has led to a decline in pattern bargaining and some dissimilarities in employment practices in different locations. The employment practices in the bottling plants, for example, are now different from those in the new tonnage plants.

The restructuring of BOC India has involved long negotiations with its trade unions. The unions initially opposed VRS, closure, and divestment of units, and in some locations there have been some legal complications. In the Ghatkopar plant, for example, the union moved Mumbai High Court against the state government's permission for its closure in 1998. The court ordered reopening of the factory and payment of back wages. This led to complications and delayed closure of the unit. The divestment of non-core business involved long negotiation with the workers and guarantees by both new and old employers for retaining existing terms and conditions of employment.[22] In the initial years of restructuring, there were growing conflicts with the unions, but over time the conflicts declined. The long-term wage agreements in 1992, 1996, and 2000 include issues relating to labor flexibility, productivity, elimination of restrictive practices, and improvement of organizational performance. The old productivity improvement scheme has been replaced by a prosperity-sharing scheme. The agreements provide for complete interchangeability among the workers in their respective grades and in the higher grades with acting allowances. They have specific clauses on employee involvement, new workplace practices, and progressive implementation of the BOC group standards. In contrast to past practices, increases in wages are now greater at higher levels than at lower levels. In the agreements, the union and workers agreed to extend full cooperation in training, skill improvement, and workplace safety. They agreed to introduce attendance tracking through time cards, use of safety gear/apparel, training on non-working days, and avoiding delays in introduction of new machines. The unions are no longer opposed to contracting out of jobs and they are now more amenable to changes in organizational structures and practices.[23] All these indicate a departure from the past practices.

Networking and MIS

The restructured BOC now needs more coordination among its different fragmented activities than it needed in the past. The production of liquid gasses, their storage, bulk transportation, bottling of the gasses, storage of cylinders, their transportation and distribution to depots, and sales agents need to be coordinated for effective and efficient functioning of the organization. Management needs to closely monitor these activities that take place at different locations. Further, as many activities like transportation of liquid gasses and cylinders have been contracted out, the need for close supervision is now much more than what would be needed in the case of in-house operations. The new structure needs an efficient and cost-effective logistic system to deliver the products to the customers at the right place, at the right time, and at the lowest cost. In BOC India, the management introduced an MIS to monitor and control the different activities in multiple locations on a real-time basis.

BOC India has transformed its business through inter-enterprise computing by linking their computer system with their bulk customers, contractors, and dealers. Its internationally renowned MIS system is an integrated system for sales, distribution, production planning, finance, materials management, and HRM. It provides online and real-time information for critical management decisions. The inter-enterprise computing enables them to forecast demand for products and helps dealers to strengthen their supply position, reduce inventory, and improve product availability. When a truckload of cylinders reaches a dealer, a stream of computer bits is sent across the network all the way to the depots, transportation system, bottling plants, and tonnage plants. This puts into motion a series of activities that result in the cylinders being replenished. In the past, different parts of the organization and their customers exchanged funds, information, and knowledge by physical means through paper documentation, such as letters, reports, invoices, computer printouts, checks, face-to-face meetings, and telephone calls. Consistent with this arrangement was a computer system that was internal to each part. In contrast, the new system now extends all over the organization and includes customers, dealers, and other partners. This has speeded up communications between different paths with reduced costs. The HRM system is a part of the integrated system. The changes have created new kinds of relationships between the organizations and their people.

Introduction of HRM Practices

Since the mid-1980s, HRM has emerged as an exciting new approach to managing people at work. It is a "distinctive approach to employee management which seeks to achieve competitive advantage through strategic deployment of a highly committed and capable workforce, using an integrated array of cultural, structural, and personal techniques" (Storey 1992: 5). The HRM approach has many different connotations depending on who is using it and for what purpose. It combines a whole bag of strategies ranging from selection of employees to rewards and continuous improvement. It emphasizes extensive communication, employee participation, and flexibility in labor deployment. In BOC India, the management adopted the HRM approach to manage its highly skilled employees in the new plants and introduced some of the HRM practices in its restructured old plants. Introduction of new technology needed employees with new skills and old skills became redundant. The tonnage plants, for example, recruited qualified engineers to run sophisticated equipments in place of homegrown skilled hands used in the old plants. As the new technology increased production, it recruited new marketing and sales personnel. With reduced manpower and increase in the proportion of highly skilled employees, the management introduced the HRM pattern employment relations for employee management in BOC India.

Prior to major restructuring in the 1990s, employment relations in BOC India was characterized by a bounded amount of conflict between capital and labor. The workers were paid well primarily because of the "union wage effect" and unions believed that their continuous struggle helped to improve conditions of employees. In the protective environment, the company was making money, but there was enough scope to improve performance. The restructuring program reduced workforce drastically with redistribution of work through transfer, retraining, and redeployment. This created a sense of uncertainty among its employees. Tackling post-restructuring issues in a way that could create a sense of stability, maintain employee morale, and re-establish employee commitment to the company's objectives became an important issue. In order to achieve this, the management introduced HRM practices. It established a system of continuous communication with the employees with increased emphasis on close ties among the employees. The reduction in manpower was accompanied by reduction in the organizational hierarchy. The earlier concept of detailed designation has been done away with, employees are now identified by grades only, and the number of grades has been reduced.[24] Movement from one job to another is now easier, permitting movements both within and across grades. New employees with computer skills have replaced old employees with traditional skills. The employees now have better ability to adapt to future changes, both within and outside the company. The sharing of the benefits of higher productivity and wage increases has helped to reinforce employee confidence.

In BOC India, there has been increased emphasis on skill development, revitalization of human capital, de-layering of the organization, and teamwork. Initiatives were taken in training and development, competency mapping, and career planning, with particular focus on strengthening sales and marketing and providing it with new skills to effectuate a culture of customer service. It launched a survey on employee involvement and devised a reward scheme based on the survey results (Banerjee 2001: 41). Along with retraining of existing managers, competent young professionals have been recruited to look at things differently and explore new areas of improvement. The principle of accountability, collaboration, transparency, and stress (ACTS) is now an integral part of the work culture. A new performance management system has been introduced to reward outstanding performance of individuals and teams. The management introduced the team concept to build an effective group processes. As every individual became indispensable due to reduction in workforce, the teamwork has helped in dealing with uncertainties like absence of a group member. The members of groups after reorganization now need new survival skills that emphasize skill, quality, and performance improvement (Banerjee 2001: 43). In the new plants, employment relation represents the HRM pattern. In the unionized plants, the management has introduced some HR practices and has increased employee and union involvement in matters of mutual interest, such as safety and quality improvement.[25] The changes have led to improvements in their operations and performance. In these plants, employment relations have shifted from the traditional pattern to a form of the joint-team-based pattern.

Transformation in Employment Relations

Employment relations in BOC India is now markedly different from the traditional arrangements that existed in the early 1980s. The company has experienced many changes in its IR environment over the years. This has changed its functioning and employee management. Over time, its employment relations have changed and the most dramatic changes had been in the 1990s. All the plants of BOC India have seen introduction of new technology, large-scale reduction in employment, and contracting out of non-core activities. There have been fundamental changes in the operations of many parts of the organization as well as in the relationship between different parts. It has closed down many of its unviable units, established new tonnage plants, and converted most old composite plants into bottling plants. In the new tonnage plants, the majority of direct employees are engineers and managers and they do not have any blue-collar workers. The old plants have also changed; they now only bottle gases, and have fewer employees. Many employees have left with VRS and some highly skilled new recruits have joined in different locations. This has changed its structure of employment. In the past, all plants were unionized, now new plants do not have any union. In the past, pattern bargaining determined employee wages and benefits and employment relations resembled the bureaucratic pattern with bounded amount of conflict between capital and labor. In the restructured company, the new plants have the HRM pattern of employment relations and the bottling plants have the joint-team-based pattern. As new plants have come up with new technology, new employees, and new employment practices, the changes appear to be dramatic and discontinuous.

In both old and new plants, there are some similar shifts in management strategies (for example, strategies toward contract workers). Further, the integrated MIS has increased coordination between different plants. In spite of these converging forces, the employment relations in the old plants are markedly different from those in the new plants. The differences are in terms of a number of practices. First, the new plants have more contractor workers than the old plants. All plants have adopted the core-periphery model in employment relations with direct employees performing the core jobs and the contract workers performing the non-core peripheral jobs, but the proportion of contractor workers is much more in new plants than in old plants. Second, there are differences across plants in the types of core employees. In the new plants, the core represents highly skilled technical and professional employees, but the old plants still have large number of blue-collar workers. Third, there are differences in management of human resources.

The new plants use modern HRM techniques with extensive communication, employee involvement, and teamwork. In the old plants, too, management has tried to adopt some of these practices, but they are less developed and they still have some legacies of the traditional practices. Fourth, there are differences in management strategy toward unionization–union-avoidance in the new plants and union-substitution in the old unionized plants. Finally, the new plants with highly skilled and better educated workers have more labor flexibility than old plants having large number of low skilled workers. The changes have created new kinds of relationships between the organization and its people.

BOC India has seen dramatic changes in its employment relations over a short period of time, which indicates "transformation" in its employment relations system.[26] The term "transformation" is used here to mean rapid, fundamental, and discontinuous change in employment relations system (Erickson and Kuruvilla 1998).[27] It is distinguished from non-fundamental and incremental changes. The key element in deciding whether a transformation has occurred is whether or not there have been changes in the deep structures of the employment relations system. The changes that do no involve change in the deep structures cannot be labeled as a transformation. In other words, the main issue is whether there has been serious reconsideration of the network of fundamental and interdependent choices that determine the basic structure of employment relation systems. The fundamental changes in employment relations in a firm can occur in two ways, in a gradually adaptive way or in a discontinuous revolutionary fashion. The key defining features of a "discontinuous" change are the speed of the changes (relative to the previous periods of change) and an increase in diversity. The changes are in terms of changes in various elements of employment relation systems and the relationship between the elements. The elements here are employment rules, management style, structure of work organization, pay procedure, job security, and employer–employee relations. The rapid change in employment relation systems in BOC India with changes in the deep structures of its employment relations indicates transformation in its employment relations system.

Notes

1. The term transformation is used here to mean rapid, fundamental, and discontinuous changes in employment systems as described by Erickson and Kuruvilla (1998). It is distinguished from the non-fundamental and incremental changes.
2. There are many examples of lockouts for long periods. In West Bengal, for example, 266 units involving 32,000 workers were under lockout for more than a year in 2005 and more than half of them were under lockout for more than 10 years.
3. They closed plants in Ranchi, Kanpur, Guwahati in 1991, a plant in Delhi in 1996, and Ghatakopar-Mumbai plant in 1999. The Kanpur unit was closed after obtaining government permission. They locked out the Asansol unit in 1998 and reopened after two years with only three workers.
4. It sold the health care division to the Indian associate of a health care major, Instrumentarium Corporation, which is now part of Datex-Ohmeda (India) Private Limited (BOC India 2001).
5. There are some state amendments. In West Bengal firms with fifty or more workers need permission.
6. Most agreements have general clauses on cooperation for modernization, but few have specific clauses. ITC, Tribeni Tissue agreement in 1993 had specific clauses on implementation of modernization program (Das 2000).
7. Only four employees in the Taluja plant in Maharashtra are paid according to the union agreements, but they are not union members.
8. The division contributes 96 percent of total sales (82 percent industrial gases and rest medical gases).
9. The Tarapur plant built in 1989 has a daily capacity of 100 tons. The Taloja plant built in 1994 has daily capacity of 110 tons. The Jamshedpur plant built in 1998 has a daily capacity of 1,290 tons.
10. The bottling plants or compressor units (twenty numbers) are located all over the country. The cylinders from the bottling plants are distributed to over thirty-nine depots/warehouses and finally supplied to dealers and customers.
11. Every day, 100 tankers carry more than 300 tons of liquid gases and cover about 2,500 km.
12. Of the 630 direct employees in BOC, about half are in the managerial category, which in the past was only 10 percent. Employment in the gases division dropped from 4,000 in 1989 to 500 in 2003.
13. The Industrial Disputes Act 1948, for example, puts several restrictions on firms with 100 or more workers, but most contractor firms being small in size do not face such restrictions.

14. Most firms have large number of contractor workers engaged in loading/unloading (example, about 30 percent in Mitshubishi Chemicals, and about 60 percent in Hind Lever Chemicals).
15. The agency fee varies across firms. In BOC India, it is about 8–12 percent of the wage costs.
16. Section 2c of the Contract Labor (Regulation and Abolition) Act, 1970.
17. The Supreme Court judgment in the Air India case (1997) observes that Section 10 of the Act clearly indicates the inherent legislative intent of making the erstwhile contract laborers direct employees of the employer on abolition of the intermediary contractor.
18. The Union Budget 2001–2002 proposed to facilitate outsourcing and contractual appointments.
19. After bifurcation of the AITUC and formation of the CITU, the unit had two unions for a brief period, but finally the AITUC union became non-functional. In the early 1970s, a new union affiliated to the INTUC was formed, but it became non-functional by 1977.
20. In the Kolkata factory, the regular workers' union represents the contract workers. The Taloja plant does not have any union of contract workers, but some security workers provided by the Maharashtra Contractor Workers' Board are members of a union.
21. Non-members in categories that are covered in the union agreement are paid according to the agreement (for example, Taloja plant).
22. Esab India took over the welding business as a going concern. The sale agreement included specific clauses on retaining the terms and conditions of services of the employees.
23. In 1995, the charter of demand included demands for abolition of the contract system and absorption of contract workers in perennial jobs, but there was no such demand in 1999.
24. The number of grades was brought down from seven (sixteen) to three in office and from eleven (thirty-three) to five in the factory by the 1992 and 1996 settlements.
25. The exercise of obtaining ISO-9000 certification that started in 1992 involved all employees, irrespective of their grades and positions. By 1995, all its units received ISO-9000 certification.
26. There are similar changes in employment relations in many other companies in India. Examples of such firms in West Bengal include Texmaco, Alstom Power, ABB, and ICI.
27. Erickson and Kuruvilla (1998) applied the concepts in their discussions of national systems; they can also be applied to discussions on transformation of employment system of a company or a firm.

Chapter 6

Employment Relations in IT-enabled Services

INFORMATION AND COMMUNICATION technology (ICT) has rewritten the agenda for the industrial world. Old ideas about how to manage organizations and their people are withering away and new ideas that emphasize IT and knowledge management are replacing them. According to the new ideas, flow of intelligence, ideas, and knowledge are now the main contributors of economic development and corporate profits. The key strategy is to increase firms' ability to collect, process, and disseminate information in a way that can improve organizational performance. In recent times, there has been an explosion of information and knowledge, and organizations now need to manage them effectively. The changes have been in all spheres of management and more so for management of human resources, as HRM is profoundly information intensive. Firms differ in their use of IT. Most modern firms today use IT to improve organizational efficiency, but few utilize it as their core activity and few have an integrated MIS that links all individuals with the system. Of particular interest are the IT firms. They provide IT services—hardware or software or information processing services. ITES sector (like the customer call centers), which is a sub-sector of the IT software and services sector, covers a wide range of services that are possible to be rendered cost effectively only by using IT.

Over the past decade, the ITES sector in India has seen phenomenal growth. It has logged the highest growth among the software and services segments and there are indications that the growth will continue. India has emerged as a preferred location for organizations in developed countries planning to outsource their ITES. The world market for ITES is expected to grow further and India is expected to capture a sizable portion of the market. The study of employment relations in the ITES sector is important for a number of reasons. First, the ITES firms provide human-intensive services and engage a large number of employees. Second, unlike the IT software firms that engage IT professionals, the ITES firms engage employees with general education. Third, as the services are delivered over telecom networks to customers that are often outside the country, it creates linkages that reinforce global influences. Fourth, it creates new forms of work organization with management control using IT-network and new workplace practices. Finally, the sector is emerging as a key business opportunity for the export-driven market. This chapter describes employment relations in the ITES firms and compares them with the firms in other industries in India and with the ITES firms in other countries. It examines use of IT in management of HR.

Growth of IT and IT-enabled Services in India

The Indian IT industry has grown exponentially since early 1990s, both in absolute terms and in terms of share of GDP. It accounts for about 12 percent of the employment in the organized private sector.[1] The sector has even shown substantial growth during the global slowdown and there is still considerable room for further growth. IT essentially refers to all kinds of digital processing, storage, and communication of information. The basic distinction within the IT sector is between hardware and software services. The former refers to physical components of processors, storage devices, and communication devices, while the latter refers to instructions that govern the flow and processing of information in digital form. Many Indian firms perform hardware assembly and maintenance tasks, but the software segment is much more robust than the hardware industry. Many firms in developed countries are outsourcing their software requirements to Indian companies, and Indian software majors are gradually moving up in the value chain in terms of capabilities and breadth of solutions offered. According to the National Association of Software and Services Companies (NASSCOM), one out of every four global giants outsources its critical software requirements to India. Of the total annual revenue in software services, the software exports contribute to about three-fourths of the gross revenue and the domestic software market accounts for one-fourth of total revenue. Apart from the high-growth export segment, the domestic software market is also growing steadily and is expected to grow faster in the next decade (NASSCOM Foundation 2008).

ITES includes human-intensive services that are delivered over telecom networks or the Internet to a range of business segments and verticals. It includes a variety of services ranging from call centers and other customer interaction services, insurance claims processing, payroll processing, medical transcription, and back-office operations. According to a Nasscom-McKinsey study, India is well positioned to derive benefits from the ITES market and become a key hub for these services. The importance of the sector is reflected in its potential to create employment. The sector accounts for 23 percent of the revenue in the IT services sector, but its share in employment is 35 percent (NASSCOM 2002). The potential of employment generation through ITES in India is to be viewed in the broader scenario in the Indian economy. Since the 1980s, there has been slow growth in the organized sector employment, but this sector has shown impressive growth in the organized sector employment. This is particularly important in the context of increasing supply of educated youth seeking employment. The labor-intensive nature of the ITES sector and its recent phenomenal growth in India make this sector particularly important for the study.

India's software export boom is attributed to its comparative advantage. Its strength lies in low employee costs, availability of a large pool of workers with software and language skills, and supportive government policies. The existence of technical education institutions like the IITs, the ubiquity of UNIX in the academic environment, and the relatively low cost of education have helped in the development of the industry in India (Singh 2002). Indian IT workers are ranked high in terms of capability, quality of work, and work ethic in the international market (Fiveson 2001). Average inbound, outbound, and web support programs cost much less in India as compared to the United States (outsourcing to India gives a savings of about 40 percent). In India, labor costs are low, but productivity levels are comparable to those in the developed countries. In certain ITES categories, such as back-office operations, Indian centers have achieved even higher productivity levels than their western counterparts. India's unique geographic location also helps in reducing turnaround times in certain operations like data conversions by leveraging time zone differences. The favorable and progressive government policies, such as tax holidays, incentives, and infrastructure facilities for setting up ITS and ITES centers have helped in the industry's growth. The industry has developed in a much less restrictive environment than firms in the manufacturing sector or traditional firms in the service sector. Further, as most domestic firms have developed independent of traditional business houses, they are free from the bad habits of those business houses developed over many decades of operating in a protective environment (Kapur 2002; Singh 2002: 17). All these factors have contributed to the high growth of India's IT and ITES industry.

There are different types of ITES firms, and often the different categories overlap as firms can have more than one activity.

The three broad segments in the spectrum of ITES in India are: (*a*) customer interaction services, including call centers, (*b*) back-office operations/revenue accounting, data entry, data conversion, including finance, accounting, and HR services, and (*c*) content development/animation/engineering and design and Geographical Information System (GIS). The current trend indicates that these three sub-sectors will remain important even in the next decade. Of the three major segments, the third segment needs employees with specialized computer skills, while the first two are labor-intensive and do not need any specialized technical skill [for example, the Customer Service Representatives (CSRs) in call centers or data operators in back-office operations]. The customer service centers have trained employees and access to requisite databases, Internet, and other online information infrastructure round the clock. They provide support in areas, such as marketing, selling, technical help, and so forth. In back-office operations, firms generally handle data for verticals, such as banks and civil aviation. They receive raw data or paper documents and do data entry and necessary reconciliation. This chapter examines employment relations in ITES firms with examples of customer service centers and back-office operations.

Employment Relations in Call Centers: The Debate

Employment relations can be organized differently in different firms and management can choose from different alternative models of employment relation. Various factors, such as physical technology, social environment, conditions of labor markets, and government regulations limit their choices. Broadly, there are two models for organizing work—the industrial model and the salaried model (Box 6.1). Of the two models, the industrial model describes much of the blue-collar work, while the salaried model characterizes much of the white-collar work (Osterman 1987). In the ITES firms, the jobs are no doubt white-collar jobs, but their work organization does not represent a pure salaried model.

Box 6.1: Industrial Model and Salaried Model of Work Organization

> In the industrial model, work is organized into a series of tightly defined jobs with clear work rules and responsibilities for each job. Management's freedom to move workers from one job to another is limited by seniority provisions and some times by workers' willingness. Wages are attached to jobs and jobs are clearly defined. Everyone knows who is doing what work, and who is entitled to what wages. In contrast, the salaried model is more flexible with more personalized administrative procedures. Individuals have job descriptions, but the immediate superiors can change them. The flexible job description in the salaried model allows a greater role of personal qualities and merit considerations in wage setting. The industrial and salaried models are primarily models for organizing blue-collar and white-collar work, respectively, but the salaried model is also seen in some manufacturing firms and the industrial model is also found in some white-collar work.

Source: Osterman (1987: 47–51).

Most IR and HRM research emphasizes blue-collar work and examines employment relations in manufacturing industries. Only a few studies examine the service sector or the salaried model. The salaried model, which is equally important, not only describes employment patterns of large numbers of workers in the service sector, it is also seen in some innovative employment settings in the manufacturing sector. Further, some of its characteristics represent the general direction in which management is trying to reorganize work. Within the salaried sector, the ITES firms are particularly important because they emphasize the use of IT and knowledge management in employee control. The emergence of the IT sector in India has to be studied in the context of changes in the Indian economy and the spread of new HR practices. India's integration with the world economy began only in the 1990s and India is also a latecomer to HRM. Indian industry is more familiar with HRD, a concept that focuses on improving the skills, knowledge, and attitudes of individual employees (Ramswamy 2000: 217). In this background, the ITES industry is an excellent sector to study the spread of HRM practices and use of IT in employee management in India.

Employment relations in call centers is described by two contrasting images. The first image emphasizes the constraining nature of the work setting, an appropriate metaphor being electronic sweatshops or the panoptical wired cage (Frenkel et al. 1998: 957). According to this view, the employees are connected to IT that automatically allocates work, facilitates its completion, and monitors employee performance. Work is deskilled and monotonous and is conducted in relative isolation from their colleagues but under close supervision of management. A contrasting positive image of call centers sees workers as semi-professionals, where workers are empowered and work is customized to customers' needs. This improves workers' knowledge and skills, and the semi-professional status of workers provides favorable work relations. Frenkel et al. (1998) argues that neither the deeply pessimistic view nor the strongly optimistic view is a fair representation of employment relations in call centers. Instead, a complex hybrid form of work organization represents the real picture that provides for both routinized and customized responses. The practices in call centers are different from those in the ideal bureaucratic model. The employment system is best described as "mass customized bureaucracy" (Frenkel et al. 1998). It has some aspects of the bureaucratic model but departs from it in other respects. This hybrid form is characterized by precise hiring criteria, training for job proficiency, limited career opportunity, and a greater element of performance/skill-based pay. The control relations are characterized by strong reliance on IT and facilitative supervision referred to as "info-normative control."

How IT-enabled Firms Differ from Other Firms

Most studies in management methods, work reorganization, employment practices, and IR began in the manufacturing setting. Many of these studies argue that their models are universal and apply equally to all work settings. However, there are now arguments that there exist other models of employment relations, and that different models are suitable under different circumstances.

The differences in the employment practices between the manufacturing and service sector firms are partly because of differences in the nature of work in the two sectors (Appelbaum and Batt 1994: 98–99). The way work is organized in the service-producing firms is different from those in the goods-producing industries. In a manufacturing plant, a group of workers are directly involved in production or assembly of a final product (such as an automobile or a mobile phone) and no one worker is responsible for producing an entire product. In contrast, service contact work requires an individual employee to work with an individual customer. An employee here is like a craft worker in goods production, where the customer–employee link is as important as the employer–employee relationship. The way to improve performance here is to increase the breadth and depth of the workers' skill so that they can handle most or all of the customers' needs. Quality control is relatively difficult in the service industry because services are delivered as and when produced and there is no scope for pre-inspection. Given its importance and problems of measurement and control, performance measurement takes a dominant role and often includes measurement from customer's point of view. This is particularly important in firms that aim to provide high-quality services (Appelbaum and Batt 1994: 105–106).

Work organization in call centers, in contrast to most large firms in the service sector, is relatively new, physically different, and dominated by the use of IT facilities. Every aspect of work is monitored and controlled by using IT. The CSRs work in large, open-plan offices seated in cubicles divided by shoulder-high partitions. They are integrated into the networked computer/telephone systems through their headphones. While speaking to a customer on the telephone, they read and enter data into a personal computer that is networked within the organization, and sometimes it extends to other organizations. Most often the CSRs are required to answer incoming calls or make outgoing calls. They are required to provide customers with product and procedural information, process customer transactions, and attend customer queries in a responsive, accurate, and timely manner. In call centers, work is so designed that there is less emphasis on a particular narrow function by a worker and more focus on the customers. In this setting, jobs of front-line workers are expanded to allow them to handle a customer request independently without contacting their supervisors. In this customer-oriented structure, each manager controls total transactions for a particular set of customers. The work settings of call centers in India described earlier are similar to those seen in other countries.

Jobs of CSRs are organized around particular markets, or geographic area or particular types of business customers. A sense of teamwork and cooperation arises from their training, which aims to improve communication among workers and between workers and managers. Electronic monitoring, including spot checks of phone conversations by supervisors and daily evaluation reports, ensures quality of services (Appelbaum and Batt 1994: 107–108). Typically, for every ten to twenty CSRs there is a team leader, and one supervisor for three team leaders. The supervisors report to the managers, who are responsible for an account or a business customer. In call centers, management expects the CSRs to handle their customers in accordance with specified service standards and guidelines. The CSRs have some discretion in their work, but they must conform to the company procedures and policies and provide services that leave customers feeling satisfied and valued. While the first condition ensures standardization and cost-minimization, the second aims at fostering customer loyalty and service quality.

The customer-contact service centers differ from manufacturing organizations and arguably these differences shape their employment relations. In manufacturing organizations, for example, the front-line workers produce a tangible product in relatively close physical proximity of one another and their work is interdependent. Improving performance depends on improving coordination between the workers and understanding how what is done at one point in the process affects work in another point. By contrast, successful performance in customer-contact jobs requires individual workers to develop a close relationship with a customer. In this setting, a low-cost strategy means: low-wage workers, designing narrow jobs to accommodate such workers, and using company rules and technology to control their work. This approach creates dissatisfaction and poor service, high turnover, and lack of continuity between the employees and the customers. In customer-contact services, the way to improve service is to move away from the impersonal and assembly line mentality to a more "professional" or personal model of client contact. Front-line workers need to have the ability to handle multiple issues to reduce the time for solving a problem in a way that does not require talking to more than one person. To achieve this, workers need a deeper understanding of the services that the firm offers and command over information or computer systems to answer customer questions with accuracy. The advantage of teamwork in this setting is primarily the mutual gains achieved by employees in learning from one another, in problem solving, and in supporting each other (Appelbaum and Batt 1994: 109).

There are other specific issues for the customer contact centers in India. They are located in India, but they sell their services in other countries (mostly in the United States). This export of services is different from the export of products by manufacturing firms. Here, the services are produced and exported to customers at the same point of time and the employees are in direct contact with the customers. Considering the location differences, there are three important issues relating to the employees. First, as most customers are located in the United States with a time delay of about twelve hours, the service centers mostly operate at night and only a few employees work during the regular office hours. Inconvenient working hours lead to problems in keeping employees in good physical and mental health. In general, there are two shifts; one starts in mid-night and the other early morning. Second, as the holidays in these firms are same as holidays in the United States, employees cannot get leave even on national holidays when their relatives and friends enjoy their holidays. This increases the need to develop friendship with fellow employees. Third, as the CSRs directly deal over phone with customers who are members of a different culture, they have to learn the key cross-cultural differences between India and the United States. They have to understand the customer accents, common American word usage, slang, and idioms. In work, CSRs are expected to identify themselves closely with the American society. They are thus called "virtual aliens" (Tapscott 1995: 5).

Most employees in the call centers work as CSRs or agents and a substantial number of them are female employees (Table 6.1). Only few of the employees in call centers work in higher positions and few technical workers are engaged to maintain the IT facilities. In addition to creation of jobs for CSRs and at higher positions, call centers also create indirect jobs. They engage contract workers in low-skill activities, such as security, housekeeping, canteen, and transportation. In the software technology parks, the software park management provides some of the services centrally in exchange for a service charge. In general, the number of contractor workers is about 15–20 percent of the regular workers. The contractor workers in customer service centers or those engaged by the software park management are no different from those in other types of firms. The primary focus of employee management in call centers is for the CSRs, who represent the majority of workers in call centers. All studies on call

Table 6.1: Employment in IT-enabled Service Firms

Name of Firm	*Location*	*Type of Service*	*Employees*	*Agents*	*Female Agents (%)*
BNK International	Kolkata	Call center: inbound and outbound calls	155	120	45
First Ring India Pvt. Ltd.	Bangalore	Call center: inbound and outbound calls	900	830	38
HSBC Data Processing	Hyderabad	Call center and back-office operations	2,000	1,800	50
24/7 Customer.com	Bangalore	Call center: inbound and outbound calls	700	600	30
Data Core of DCL	Kolkata	Back-office operations	180	150	100
Vishnu Solutions	Kolkata	Call center: outbound calls	200	180	35

Source: Based on data collected from individual firms.

centers, therefore, focus on employment relation issues relating to the CSRs.

Case Studies of Call Centers

The Indian ITES had its roots in the mid-1990s, when several ITES companies were established in different parts of the country. The companies such as American Express, British Airways, and GE Capital established their captive units for customer support and transaction-processing services.[2] Some of the ITES firms are captive units of MNCs handling customer services for the parent company (for example, HSBC), some are arms of the ITES firms in the developed countries doing jobs for different offshore firms (for example, 24/7 Customer.com), and some are independent firms that handle jobs for a number of clients (for example, BNK International). Along with the differences in ownership patterns, ITES firms also differ in their organizational structure and these differences have substantial influence on their operations.

ITES firms differ by their activities and nature of work. Some operate purely as call centers and handle different types of calls, some do back-office operations, and some perform both the functions. Whatever be the activity, all ITES firms do some data processing. However call centers do less data processing than firms having back-office operations. Call centers differ by the types of calls: some handle only inbound calls, some handle only outbound calls, and some handle both inbound and outbound calls. In brief, the ITES firms in India differ from each other depending on their ownership, relations with clients, and types of functions. The issues in employment relations for the CSRs recruitment, training, career structure, reward systems, monitoring, and evaluation are discussed here based on the case studies of a number of firms. The firms differ in their nature of work, type of customers, relationship with customers, organizational structures, and methods of marketing their services (Box 6.2).

Box 6.2: IT-enabled Service Firms Differ by Activities

1. Data Core, Kolkata, established in the 1990s, does only back-office operations outsourced by its counterpart in the United States. It is a subsidiary of DCPL.
2. HSBC Data Processing India, a wholly owned subsidiary of HSBC, started its operations in year 2000. Its three units (two in Hyderabad, one in Bangalore) with about 3,200 seats do data processing for bank services, such as mortgage and worldwide payments and manage inbound calls from HSBC customers.
3. BNK International, Kolkata, is an independent vendor. It has 120 seats and deals with both inbound and outbound calls. It can receive all types of calls, that is voice, fax, e-mail, chat, and so forth, and has fully equipped back office support system.
4. First Ring India, Bangalore, subsidiary of a US company, handles inbound calls for credit card holders and outbound calls for financial and marketing services of credit card companies. Its US partner closely monitors the programs and expatriates fill up the senior positions.
5. 24/7 Customer.com, Bangalore, with 700 seats does inbound and outbound calls for telecom, hotel, car rental, and merchant services. It started as an e-mail support and e-commerce company in year 2000, but then shifted to voice transcription and call center activities.
6. Vishnu Solution, Kolkata, handles only outbound calls. It does telemarketing for their clients, who have provided a database of phone numbers. The agents are expected to sell at least a minimum percent of the calls.

Source: Based on the information collected during the field visits of the centers mentioned in Table 6.1.

Selection and Recruitment

Discussions on structure employment relations in a firm typically center on selection and recruitment, training and retraining, grievance redress mechanisms, monitoring and evaluation, and rewarding of employees. Selection and recruitment decisions involve a number of issues, such as determination of jobs to be filled, skills and knowledge required, sources of recruitment, and criteria and procedures to be followed. Firms need to decide whether to hire from outside or inside the organization. Prevailing legal and social norms, labor supply, organizational size, technology used, and labor market conditions influence the selection and recruitment decisions. In call centers, recruitment of CSRs is a major HR activity and it takes up major part of HR managers' time. This is because most firms are new and have high turnover of CSRs. In India, traditionally most firms have very low turnover, but call centers have high turnover because of the nature of work and limited promotion opportunities. As most applicants for CSR posts are inexperienced and lack the required profile, there are low success rates in tests and interviews.[3]

The first step in the selection and recruitment process is the analysis and assessment of the knowledge and skills required for the jobs. The expected qualities of the CSRs are presented in Box 6.3. The minimum academic qualifications of applicants vary across firms: some recruit college graduates only, while others recruit both graduates and non-graduates. Computer knowledge is not essential, but it is a desirable qualification. Finally, the CSRs must be able to maintain the more schedule including working at night.[4]

Once, the characteristics required to fill the jobs are known, firms need to decide the sources from which they can recruit the

Box 6.3: Qualities Required for Recruitment as CSRs

CSRs must be able to acquire contextual knowledge to accomplish their tasks. Particularly important is the social skills in relation to customers and to a lesser extent in relation to other employees of the organization. They must be able to communicate effectively with the customers with clear, conscious oral expression, and neutral accents. They must be able to remain calm under pressure in the face of a continuous stream of customer calls with a friendly, positive, and tactful attitude, while simultaneously remaining personally disengaged, and hence protecting themselves from customer abuse. The CSRs must be active listeners, that is attentive to explicit and implicit cues given by the customers. Being patient and empathetic is particularly important, when customers are upset. They must be able to clarify and pinpoint customer requirements and have analytical skills to resolve customer problems. Further, sales skills are important in organizations selling products.

Source: Based on the information collected during the field visits of the centers mentioned in Table 6.1.

right people. As CSRs represent the lowest category of employees in call centers, they are mostly hired from external markets according to the criteria that prioritize skills, competency, and other personal attributes. Except in new firms, recruitment in most supervisory positions is by promotion.[5] This is mainly to create promotion opportunities for the CSRs and make their jobs attractive. Some firms have even declared that team supervisors, senior team supervisors, and quality assessment people will be recruited only through promotion (First Ring, BNK International, and Vishnu Solutions).

In most firms, recruitment and selection is done in-house. Open advertisements and personal contacts are the main methods to attract applicants. Most customer service centers follow rigorous methods for recruitment of employees. Typically, the selection process starts with screening of applications by short-listing of likely candidates from their resumes. It is followed by tests, interviews, and group discussions. In call centers, telephone interviews are often an integral part of the selection process. Firms differ in types of tests and interviews and in their sequence, but all firms follow a step-by-step process and most firms have multiple interviews and over-the-phone assessments. The candidates who succeed in one step become eligible for the next step. Some firms start the selection process with written tests (HSBC, First Ring), some with personal interviews (Vishnu Solutions), some with telephone interviews (BNK International), and some even with group discussions (24/7 Customer.com). Speech evaluation and script reading are often part of the selection process, when it is checked whether the applicants' accents are discernable and without mother tongue influence. In HSBC, as workers need numerical skill, the selection process starts with innumeracy and value reasoning. It is followed by local interviews, and then telephone interviews and then with people in the UK-HR department.

Employee Training

Training programs in call centers like in other firms aim to bring changes in knowledge, skills, attitudes, and social behaviors of employees so that they can handle their jobs fast and effectively. They focus on developing (*a*) fluency in English with proper accent, (*b*) social skills and positive attitude, (*c*) interpersonal skills, (*d*) communication skills, (*e*) basic computer knowledge, (*f*) analytical, organizational, and problem-solving skills, and (*g*) ability to handle sensitive situations professionally. The objectives are to bring employees' English skills to a clear level of understanding, improve listening skills (not to make assumptions), enhance customer service skills (while some customers may like to talk, some may like to finish fast), and improve understanding of cross-cultural differences and desired accents (American accent for customers in the US). The training programs differ across firms. They are not very exhaustive in firms dealing only with back office operations (Data Core), but firms dealing with inbound calls have elaborate training programs. In general, firms providing similar services have similar training programs. The training programs are mostly for the new recruits as CSRs and are typically for six weeks. Table 6.2 briefly describes a typical training program. In the induction training, the trainees are trained in some general skills like customer-relation skills and basic computer and communication skills. They are also exposed to various business divisions, functional departments, work centers, company products, systems, and procedures that are specific to the firm.

The training courses typically include practical exercises, role-plays, and reinforcement by peer discussions. A "buddy" system where novices sit and learn from experienced CSRs is common in many firms. Additionally, there is side-by-side coaching: where monitoring and analysis are undertaken with supervisors or team leaders sitting alongside the CSRs, listening to calls and afterwards evaluating them and suggesting then how the calls can be improved. All call centers have in-house training facilities. Most often, the trainings are done in-house with the help of some external agencies. For example, HSBC conducts in-house training programs with the help of some process experts from the UK. In BNK International, the American Society for Training and Development conducts the trainings. In Vishnu Solutions there are two trainers from SCL Info Systems. Most often the clients are not involved in training, but sometimes they send special training modules and verify quality of training.[6]

Table 6.2: Training Plan in a Call Center[7]

Focus Areas	*Training Deliverables*
1. Call center overview	• Factors that make a call center successful
2. Computer skills and telephone skills	• Basic computer skills, data entry, and data retrieval • Steps involved when handling a call
3. Voice and accent training • Voice modulation and pacing of speech • Regional accent reduction • American accent recognition and adoption	• Speaking ability • Accent neutralization for clear speech • Word, phrase, and sentence simplification and structuring • Voice clarity • Understanding accents of customers • Common American word usage, slang, and idiom familiarization
4. Customer communication • Communication skills • Telephone etiquette and techniques • Service orientation to US • Quality of calls • Handling difficult customers	• Control of calls, understanding customer query through effective listening and summarizing • Awareness of expectations of customers • Competence, error-free and timely service • Standards of performance expected for each call • Dealing with difficult situations, damage control, handling irate, demanding, or talkative customers • Dos and don'ts on telephone
5. Writing and summarizing skills	• Writing techniques • Comprehension ability • Communication recovery techniques
6. Cross-cultural orientation • Factors that differentiate Indians from westerners	• Cultural overview of America • "Thinking like an American": key cross-cultural factors that differ between India and US • Understanding Western culture and Western concept of task and relationship

Source: Based on training plan in BNK International.

Compensation and Rewards

The CSR compensation systems take into consideration both position-related features and performance-related criteria. The non-variable part of the compensation consists of a base salary based on qualifications, years of service, and competencies, and allowances like night shift allowance and free food.[8] The base pay and allowances conform to three equity parameters: external equity (fairness vis-à-vis other call centers in the area), internal equity (fair deal in comparison to colleagues), and individual equity (rewarding an individual for his unique contribution). A CSR's compensation initially depends on the individual's initial attractiveness to the organization, subsequently it depends on performance (annual increments of individuals) and general movement of the local labor market. The CSRs represent the lowest category of employees in ITES firms and receive the lowest level of wages in the organization. The team leaders get about 20–30 percent higher wages. The initial wages are fixed on the basis of prevailing wages in similar firms. Their annual increments are then based on firm's performance and their individual performance. In all firms, a large part of the CSR's compensation is performance-based in the form of incentives. Most firms set monthly or weekly targets for individuals depending on the CSR's experience, skill, and types. If they fail to achieve the minimum levels repeatedly in consecutive months, they not only receive lower wages, they are warned about their performance. For high performers, incentives represent a major part of their earnings. Most often, the CSRs are rated based on productivity, quality, punctuality, and adherence to the schedules and are paid incentives based on their individual ratings. In many firms, employees are assessed and graded annually in terms of unsatisfactory, satisfactory, high achievers, and excellent based on the targets achieved. On the basis of their achievements, they receive monetary rewards and even company shares at lower rates. Many firms monitor performance daily and some even monitor hourly performance and pay hourly incentives.[9] In all ITES firms, annual bonus is performance-based.

The CSR reward systems often include non-monetary recognition. Non-monetary rewards, which are generally uncommon in traditional industries, are common in call centers. Most call centers have well-established and formal systems of non-monetary rewards. These rewards aim to motivate employees, build their self-esteem, and create a positive work culture. Non-monetary rewards take the form of treats (such as dinner with the boss), knick-knacks (different decorations/pins), awards (certificates, trophies), social acknowledgment (recognition at get-togethers), tokens (vacation trips), on-the-job rewards (special assignments), or outings for group members (picnics). There are awards like "agents of the month" and "champion of the company." Firms differ in the types of rewards and awards, but all the programs and schemes aim to motivate employees toward company's objectives.

Performance Measurement and Management

Performance monitoring occupies a central role in call center operations. The performance-related information on individuals and groups provided by the IT-network on a continuous basis is used as the objective data to establish and reinforce performance norms. Management expects CSRs to perform their job in a timely manner by observing company norms and in a way that leaves customers with a feeling of satisfaction and value. Management uses "informative control" based on IT and clear definition of working norms (Frenkel et al. 1998). In this system, every step taken by the CSRs generates information and performance data, which is stored and transmitted through the networked personal computers and is used to monitor individual CSR's work on a real-time basis. In call centers, performance appraisal is a central feature of employee management. It has both formal and informal components. Informal performance appraisal is a continuous process and includes feedback mechanism. In this approach, the team leaders or supervisors, who work as facilitators, inform the CSRs about how well they are doing their work. For example, the supervisors spontaneously mention that a particular call was well performed or poorly performed. Because of the close connection between employee behavior and feedback, the informal system quickly encourages desirable performance and discourages undesirable performance. Formal performance appraisal usually occurs annually/bi-annually and is linked to monetary rewards.[10]

A performance appraisal system, to be effective, requires a clear statement of what the organization needs to achieve and how the responsibilities of individuals and groups fit within the organizational goals. In most call centers, there is clear statement about what is expected from the CSRs. Their tasks are very focussed and their performance is measured based on a set of numbers generated by the networked systems. It is measured for groups and individuals, both separately and jointly. Most often, the criteria for determining performance-based incentives are centralized and governed by a few simple rules that are easily understood by the CSRs (Frenkel et al. 1999: 116–117). In general, the performance matrix is defined using a set of indicators like average handling time. Targets are fixed and the CSRs are expected to achieve the targets. If an individual cannot attain the targets repeatedly then he/she is taken out of the program. The writing on the wall is very clear: "If you cannot attain your numbers then you are in trouble." In call centers dealing with outbound calls, the CSRs are expected to sell a minimum percentage of the calls and their daily performance is measured by the percentage of successful calls or sales per hour (for example, Vishnu Solutions and 24/7 Customer.com). Besides meeting the targets, adherence to company guidelines is an important aspect of performance measurement. The agents, for example, need to use documented legal terms so that customers are not misled and there are no legal complications.[11]

Employee Motivation and Grievance Redress

The inherent nature of jobs in call centers is monotonous, and for many CSRs the jobs lack challenge. The monotonous nature of the jobs and lack of challenge lead to high attrition. In countering the tendency for the work to become socially isolating (in relation to colleagues) and stressful (owing to constant customer interaction and occasional customer abuse), managers in call centers try to promote and encourage close social relations among the front-line workers, and between workers and supervisors, to ensure social and psychological support. In order to achieve this, there are program-wise parties at company expenses, program-wise cultural clubs, and theme days. Often the groups are based on CSRs' residences so that team members staying in a local area can easily organize such programs. Most call centers organize periodic pulse checking, employee satisfaction surveys, or employee perception surveys to monitor employee satisfaction.[12] They have arrangements to receive suggestions for improvement of employee support services, such as transport and meals. The results of surveys and the suggestions are used to refine policies and programs for reduction of employee grievance and promotion of employee motivation.

Most call centers follow an open-door policy for grievance redress. Employee manuals and websites clearly document the dos and don'ts for CSRs. They include policies on medical, transport, dress code, and so forth. Senior managers are easily available if any employer wants to meet them. In all call centers, the senior managers try to maintain close contact with the CSRs and have arrangements to listen to employee grievances. At 24/7 Customer.com, for example, a senior HR manager is available on alternate days to listen to employee grievances. Once in a fortnight, the heads of the departments meet workers in the absence of supervisors. There is a 24-hour help line for the employees and if any call is made, an HR manager gets in touch with the concerned employee. There is a committee with active female members for the prevention of sexual harassment. Most call centers have special focus on grievances relating to canteen facilities, night transport, and security issues, which are particularly important for night work and often major sources of employee grievances.

In call centers, several constraints limit employee satisfaction. One of them is the limited scope of employee discretion. There have been attempts to increase employee discretion, but the detailed guidelines on how to perform each task and how to deal with customers limit employee discretion. In manufacturing settings, team concepts have helped in improving relationship with co-workers, increasing employee discretion, and employee commitment. ITES firms also have teams, but they are not cohesive; they are more like groups of employees working for specific clients. Employee control is based on management-inspired norms and employees are mostly judged based on individual performance. The nature of the work puts more emphasis on individual performance than group performance. The CSRs do not need the help of team members to complete their tasks. In fact, as peer pressure works in favor of high achievers, there is tension within the groups and sometimes dissatisfaction among the CSRs. The monotonous nature of work, unusual work schedules, health problems associated with night work, and lack of promotional opportunities limits employee satisfaction and increase employee turnover.[13] Most call centers have high quit rates, which is a serious problem as it adversely affects company performance.[14] Further, firms that have high quit rates also have high absenteeism. Quit rates is, however, lower in firms that only have back-office operations.[15] The high quit rates indicate dissatisfaction amongst workers. However, the employee recreation programs and group programs have helped to lower quit rates.

None of the call centers in India has any union. This is in contrast to high level of unionization of call center workers in the developed countries (Batt 2000: 16; Frenkel et al. 1998: 959). In all ITES firms in India, management has adopted union-avoidance strategies. This is evident in the designations of the CSRs. The designations like Call Center Executives (HSBC), e-Relationship Officers (24/7 Customer.com), Customer Care Executives (BNK International), and International Tele-Marketing Executives (Vishnu Solutions) project them as managerial staff. This helps firms to avoid class conflict in a number of ways. First, in a status-conscious society, it creates a feeling of being at a higher level in the social hierarchy than the blue-collar workers. Second, in India, the executives belonging to management categories cannot be part of workers' unions. Finally, they are not considered as "workers" under the Industrial Disputes Act 1947 and thus cannot get protection under the Act. All these help call centers to remain non-union. In call centers, the manual jobs like as office maintenance, sweeping, canteen, and security have been contracted out, but the contract workers also do not have any union.[16]

Conclusions

Employment relations in the ITES firms are different from those in the traditional manufacturing firms and even from other service-sector firms. The main distinctive feature is the extensive use of IT in selection, training, job allocation, monitoring, performance evaluation, and computation of rewards. Most ITES firms have introduced HRM practices like performance-based pay, empowerment, and employee communication, but they have not been able to increase employee discretion or their opportunities for promotion. Their employment relations system does not represent the ideal HRM pattern. They represent a distinctly new HRM approach in managing people at work. A complex hybrid form of work organization represents the real picture of the employment system in the ITES firms. It is best described as "mass customized bureaucracy" that has some aspects of the bureaucratic control and HRM practices, but departs from the ideal HRM pattern in other aspects (Frenkel et al. 1998). This hybrid form has more exacting hiring criteria, and emphasis on training and performance, and knowledge/skill-based pay, but has limited career opportunities or employee discretion.

Most industrial sectors have multiple dominant patterns of employment relations (for example, textile industry), but the ITES sector is relatively homogeneous and exhibits only one dominant pattern of employment relations. It is a type of the HRM pattern. The pattern is, however, different from the HRM pattern in the manufacturing industry or the HRM pattern in other service sector firms. In the manufacturing industry, the HRM pattern evolved from the industrial model of employment relations, while in the ITES it developed from the salaried model. Although the employment relations in the ITES firms developed from the salaried model, its work organization does not represent the simple bureaucratic model it represents a "mass customized bureaucratic" form of work organization (Frenkel et al. 1998). The main difference is in the strong reliance on IT for supervision and control. It has some characteristics of the bureaucratic model, but it differs in matters like limited career opportunity and employee discretion. The emergence of this hybrid pattern has introduced a new pattern of employment relations, and has thus contributed to growing variation in employment relations in India. Further, as the ITES firms are adopting global practices in employee management similar to those in other countries, they are contributing to global convergence in employment relations.

Notes

1. The share of IT services in GDP has grown from 1.2 percent in 1998 to 3.2 percent in 2000 and 5.2 percent in 2007. The export earning has grown from USD 1.8 billion in 1998 to USD 40.4 billion in 2008. The direct employment in the sector was about 2 million in 2008. The direct employment in the sector has grown at a rate of 26 percent in the last decade. Further, about four indirect jobs are created for every job created in the sector (NASSCOM Foundation 2008).
2. Some health care, back-office operations, and customer-relations management service companies, however, existed earlier.
3. In 24/7 Customer.com, Vishnu Solutions, and First Ring, only about 5–8 percent of the applicants called in the first test were finally selected. IT-enabled firms differ in their recruitment and selection strategies depending on their type of function. Firms that operate as call centers require people with different skills than those involved in back-office operations. High attrition rate is a major problem in Vishnu Solutions and 24/7 Customer services. However, turnover is low in back-office operations (for example, Data core, which does back-office operation).
4. In First Ring, among the CSRs 70 percent are graduates, 20 percent are diploma holders, and 10 percent are undergraduates. In Vishnu Solutions, everyone is a graduate. Interestingly the selection process in this unit includes interview of parents (particularly for girls) to get the parents' consent for night work.
5. In call centers, the recruitment through promotion is common in all countries mainly because of low promotional opportunity (Frenkel et al. 1999: 125).
6. In 24/7 Customer.com, some clients wanted to evaluate the CSRs before they go on line; but it was not about selection of individual employees.
7. Source: BNK International, Handbook 2003.

8. At 24/7 Customer.com, food is supplied free. There is special attention to the quality and variety of food served. At First Ring, the basic wage is Rs 4,500, and the night shift allowance is Rs 2,500. Including incentives, a CSR gets about Rs 12,000 after confirmation. Annual increase in salary in the recent past was nearly 10 percent.
9. Frenkel et al. (1999: 110) found that some employees received incentives twice the base salary. This is also seen in our case studies. In First Ring, about 60 percent of the total wage is incentive. The CSRs are rated on a scale of 1–5. For ratings 1 (poor) and 2 (partially meeting expectations), there is no incentive. Incentives are 80 percent for rating 3, 100 percent for rating 4, and 120 percent for rating 5. If an employee has a ranking of 5 in all items of performance measurement, his overall ranking is "virtual 6" and incentive is 150 percent. In Vishnu Solutions, a CSR who achieves two sales-per-hour gets incentives.
10. At 24/7 Customer.com, performance appraisal is once a year by the supervisors and then reviewed at a higher level. All decisions on wage increases or promotions are based on individual performance. At First Ring, performance appraisal is twice a year and good performers are rewarded.
11. Most often, a percentage of calls are checked for possible legal complications. At First Ring, the checking is done for 100 percent outbound calls and 10 percent inbound calls.
12. 24/7 Customer.com, has a pulse checking by supervisors in every quarter, an employee satisfaction survey every six months, and an employee perception survey every year.
13. Some take these jobs to improve their verbal skills and consider the job as a step toward future work life. Some even feel that it will help to improve performance in Test of English as a Foreign Language (TOEFL), and Graduate Record Examination (GRE).
14. There are also problems of low turnover. According to an official at HSBC, a certain level of turnover helps to improve promotion opportunities (about 6 percent turnover is considered to be ideal).
15. Quit rates are between 15–50 percent in call centers, it is lower in firms with back-office operations (2–6 percent). It was 15 percent in First Ring, 20 percent in 24/7 Customer.com, and 30 percent in Vishnu Solution in 2002. In HSBC and Data Core, quit rates are less than 5 percent.
16. Attempts to form trade union in Hyderabad Software Technology Park were not successful.

Chapter 7

Multinationals—Convergences and Divergences in Employment Relations: A Case Study

CHANGES IN EMPLOYMENT relations over the last two decades indicate growing similarities in employment relations across countries. This global convergence is partly due to international diffusion of managerial and organizational techniques and practices. FDI and global market forces mediate the diffusion process (Taira 1992). If certain HR practices improve productivity and efficiency of some firms, they spread naturally via market forces to other firms within and across countries (Amante 1995: 645). The development and spread of Japanese and American HRM practices in workplaces all over the world illustrate this diffusion. The diffusion process is constrained or facilitated by various exogenous and endogenous factors, including global strategies adopted by MNCs (Caligiuri and Stroh 1995). The transfer of employment relation practices from one country to another leads to convergence in employment relations across countries. It also leads to divergences in employment relations within the countries.

As a unit in a country adopts practices from another country, it adds to global convergences in employment relations. If the practice adopted was not in existence in the recipient country, it adds to divergence in employment relations within the country. Multinational Enterprises (MNEs) accelerate the convergence–divergence process through transfer of knowledge and practices from one country to another, particularly from their units in home countries to their units in host countries.

Globalization with opening up of borders to flows of trade and investment is increasingly pushing firms to adopt management practices that have been successful in other countries. This has made the studies in comparative and international employment relations increasingly important. The academics and professionals in the field are now interested to know about the emerging similarities and differences in employment systems across firms and across countries. The issues are particularly important for MNCs, as they manage their employees located in different social and political environments. The most important question they face in managing HR internationally is the global–local question: whether they should adopt globally uniform corporate employment relation policies or tailor them to suit local environments. Numerous researchers have examined transfer of American and Japanese employment practices to other countries. Most of these studies are for the developed countries, some for the NICs in Southeast Asia, and only few for other developing countries[1] (Amante 1995; Florida and Kenney 1991; Smith 1983; Thurley 1983; Wasti 1998). Some studies have examined employment practices in Indian firms, but none have examined transfer of the practices or the global–local debate. This chapter examines the global–local issues for Japanese multinationals in India and finds their implications for the convergence– divergence debate in employment relations.

Multinational Corporations in India

The liberal policies favoring open markets and foreign investments introduced in the 1990s have increased involvement of MNCs in India. As MNCs are market driven and strategically oriented, their increasing influence has changed the organizational forms of

Indian companies. In the past, firms in India were characterized by family dominance in the private sector and "bureaupathy" and welfare orientation in the public sector.[2] Some MNCs entered the Indian market before economic liberalization, but despite being managed by their parent companies, they were smaller in number and restricted in their operations or influence. They had insignificant impact on the domestic companies. In contrast, MNCs that entered in the post-liberalization phase have far more freedom to adopt new management practices. Their number itself has made them highly visible and a force to be reckoned with. By 2000, the Indian market was flooded with well-known product brands and over 3,000 MNCs; they either established wholly owned subsidiaries, or joint ventures, or entered strategic alliances with domestic partners (Sinha 2004: 37). The result has been increased influence of MNCs in Indian economy in the post-reform period.

The immediate impact of liberalization can be seen in the increased inflow of FDIs. The number of foreign collaborations per annum and the value of foreign investment increased dramatically in the post-liberalization period compared to those in the pre-liberalization period. The investments are from different countries that have different cultures and different dominant workplace practices.[3] The increased inflow of foreign capital and technology and increased exports, among other factors, had an invigorating impact on industrial growth. The performance of private-sector firms improved tremendously and, of them, the MNCs performed better than the domestic firms.[4] MNCs with greater financial capabilities, better paid personnel, better access to technology, and established networks in the international market are always in a better position to compete. They are relatively large, more prosperous, and vertically integrated. They have a special edge over Indian companies because of their knowledge, technological strength, reputation, breadth of products, and range of services. Many Indian companies established alliances or joint ventures with them for capital, technology, or access to international markets, and many others started to emulate MNCs' principles and practices and wanted to function and look like multinationals. Overall, the MNCs that entered the Indian market in the post-reform era have had substantial impact on employment practices of Indian firms.

Management in MNCs is founded on the belief that the principles and practices of management that they have evolved over the years are universally effective and transferable. Underlying this belief is the worldview that although different societies are at different levels of economic development and modernization, they are evolving to be alike. As almost all multinationals initially developed in the west, this belief actually implies that as societies get industrialized and modernized, people's values, attitudes, habits, and lifestyle would converge to a single pattern characterized by the industrialized culture of the west (Kerr 1983; Meyer 1970). It also means that the world would become unipolar and MNCs, as carriers of the industrialized culture of the west, would show the future nature of work organizations (Sinha 2004: 38). However, there was a dent in this Western worldview when the Japanese work organizations integrated their collectivist cultural values and social habits with the Western principles and management practices. Consequently, there are now two models for designing and managing employment relations in MNCs—the American model and the Japanese model. Over the years, with the dispersions in the nationality of MNCs and emergence of different models of effective organizations have increased complexities in management of MNCs.[5]

Management in MNCs is based on a set of common principles and practices aimed at increasing market share, enhancing productivity, and improving profitability. MNCs maintain their competitive edge by setting goals of high product quality, low product costs, and high customer satisfaction. They realize these goals by adopting macro-level measures, such as acquisitions, mergers, joint ventures, alliances, and networking, and these are supported by micro-level management practices. They introduce employment practices that include a set of values and orientations like discipline, punctuality, meritocracy, rationality, individualism, egalitarianism, risk taking, creativity, and interpersonal relationships. Along with these are some of the Japanese practices like teamwork, QCs, TQM, and *kaizen*. As the Indian market opened up in the 1990s, the MNCs that were already present in the country increased their shareholdings and new MNCs entered the Indian market by establishing fully owned subsidiaries or joint ventures. Initially they favored joint ventures, but over time, the trend shifted to setting up wholly owned subsidiaries.[6] Both joint venture and wholly owned subsidiaries are important for the study of employment relations, but the global influences are more visible in wholly owned subsidiaries that have more freedom to adopt new practices. As both global and local practices influence employment relations in MNCs, the study starts with a discussion on the global–local debate in employment relations.

Global–Local Debate in Employment Relations

Employee management in MNCs in India has to be studied in the context of previous studies in strategic HRM and strategic international human resource management (IHRM). Numerous researchers have attempted to respond to the IHRM issues by extending existing HRM theories in the global context. They assume that IHRM has the same main dimensions as HRM in a national context with only some additional features. The basic theoretical proposition in most of these studies is that to maximize organizational effectiveness (OE), there must be a fit between business strategy and HR practices. Over time, however, questions have been raised about validity of the HRM-OE model. In the global context, some authors argue that a more contextually diverse and elaborate model of HRM holds greater prospects in the 21st century and can better explain why HRM policies differ across firms (Brewster 1999; Kochan 1999; Purcell 1999: 255; Wright et al. 1999). They argue that high-commitment management practices cannot have universal applicability either in theory or in practice once the segmentation of the labor force into core and periphery is taken into account. The extension of the HRM field internationally requires a research agenda that is less sensitive to specific organizations and more sensitive to industry, institutions, and regulatory mechanisms. It needs to adopt a richer theory to incorporate important contextual factors, such as culture, ownership structures, labor markets, the roles of state and trade unions, and segmentation of the workforce into core and periphery (Bloom and Milkovich 1999: 283). They argue that the field of study "should move beyond the very linear, predictable top–down model of strategic HRM to one which is more dynamic and accounts for multiple decision being made simultaneously at all levels of the organizations" (Wright et al. 1999: 198)

MNCs are involved in worldwide management of people who work in different environments. For them, the most important issue is: how can a corporation operating in diverse socio-cultural environments establish its HR policies? In other words, how the various operating units of an MNC across the world can be differentiated and at the same time integrated, controlled, and coordinated (Brewster 1999: 3). The tension between differentiation (local adaptation) and integration (internal consistency) otherwise termed as the "global vs local dilemma" is influenced by various exogenous and endogenous factors. The exogenous factors include industry characteristics, such as nature of business, technology available, nature of competitors, and country-regional characteristics, such as political, economic, cultural conditions, and legal requirements. The endogenous factors include structure of international operations, international orientation of headquarters, competitive strategy used, corporation's experience in international management, intra-organizational network, its international entry mode, and organizational and industry life cycles (DeCieri and Dowling 1999; Schuler et al. 1993). These factors influence MNCs' strategic IHRM issues, functions, policies, and practices, and influence realization of their concerns and goals. These factors, along with global strategies adopted by MNCs, influence the transfer of HR practices to their subsidiaries. Further, not all HR practices are equally transferable. The practices that are mandated by local regulation and shaped by strong local convention or have well-defined local norms generally adhere more closely to the local practices. But, the practices that have diffused or poorly defined local norms are less likely to conform to local norms (Rosenzweig and Nohria 1994). This chapter examines the global–local issues in employment relations and more particularly whether MNCs adopt employment practices that are similar to their home-country practices or tailor them to suit local environment.

Employment relations in MNCs are influenced by the local employment practices and by the global employment practices of MNCs. Multinationals operating in India brought with them a global perspective of principles and practices of management that are claimed to be universally valid. In addition to their global perspective, the imprints of their home culture are also clearly visible. Home-country culture varies across countries from being very tight in getting performance to being value driven, where performance requirements are balanced with peoples' needs (Sinha 2004: 262). It is influenced on the one hand by the universally applicable management culture and also by the home-country culture of organizations that become multinational. The societal cultures of American, Scandinavians, Japanese, and Indians differ from each other. Americans are very high on individualism, and relatively low but still high on power distance, while Japanese are high in collectivism and power distance. Despite the differences in home cultures, product profiles, time of entry, size, and nature of Indian operations, all multinationals adopt some common strategies in establishing systems and procedures that foster a culture of high performance (Sinha 2004: 106). However, their home culture always has a distinct impact on how the systems and practices are made to work. This chapter examines the influence of home-country culture and employment relation practices in a Japanese transplant. Japanese multinationals in India are not expected to follow each and every dimension of Japanese employment practices, and neither are they expected to match all the practices of local firms. The question is: to what extent are the employment practices in Japanese multinationals typically Japanese and to what extent are they similar to the practices of local firms?

MCPI: Case Study of a Japanese Transplant

Most MNCs that entered the Indian market through joint ventures or subsidiaries in the pre-liberalization period were either European or American. Japanese FDI in India was always low and represented a small percentage of Japan's total global investment. However, it has been steadily increasing since the opening of the Indian economy[7] (Phillips 1992). This chapter examines global–local issues in employment relations by presenting case study of a Japanese transplant, Mitsubishi Chemical PTA India (MCPI), a subsidiary of Mitsubishi Chemical Corporation (MCC). MNCs differ by their country of origin.[8] A Japanese multinational has been chosen for the study because Japanese manufacturing and employment practices have distinct characteristics that can be easily distinguished from others. As personnel strategies employed by Japanese firms are allied to their production strategy and manufacturing practices (Morris et al. 2000: 1050; Oliver and Wilkinson 1992), the discussion thus includes both Japanese manufacturing practices and employment practices. The next section presents Japanese manufacturing practices at MCPI, and the following section compares them with the practices in some Japanese joint ventures and non-Japanese firms. Many firms in India, Japanese or non-Japanese, have adopted Japanese manufacturing and employment practices, but in MCPI the practices are more developed and better planned.

The name "Mitsubishi" connotes "excellence." The first Mitsubishi Company, established in 1870, was a shipping firm that diversified into various activities over the years. The company always played a central role in the modernization of Japanese industry. In 1946, Mitsubishi Corporation split itself into independent companies under the post-war government policy of industrial decentralization. The new independent companies used their accumulated knowledge and strengths to pursue growth under separate district businesses. The independent companies borne from the same root still possess a similar corporate culture with continuing link between the companies. The Mitsubishi Group, one of the six big keiretsu in Japan, now has twenty-eight major companies as represented in the Mitsubishi Friday Club. They are today Japan's industry leaders in several sectors (*The Economist* October 23 1999). MCC, a major company in the group, is one of the world's top ten chemical companies.[9] Its Purified Terephthalic Acid (PTA) business is more than thirty years old and it is the second largest PTA manufacturer in the world, with production and sales bases in various countries. Its Haldia plant started production in April 2000 and achieved 100 percent capacity utilization within a year (MCC PTA India 2001).

Employment relations in MNCs and more particularly the adoption of global or local practices are influenced by a number of exogenous and endogenous factors (DeCieri and Dowling 1999; Schuler et al. 1993). The factors and their status for MCPI are presented in Table 7.1.

Table 7.1: Factors that Influence Global–Local Dilemma

S. No.	*The Factors*	*Status of the Factors for MCPI*
1.	Industry characteristics	MCPI is a chemical plant with continuous operation. It uses state-of-the-art technology and it is world leader in PTA business.
2.	Location of plant	Haldia in West Bengal has a high level of union activity dominated by left unions and it operates in an environment of restrictive labor laws on layoff and retrenchment.
3.	Structure of international operations	MCC along with five Japanese trading companies have 95 percent of MCPI shares. It is almost like an international division of MCC.
4.	Headquarters' international orientation	Strategic decisions are taken at the headquarters and expatriates hold all the key posts. High-speed leased lines maintain constant communication with headquarters.
5.	Competitive strategy	MCC follows a combination of innovation and quality enhancement as its competitive strategy.
6.	Experience in international business	It has long experience with plants in the United States (twelve), Asia (outside Japan: sixteen), and Europe (five).
7.	Intra-organizational network	Besides strong link with the headquarters, MCPI has direct interaction with the Mitsubishi plant in Indonesia.
8.	International entry mode	MCPI was established as a new venture of MCC; its present structural form has not evolved over the years.
9.	Organizational and industry life cycle	MCC is in a developed stage of its organizational life cycle. There is emphasis on both integration between different units and sensitivity to local environment.

Source: Based on Schuler et al. (1993); DeCieri and Dowling (1999).

MNCs have several choices in structuring their international operations. These include: exports, sales office, FDI, foreign production, global production structure, multi-divisional structure, licensing, franchising, and industrial joint ventures. Each structural form has different implications for management of HR. For example, the export form involves a limited HRM role, while a divisional structure form requires more fully developed HRM practices (DeCieri and Dowling 1997: 26). As MCPI is an international division of MCC, its strategic IHRM policies and practices are oriented toward home-country policies and practices. Key decisions are made at the center, where knowledge is developed and dispersed as needed. Similarly, the greater the foreign participation of a multinational corporation, the more is the home country influence on HRM policies. The greater the headquarters' international orientation, the greater is the influences (Bangert and Poor 1993; DeCieri and Dowling 1997: 26; Dowling 1989). The discussions indicate that MCPI is more likely to exhibit strong influence of Japanese employment practices.

Japanese Manufacturing Practices at MCPI

Over the last two decades, Japanese manufacturing practices have assumed a significant role in developed countries' manufacturing. They have contributed to Japanese preeminence in many sectors, including the automobile and electronics industry (Mark 1992). The practices include TQC, JIT production, *kaizen* for continuous improvement, and 5S for housekeeping. In this section, we examine the extent to which MCPI has implemented these practices.

***Kaizen* Proposal System**: MCPI introduced *kaizen* in its first year of commercial production and over time it has gained momentum. In all departments, employees have been trained and coordinators have been appointed. The MCPI newsletter, "Enter Kaizen," describes *kaizen* as a way to maximize overall effectiveness and reliability of man and machine through teamwork, trust, and sustainable growth. *Kaizen* improves employee commitment and participation.[10] Employees by offering ideas, feel involved in management activity, feel satisfied, and find their jobs more interesting and stimulating. The process is slow, but it leads to continuous improvement. If everybody tries to make his/her job a little bit easier, makes working environment cleaner, or improves product quality a little bit, then many problems will become clearer and easier and gradually, an easier workplace will emerge with best products. The proposals need not be excellent to impress others; one might only identify the problems and others may help to solve them. At MCPI, the proposals are graded in five categories for rewards (excellent, very good, good, fair, and consolation) based on their originality/feasibility, time to implement, costs, resources required, elimination of waste, irregularity, or strain. Attractive proposals are published in the MCPI newsletter with employee's name and photograph.

5S for housekeeping: *Kaizen* values both process and results. Any *kaizen* project to be successful needs to implement good housekeeping practices. 5S is an integrated Japanese concept for housekeeping and workplace management. It is named by taking first letters of five Japanese words: *Seiri* (sorting), *Seiton* (arranging), *Seiso* (cleaning), *Seikestu* (systematizing), and *Shitsuke* (discipline). It was first introduced in office work starting with conference room, but over time it has been extended to other areas. It is claimed that 5S is a silent informer of a company's attitude toward quality and it often tells us more about a company than its financial statement. At MCPI, 5S involves all employees, including contract workers. Every Friday, work stops in all desks for half an hour and everyone, starting from the managing director to the unskilled workers, gets involved in cleaning their workplaces.

Quality improvement programs: The QC movement in India is only a decade old and in reality it has only scratched the surface. It has, however, drawn the attention of most modern firms. At MCPI, the quality control groups are registered and compete with each other for two rewards—gold and silver winners.[11] The group members meet on a regular basis to identify, analyze, and solve quality, productivity, cost reduction, safety, and other problems in their work area. The objectives are to improve performance and enrich workers' work life. QC is a participative philosophy woven around quality control and problem solving at the bottom level, involves employees at all levels, and needs quality management of people. It is a departure from the traditional approach of mass production that separated workers and management into two different blocks leading to mutual suspicion and distrust. In this approach, problem solving is no longer an exclusively management privilege; workers can also solve problems and recommend solutions. MCPI has implemented TQM with organization-wide commitment to do things in the right way and strive for continuous improvement. It emphasizes participation and involvement of each and every employee in improving product quality and customer satisfaction. MCPI has also plans to introduce Total Productive Maintenance (TPM).[12]

The interrelated programs, *Kaizen*, QC, TQM/TPM, teamwork, and 5S, are all integral parts of the Japanese management system in operation at MCPI, Haldia. The workplace management system implemented in MCPI is represented in the "House of Gemba (workplace) Management" (Figure 7.1).

Figure 7.1: House of Gemba (Workplace) Management at MCPI

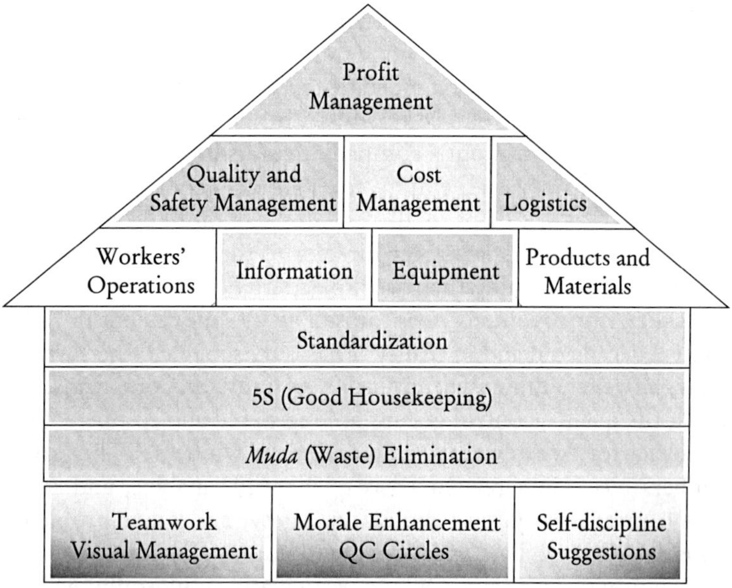

Source: Kaizen Institute (2010).

Japanese Manufacturing Practices in Other Firms

Are Japanese manufacturing practices common only in Japanese plants in India? There is no comprehensive study on the spread of Japanese manufacturing practices in India; however, there are some scattered evidence. Mathur (1991: 92–96) in a study of industrial restructuring of firms, presents case studies of two Japanese joint ventures: Maruti Udyog (a joint venture with Government of India established in 1981) and DCM Toyota (a joint venture with a private partner established in 1984). Both of them introduced Japanese manufacturing practices like the "*kaizen*" suggestion scheme, quality circles, "*kanban*" (JIT inventory), 3M for elimination of waste, and 4S for housekeeping. Over time, the QCs became inactive and the practices became diluted with the withdrawal of workers' cooperation. Both the plants were established in the pre-liberalization period. They introduced Japanese manufacturing practices, but could not sustain them in their full form.[13] Hitachi Amtrex, a Japanese joint-venture with a local partner, was formed in 1998. In this plant, the emphasis is more on improving existing practices rather than an introducing Japanese manufacturing practices. Its work organization was not team-based, but it has problem-solving teams. The teams and individuals in the teams are graded and financial rewards arc paid based on individual score, team score, and company profitability. The management introduced a new practice to avoid lapses known as "no-excuse management" and "no excuse review."[14]

Japanese manufacturing practices have not remained restricted to Japanese firms; they are also seen in some non-Japanese multinationals and Indian firms. The Japanese practices "*kaizen*" and "*muda*," for example, are well established in Jayashree Textiles, Rishra, West Bengal. At Ingersoll-Rand, a US multinational, *kaizen* is well developed and offers attractive rewards for good suggestions. Hindustan Lever, a subsidiary of Unilever, has adopted TPM, autonomous work groups, and *kaizen*. Alstom Power and Infar India have suggestion schemes similar to the *kaizen* scheme, but they are not called "*kaizen*." Alstom Power also has problem-solving teams with emphasis on cycle-time reduction, cost reduction, skill improvement, and equipment upgrades. Whether firms in India are adopting Japanese manufacturing practices or not, there is clear evidence that all firms irrespective of their sector now put more emphasis on quality and productivity.[15] The terms customer satisfaction, complaint resolution, information exchange, QCs, six-sigma, and benchmarking are now seen in many company reports and collective bargaining agreements.[16]

Human Resource Management at MCPI

Employment practices at MCPI indicate that the company has adopted the HRM model of employment relations to manage its regular employees. They are the core employees and about half of them are in the managerial category.[17] Its HR strategy indicates close link with its business strategy and its manufacturing practices. HRM involves several processes and functions. Together they are expected to help in achieving the company's business goal. In this section we discuss the most important HR processes and functions at MCPI under the following groups: (*a*) selection and recruitment, (*b*) training, (*c*) compensation, (*d*) performance appraisal, (*e*) cooperative relation with the employees, and (*f*) employee communication. Apart from the regular employees there are other groups of people like the contractor workers who also work for the organization and contribute to the achievement of the company's objectives. The issues relating to management of contractor workers are discussed in the next section. This is followed by a discussion on workers' committee of the regular workers and unions of the contractor workers.

1. **Selection and recruitment:** At MCPI, the operators have been selected from the local polytechnics or ITIs or they are science graduates. The selection process is rigorous and includes advertisements, short-listing of applications, written tests, and interviews. The minimum qualification for the lowest two grades is class ten, but most existing operators are graduates. For the higher grades, the operators are honors graduates or have diploma in engineering and are generally recruited by promotion. The recruitment of managerial and non-managerial

staff follows the same procedure, but there is no written test. There is a probation period for six months to one year. MCPI thus follows a local approach for recruitment and selection. This confirms Torrington's (1994) argument that recruitment and selection are based on local conventions and legal requirements. It is a "national activity, not an international activity."

2. **Training:** Like most MNCs, MCPI has extensive plan for employee training. The training programs aim to bridge the gap between formal education and skills and those required in actual work and more particularly those required by the company. The senior managers and engineers have received some specific training from outside, but the operators are mostly trained by using internal resources.[18] They learn from each other and from their seniors. In MCPI, all workers including contract workers receive occupational safety and fire-fighting training. Introduction of Japanese manufacturing practices required extensive training on QCs, TQM, *kaizen*, and so forth, which was mostly done through workshops and in-house programs. The training programs are mostly based on plant requirements. There is no attention to individual development followed in some firms adopting the HRM model.[19]
3. **Compensation:** Like most multinationals in India, wages at MCPI are much higher than prevailing wages at local firms. Wage rates are not seniority-based; they depend on skill and knowledge. This is a departure from the traditional seniority based approach in Indian firms, where employees were put into different wage scales with annual increments. A weak form of seniority-based wages may emerge over time, but it is still not a strategic HRM component. The operators at MCPI are divided into five categories depending on skills required and wages paid. The basic wage of the highest category of operators is twice that of the lowest category operators. There is no annual bargaining like the *nenko* system in Japan, but the workers' committee is involved in wage discussions. The regular workers enjoy lifetime employment. This is not a reflection of Japanese employment practices supported by the human capital and motivational approach (Shimada 1983); it is guaranteed under the Indian labor laws.

4. **Performance appraisal:** There are two types of performance appraisal in large Japanese corporations—the *satei* system, where the immediate supervisors assess individuals and include subjective assessment of personality and behavior; and the objective assessment based on performance that includes skill acquisition (Endo 1998; Morishima 1995). MCPI's performance appraisal system is more rigorous for the managerial staff than for the operators. There is an interim review after six months, which is an advisory meeting with the reviewer, when the extent of achievements of targets, areas for improvement, and so forth are discussed and recorded. The annual appraisals have two parts: ratings on job targets and ratings on critical attributes such as job knowledge and discipline. The ratings determine their "performance-evaluated perquisite," increments, promotions, and so forth. For the operators, there is no interim review; their annual reviews and annual payments are based on some critical attributes: some objective like attendance and some subjective like discipline and attitude toward work.
5. **Cooperative relationship with employees:** Japanese HRM practices emphasize cooperative relationship with the employees.[20] Following this approach, MCPI has adopted strategies to build and sustain a strong, managerially driven corporate culture. In MCPI, no employee is called "worker," instead there are designations like member production, member maintenance, and member manufacturing. All the clerical jobs have been designated as executive jobs (for example, Receptionists have been designated as Executive Secretary-cum-Receptionist). With all the unskilled jobs contracted out and all regular employees highly skilled, better educated, and designated as executives, it is now easier to build a cooperative relationship with the employees. At MCPI, initiatives have been taken to avoid class dynamics that distinguishes workers from executives through a series of structural initiatives and process interventions. For example, all employees—executives and workers—use the same air-conditioned buses to the factory, they (including the managing director) take food in the same canteen.[21] This is a departure from the past practices, where most firms had separate canteens

for managers and workers.[22] In addition, opportunities have been created even outside work situations to increase personal and social contact through social and cultural events.

6. **Employee communication:** Building cooperative relationships with employees needs extensive communication with all categories of employees. It helps to prevent polarization or orientation that may lead to emergence of a power base opposed to the interests of the enterprise. At MCPI, employee communications are typically face-to-face and on a "talking things through" basis. In addition, formal meetings with the workers' committee provide forums for raising employment issues. The company newsletter regularly informs employees about company performance, corporate policy, departmental issues, team performance, and new initiatives. It regularly publishes names and photographs of the new employees, whether they are managers or operators.

MCPI follows the HRM model of employment relations with emphasis on extensive communication and strong managerially driven corporate culture. The employment practices at MCPI also indicate initiatives to introduce some of the Japanese employment practices. Socialization with co-workers, an aspect of Japanese HRM practices, is tied to Japanese collectivism that treats the corporation as if it is a family (Kashima and Callan 1994). Skill-based pay, elaborate performance appraisal systems, extensive employee communication, and emphasis on cooperative relationships with the employees indicate imprints of both global and home-country practices in employment relations.

Contract Labor: Division between Core and Periphery

Like most new firms in India, MCPI has a large number of contract workers. In fact, it has more contract workers than regular workers.[23] Of the two types of contracting, "labor-only contracting" and "job contracting," MCPI has labor-only contract, where the contractors' only task is to supply labor for some agency fee. The contract workers do all the unskilled, peripheral, and non-core jobs and some of them even perform skilled jobs alongside regular workers.[24] Their wages are lower than those of the regular workers, but higher than the prevailing wages in the informal sector or the statutory minimum wages.[25] A problem with contract workers is the lack of managerial control relative to the directly engaged workers. At MCPI this is made up for by close and direct supervision of contract workers by the shop floor managers and management-conducted training programs for the contract workers.

Engagement of large numbers of contractor workers at MCPI is to be seen in the context of engagement of large number of non-regular workers in Japanese firms. Most firms in Japan engage large number of part-time or temporary workers, but it is not so at MCPI. In India, the use of part-time workers, who work fewer hours per day than regular workers, was never popular. Most firms in the past, however, engaged large numbers of temporary or casual workers. They received low wages and lacked job security. The demands for increase of wages and their absorption in the permanent rolls of firms often led to industrial conflicts. Some labor-intensive traditional industries in India still use large numbers of casual workers,[26] but the current trend in most firms indicates a shift from this traditional practice. In place of casual workers, firms are now engaging contract workers. This is more so in new firms.[27] The contract workers serve the same purpose as the casual workers, but they are not part of firms' internal labor markets, and thus their employee management policies are different from those of the regular employees.

The engagement of large numbers of non-regular workers is certainly a Japanese practice. However, at MCPI the types of non-regular workers are different: they are contract workers. The use of contract workers is now popular in many firms in India. Most new high-technology firms, Indian or multinational, engage large numbers of contract workers. These contract workers for all practical purposes work like casual workers and serve the same purpose as the non-regular workers in Japan. The non-engagement of casual workers in Indian firms is a departure from past practices. There are three reasons for this shift. First, labor legislation and court judgments in India favor regularization of casual workers and payment of wages and benefits at par with the regular workers.[28] Second, the trade unions for regular workers always represent the casual workers, and their absorption as regular workers is always a major source of labor conflict. Finally, there are problems in the introduction of high-commitment work practices with casual workers, as only individuals with low levels of education and skills, and lower ability to learn, accept casual jobs. All the three local factors—labor legislation, the union role, and the low level of education among casual workers—have influenced implementation of Japanese practices of engagement of non-regular workers at MCPI. The engagement of contract workers is not exactly a Japanese practice, but it is adoption of Japanese practices in the local environment.

Workers' Committee and Union at MCPI

MCPI does not have any union of regular workers. This is in spite of extremely liberal policy on formation, registration, and recognition of trade unions in India and in spite of the plant being located in a region of strong union influence. MCPI has a committee of workers known as Department Representatives' Committee, whose members are elected by the operators from the different departments. It represents the operators in all discussions with the management, including wage negotiations. The committee has no link or affiliation to any union federation or political party and it has no external members in its executive committee. It is similar to Japanese internal unions and committees of workers in some Japanese transplants in the US described by Pil and MacDuffie (1999).

MCPI's unionization strategy is to avoid external unions and to promote workers' committees. There was an attempt to form an external union, but it failed because of management's strong union-avoidance strategy and its ability to convince local politicians against such union formation. The union-avoidance strategy is also apparent in its attempts to avoid class dynamics that distinguishes workers from the executives and in the cooperative relationship with the workers. The types of employees and workers engaged have also helped in this strategy (for example, clerical jobs designated as executive jobs). Further, the operators are mostly from the technical schools or science graduates, who like to identify themselves more with engineers than with blue-collar workers. Many of them regard unions as institutions for labor—a category or class with which they do not like to identify (Mathur 1991: 75). They consider themselves in a higher class on the social ladder than the unskilled blue-collar workers.[29] MCPI's unionization strategy for the contract workers is, however, different from that for the regular workers. It has a union of contract workers, which periodically bargains wages and other benefits.[30] The management realized that in a local environment where contract workers are unionized in most firms, it is extremely difficult to avoid unionization.

The formation of the workers' committee at MCPI similar to the internal unions in Japan is certainly a Japanese influence. This is in contrast to unionization status in most new multinational firms. Most new multinationals in India, particularly the US multinationals, do not have any union or workers' committee. Even most new firms in Haldia, where MCPI is located, do not have any unions. The formation of such workers committee is also seen in some other Japanese firms. For example, Maruti Udyog, started with a management-sponsored internal union. DCM Toyota did not have any union initially, but when the pressure for unionization increased the company changed its policy and took the initiative to establish an internal union. At MCPI, the initiative to form a workers' committee was a strategy to prevent formation of external unions. The union strategy at MCPI thus indicates a strong influence of Japanese practices—an influence of home-country practices. The recognition of the contract workers' union, in contrast to the almost non-unionized status of Japanese non-regular workers, however, indicates adoption of local practices. It is an influence of local convention supported by strong pressure for the formation of unions of contract workers.[31]

Discussion and Conclusions

This is a presentation of employment relations at a Japanese multinational and its comparison with the employment practices is other firms in India. It examines whether the Japanese multinationals in

India follow Japanese employment practices or adopt local practices. MCPI has been chosen for the case study because it is practically a wholly owned subsidiary of MCC with strong influence of MCC in formulation of its employment practices. The influence of home-country practices in managing people at work is expected to be stronger in the wholly owned subsidiaries than in joint ventures (DeCieri and Dowling 1999; Schuler et al. 1993). The presence of large numbers of Japanese expatriates at MCPI (seventeen of them in key positions) and the dedicated communication network with MCC, Tokyo, indicate strong headquarters influence. Here are some of findings on the employment practices at MCPI:

1. The regular workers at MCPI, as in other Indian firms, enjoy lifetime employment. This is not due to adoption of Japanese practices, rather it is because of the restrictive provisions of the Industrial Disputes Act 1948, which make layoff or retrenchment almost impossible in large firms.
2. Most traditional firms in India have seniority-based wages. In MCPI, wages of regular workers are not seniority-based; they are skill and performance-based. The wage rates and patterns are similar to those in other new firms in India. There is no wage system like the Japanese *nenko* system. In wage fixation it follows the local practices.
3. MCPI does not engage any part-time or temporary workers. Part-time workers were never common in India, but traditionally firms engaged large numbers of casual workers. This non-engagement of part-time of temporary worker is in conformity with the present practices in Indian firms.
4. MCPI has more contract workers than regular workers. Most firms in Japan have large proportion of non-regular workers in the total workforce, but the use of contract workers is not popular in Japanese firms.[32] The contract workers at MCPI serve the same purpose as the non-regular workers in Japan, such as savings in wage costs and increase in flexibility.
5. Increased use of contract workers indicates new divisions in the labor markets. Legally, the contractors should manage contract workers, but in practice the MCPI management decides about their wages and benefits and closely regulates their activities.[33]

As in most new firms, management of contract workers is an integral part of MCPI's labor management functions.

6. The absence of temporary workers and presence of a high proportion of contract workers is now common in all firms in India. At MCPI, this new arrangement has emerged from the interaction of global pressure for engagement of non-regular workers and the local legal and political constraints concerning engagement of casual workers.
7. MCPI has adopted an internal union strategy. This is in contrast to union-avoidance strategy of many new firms, particularly the US multinationals.[34] At MCPI, the formation of workers' committee is a part of the corporation's global strategy. This is in contrast to Torrington's (1994) claim that union strategy is a national activity rather than international activity.
8. At MCPI, the wage rates are significantly higher than the prevailing local rates. There is emphasis on open and transparent management, free flow of information, cooperative relationship with workers, and removal of barriers that separate workers from their managers. This is part of a global strategy, but it is not typically Japanese. It is also seen in many non-Japanese multinationals.

MCPI has introduced many Japanese manufacturing practices like *kaizen*, 5S, TQM, and teamwork. Other Japanese multinationals in India have also introduced these practices, but at MCPI the practices are better developed, better integrated, and more successful in achieving their objectives than in Japanese joint ventures. Employment relations at MCPI differ from an average Indian firm on many counts. First, the wages in most Indian firms are seniority-based, while at MCPI they are skill- and knowledge-based. Second, unlike most traditional Indian firms, MCPI does not engage any casual worker; instead, it engages large numbers of contract workers. Third, MCPI does not have any union of regular workers, but it has a workers' committee. Fourth, wages at MCPI are relatively higher than those of average Indian firms. In summary, MCPI has used a combination of global and local approaches in formulating its HRM policies. For some functions it has introduced global or home-country practices (performance appraisal and rewards), while for others it has adopted local practices (recruitment, control of non-regular workers, collective bargaining, and job security). The global–local choices in managing people at work have been influenced by the spread and strength of local conventions for each activity. In shaping its employment relations, MCPI has drawn from the emerging employment practices in Japan, but most often they have modified them to fit the local environment. On union strategy and compensation policy, they have drawn from the global strategy and fitted it to the local environment. The emphasis has been to adopt local practices that can achieve the key objectives of their global practices. Finally, MCPI, as have some other Japanese multinationals in India, has introduced employment practices that have been globally successful, but locally uncommon. Introduction of such practices have led to growing variations in employment practices (divergences) in India and growing similarities in employment relations with firms in other countries (convergences).

Notes

1. Of the 226 Japanese subsidiaries reported in five studies on Japanese multinationals, 139 are located in developed countries (mostly the US and UK) and remaining 87 are located in NICs in Southeast Asia (Bird et al. 1998).
2. In 1951, twelve business houses dominated the Indian industrial landscape. Even in 1997, their companies represented the majority of the top 100 Indian companies. Members of their families occupied crucial positions and succession to the top was normally synonymous with succession in family. Only in some companies family dominance coexisted with professionalism. In the public sector, excessive bureaucratization has prevented efficient functioning of firms. The bureaucratic style of management degenerated into a bureaupathic (bureaucratic that becomes pathological) form, which was based on mistrust of subordinates (Sinha 2004: 33–34).
3. The average value of foreign investments per year was Rs 53.62 million during 1967–1979; it became nearly 20 times during 1980–1990 and 40 times during 1991–2000. The largest investment in 2000–2001 (excluding Mauritius) was from the United States, followed by Japan, Germany, the Netherlands, Italy, and South Korea (Government of India, *Statistical Outline of India 2001–2002*).
4. The growth of profits of MNCs was 50 percent more than the domestic firms (Sinha 2004: 32).

5. Only six of the largest 50 MNCs in 1959 were non-American, while by 1993 about 60 percent of the largest 100 MNCs were non-American, representing fifteen countries (Briscoe 1995: 2).
6. Initially, many joint ventures were established, but over time one of the partners acquired greater influence. Most often, the foreign partner with better strength of capital bought out the Indian partner.
7. During 1991–1997, the Japanese FDI approval was only 4 percent of total FDI approvals in India (RBI Annual Report).
8. For example, Korean companies (LG, Samsung, Hyundai, and Daewoo) preferred to set up wholly owned subsidiaries while the Japanese companies opted for joint ventures (Suzuki, Honda, Yamaha).
9. MCC together with five major Japanese trading companies and West Bengal Industrial Development Corporation Ltd (WBIDC) (with 5 percent share) formed MCPI to set up the PTA plant with annual production capacity of 350,000 tons.
10. *Kaizen* means, "change for the good" (*kai*: change; *zen*: better). Doing things better everyday defines *kaizen*. The emphasis is on waste elimination and customer satisfaction. The newsletter "Enter Kaizen" conveys the company's programs and keeps employees continuously informed. There were eighty-one *kaizen* proposals by December 2000, 150 proposals by March 2001, and 428 proposals by June 2001.
11. There were twenty-six registered quality circles in 2001. An important aspect of QC is "making the people first" as explained by the Chairman Mr Matsushita: "we make people before we make products."
12. Japan Institute of Plant Maintenance defined TPM as a system of maintenance that covers the entire life of equipments. Because of its target to increase productivity out of the equipment, the term TPM is popularly known as Total Productivity Management (Senju 1992).
13. In Maruti Udyog, more than 400 QCs were formed, but over time most of them became inactive. DCM-Toyota, a joint venture of DCM and Toyota (equity 26 percent) also introduced *kaizen*, but the number of suggestions dropped from 1,250 in 1986 to 982 in 1988 (Mathur 1991).
14. All employees in the top and middle levels are assigned Activity Outcomes (AO) and Business Outcomes (BO) that define the goals for each individual. BO quantifies revenue generated by an individual, while his or her immediate superior sets AO. The AO scores and BO scores together give the "No Excuse score." All the shortcomings and non-performance are addressed using root-cause analysis and recovery plans.
15. Example: the wage agreement of Alstom Paharpur Works spells out the policy of continuous improvement and total customer satisfaction through timely delivery of error free product/services. If a worker does not conform to quality standards, he would be liable for disciplinary action besides loss of incentives (Agreement, October 1994).

16. For example, Reliance has introduced QCs in all plants, and some plants have introduced TQM, and some has housekeeping programs similar to 5S.
17. In MCPI, out of 313 regular employees only 153 operators belong to worker category.
18. In 2001, the senior managers of the personnel and administration department visited the Mitsubishi plant in Indonesia to learn about its personnel and HR principles and practices.
19. This is in contrast to training programs at Ingersoll Rand, a US multinational, where training programs in addition to organization's needs also focus on the aptitude and needs of individuals.
20. The Japanese Ministry of Labor identifies the stability in labor-management relations with employee consultation as the main element of industrial democracy (Nakamura 1988).
21. Concern for employees is reflected in actions of senior officials. In December 2000, Mr Akira Miura, Chairman, visited the plant; he visited the canteen and playgrounds before visiting the factory.
22. Many firms still have separate canteens for managers and workers (Alstom Power, Reliance, Jayashree Textiles), but most new firms have single canteen (Haldia Petrochemicals, Torrent) and some old firms are shifting to the single-canteen model. Alstom AEI had three canteens for senior managers, junior managers, and workers, but now it has one canteen. Infar India, Ganganagar introduced the single-canteen model to avoid religious conflict between two groups of workers in the 1970s.
23. At MCPI, there are 313 permanent employees (160 executives) and 388 contract workers (123 engaged in loading–unloading). The ratio is similar in Haldia Petrochemicals.
24. For example, the instrumentation department with five managers/engineers and one supervisor has one operator and three skilled technicians under a contractor (MCC PTA India 2001).
25. The contractors get about 8–12 percent of wage costs as agency fee. The wages of contract workers are about 40 percent lower than those of regular workers. The gross daily wage for an unskilled contract worker is, however, higher than the government-set minimum wage. All the contract workers are covered under PF, ESI, and the Gratuity Act and receive overtime at double the normal rate. The wages of the highest category of contract workers (crane operators, welders) is about 50 percent higher than those of the lowest category contract workers.
26. In the jute industry and tea plantations, about 30–40 percent of total workers are still casual workers.
27. Most new firms do not engage any casual workers (Torrent, Ingersoll Rand, Alstom Power, Hitach Amtrex, Infar). Firms that used casual workers in the past are now discontinuing the practice (Alstom AEI, Infar India, Jayashree Textiles, Alstom Paharpur).

28. The Supreme Court observed that concerned effort must be made to regularize casual workers as far as possible subject to their fulfilling the qualifications. If a casual worker is continued for a fairly long spell, say two or three years, it becomes obligatory for the authority concerned to examine the feasibility of his regularization (Supreme Court of India 1992b).
29. They even demanded to replace their present designations with more prestigious terms like "production staff," "technical staff," or "production associate."
30. At MCPI, wages of contract workers are double the statutory minimum wage rates. The wage agreement also provides for earn leave, sick leave, festival holidays, annual bonus, house rent allowance (HRA), and retrenchment benefits. There are similar agreements in other units in Haldia (Haldia Petrochemicals, April 1998; Hind Leaver Chemicals, 1999).
31. In 1998, about 22 percent of wage-employed workers were part-time workers in Japan and they represented 2 percent of organized workers (Japanese Labor Ministry Basic Survey on Trade Unions 1998). Here, local convention means practices in majority of firms in a locality and not national practices. In India, unionization of contract workers varies across states.
32. While 35 percent of all workers are non-regular workers, only 0.5 percent are agency workers.
33. For example, the management is increasingly involved in selection, recruitment, and training of contract workers, and they also manage unions of contract workers.
34. None of the new US multinationals in India has any union (example: Ford in Tamil Nadu).

Chapter 8

Employment Relations in Small Firms

NINETY PERCENT OF all workers in India work in small firms; about half of them are self-employed or owners of small firms and the other half are employed by these firms. Most studies on managing people at work focus on large firms. This is mainly because the workers, their unions, and employers in large firms are the most vocal and always draw attention of the policy makers and public more than their counterparts in small firms. However, the issues of managing people at work or employer–employee relations in small firms, in the informal sector, are also equally important. There are a number of reasons for this. First, the small-firm sector employs the majority of workers in developing countries. Second, employment relations in the formal sector cannot be seen in total isolation from the informal sector, as informal-sector activities influence formal-sector activities and vice-versa. Third, in reality, there is a continuum of production activities and it is impossible to see the informal sector as an individual entity by itself. Fourth, small firms are in a state of transition and with time some of them may graduate to the formal sector (Emmerij 1974). Fifth, while the state is easing up on regulation in the formal sector, there is increasing coverage of labor legislation in the informal sector. For example, over the years, there has been an increase in coverage of minimum wage legislation and social security benefits in the informal sector. Finally, the linkage between the formal and informal sectors is on the rise as large firms are increasingly off loading their jobs to small suppliers or small contractors.

The issues in managing people at work in small firms are not only important for the employers, unions, and workers in the informal sector, they are also important for the policy makers and the stakeholders in different sectors. In spite of its importance, there is hardly any study on employment relations in small firms. This makes the subject more challenging. This chapter starts with a description of the informal sector, its growth potential and spread, its dominance in future, and its importance in the economy. In most small firms, the system of employee control is informal and unstructured and employers are not subjected to any external influences in exercising their control over their workers. However, in some small firms institutional influences—labor legislation, trade unions, employers' associations, or regional collective bargaining agreements—do influence firms' employer–employee relations. Most labor laws in India are for the workers in the formal sector and only a few apply to the workers in the informal sector. Most small firms are without any external influence, however, in some small firms the institutional influences restrict employers' arbitrary authority and influence firms' employment relations. As some firms are subjected to these influences, while others are not, the net result is increasing variations in firms' employment relations.

Workers in the Informal Sector

Worker participation in the labor market varies from country to country and from region to region. It varies across sectors and across employments. In India, most workers work in the informal sector. While in the formal sector activities are well regulated by legislation, it is not so in the informal sector. The social security legislations (PFs, ESI) mostly apply to workers in the formal sector and do not cover majority of the workers in the informal sector. Unionization is also low in the informal sector (Das 2008: 976). The two terms, informal sector and unorganized sector, are now interchangeably used, but of them, the former term is now more popular. Hart (1973) first launched the term "informal sector" to describe the part of the urban labor force that falls outside the organized labor market. The concept has been further refined to include workers in rural areas (Jagannathan 1987; Parthasarathy 1996: 1859). The distinction between the formal and informal sectors is based on state recognition and regulation. The distinction for the factory workers in India can be made on the basis of whether or not the employing enterprise is registered under the Factories Act, 1948. Once an enterprise is registered, workers' recruitment, working conditions, wage payments, dismissals, and so forth, are formalized. Accordingly, the informal sector is derived as the residual after deducting the registered labor force from the total labor force.

The above description of the informal sector does not include the casual or contract workers who work for the formal-sector establishments. Their wages and working conditions are inferior from those in the formal sector and they do not have job security. They are more similar to the workers in the informal sector. Often, the contractors or suppliers are small firms that do not have independent existence outside the activities of the formal sector firms to which they are linked. In general, while the direct workers in large firms get high wages and have job security, the casual and contract workers are poorly paid and their working conditions are less regulated. They are more similar to workers in the informal sector and are thus part of the "informal labor market" (Papola 1992: 42).

The informal-sector workers in India work in different employments.[1] They include: (*a*) agricultural workers, (*b*) workers in small manufacturing units like hand looms, power looms, "beedi" making, tanneries, and so forth, (*c*) employees in shops and small service firms, (*d*) construction workers, (*e*) sweepers and scavengers, (*f*) casual workers, and (*g*) contract workers. The share of informal-sector workers in total employment varies across industrial sectors. It is nearly 98 percent in agriculture and low in mining or power sector. In the informal sector there are both casual (paid on daily basis) and regular workers (paid on monthly basis). Of the wage-employed workers, who represent half of all workers in small firms, about one-third are in regular employment and two-thirds are in casual employment. The recent trend shows a shift of activities from the formal to informal sector (Ascher 1987; Das 1998). In India, while the share of workers, in manufacturing, has declined over time, it has increased in the service sector, which has less potential to generate formal-sector employment than the manufacturing sector.[2]

Labor Laws in the Informal Sector

Government intervention in the labor markets originates from the belief that as members of society, people are entitled to certain rights like those emanating from the notions of liberty and equality. The state intervention varies from country to country. In India it also varies across industrial sectors as labor laws and their enforcement vary across industrial sectors. Most labor laws are for the workers in the formal sector. Some labor laws apply to workers in all industries (Table 8.1), while others apply to workers in specific industries (examples: Motor Transport Workers' Act, 1961; Sales Promotion Employees Act, 1976; Beedi and Cigar Workers' Act, 1966). Some laws cover both formal and informal sector workers, but they are not as effective in the informal sector as in the formal sector. For example, the legislation for protection of women and child labor is less effective in the informal sector than in the formal sector. The Trade Union Act, 1926, does not distinguish between the formal and the informal sector, but union coverage is very thin in the informal sector.

Table 8.1: Legislations Influencing Wages in the Informal Sector

Legislation	*Type of Intervention*
Minimum Wage Act, 1948	Minimum compensation for work. Workers in scheduled employment to be paid minimum wages.
Trade Union Act, 1926	Workers of a number of small units can form unions, which can bargain wages and other conditions of work.
Industrial Disputes Act, 1947	Unions can raise industrial disputes on wages and the conciliation machinery can intervene.
Equal Remuneration Act, 1976	Protection of the vulnerable. Equal wage for women for same or similar work.
Payment of Wages Act, 1936	Regulates the manner of payment of wages and realization in case of non-payment.

Source: The Legislations in Malik 2006.

The most important labor law for the workers in the formal sector is the Minimum Wage Act, 1948. It provides for legal action against an employer if he/she does not pay minimum wage. The Apex court has observed "the employees are entitled to minimum wage at all times and under all circumstances. An employer who cannot pay this minimum wage has no right to engage labor and no justification to run the industry" (Supreme Court of India 1992a: 504). In spite of such judgments, many informal-sector workers do not receive the minimum wages. There are several reasons for this. The scope and coverage of minimum wage legislation is often too ambitious for the administrative and financial resources available with the enforcement machinery. The number of inspectors is inadequate, they do not have adequate training or experience, and enforcement is particularly difficult in remote areas. The most important explanation for poor enforcement is, however, the concern felt by the governments that strict application might increase unemployment, force enterprises out of business, and make the workers redundant. The existence of a large number of surplus labor in developing countries means that many will be willing to work for lower wages (Gindling and Terrell 1995; Watanabe 1976: 347). Payments of wages lower than the statutory minimum occurs partly because of a lack of awareness of legal provisions and partly because the employees do not report this for fear of losing their jobs. As with other labor legislations, minimum wage legislation needs active support of workers and unions for its effective implementation, but it is often lacking in the informal sector.[3]

Labor laws that apply to workers in the informal sector influence workers' wages and other conditions of work. They also raise workers' expectations about their entitlements and induce them to demand benefits as provided in the laws. Even when minimum wage laws are not strictly enforced, they help to organize workers for collective action by creating a feeling of deprivation among the workers. This results in increase in wages. Labor laws in the formal sector also have indirect influence in the informal sector. The acts relating to payment of HRA, gratuities, and bonuses, or those relating to factory workers, apply to establishments with more than ten or twenty workers, but some informal-sector workers also receive similar benefits.[4] The influence of labor laws on the informal sector workers varies across small firms depending on types of firms, their locations, and their linkages to the formal sector. Some small firms pay minimum wages, some pay higher than the minimum wages, and some pay lower than the minimum wages. In addition to these influences, the social customs and practices like the demands for "informal minimum wage" also influence the employer–employee relations in small firms.[5]

Employer Associations and Trade Unions in the Informal Sector

Employers' associations and trade unions, when present, influence firms' employment relations. In most small firms, employers operate on the basis of an internal locus of control and without any external influence. However, whenever workers become members of trade unions or employers form their associations, they influence firms' employment relations. The extent and rationale of such influences vary across firms depending on the strength, purpose, and roles played by the unions and associations. Employers form associations to protect and promote their interests. They feel that by collectively forming such associations they can more effectively safeguard their interest against government regulations, competitors in trade and business, and labor unions. Employee management is not the primary focus of most employers' associations, but over time they get involved and influence employer–employee relations in member firms.

In the informal sector, most employers' associations are for small firms located in a region that produce same product or closely related products and often they are registered under the Societies Act.[6] In India, one can find them in different industrial sectors and in different parts of the country. The most active of them are the manufacturers' associations organized by trades like the Bleachers and Dyers' association in the hosiery industry. Some of these associations affiliate into region-wide federations or chambers of commerce. The associations perform a wide range of functions and differ in their activities. They provide business services, such as organizing seminars and buyer–seller meets, provide information and library services, hold exhibition and trade fairs, circulate trade journals and newsletters, pursue government for resources, and so forth. Sometimes, they loosely regulate prices to prevent excessive undercutting, facilitate contacts, provide services for contract adjudication, provide legal advice and assistance, and facilitate document certification for product quality (Chari 2000; Moore and Hamalai 1993: 1897; Tewari 1998). Some associations help their members in managing employees in their member firms and engage labor experts to help their members in labor disputes.[7]

In India, as in other countries, there are wide variations in trade union activities across sectors and across employment categories. In the informal sector, trade unions are weak and their coverage is thin, and majority of small firms do not have any union. Unionization in the informal sector varies across states. In West Bengal, small-firm workers in hosiery, brickfields, shops, and establishments are unionized and there are organizations looking after the interests of small farmers and agricultural laborers. Most often, efforts to organize workers in the informal sector are initiated by the political parties. The link between the political parties and trade unions is thus more prominent in the informal sector than in the formal sector. The influence of trade unions in the informal sector is now an important issue as recent trend shows a decline of unions in the formal sector and increase in union activities in the informal sector.[8] Most trade unions of small firms represent large numbers of firms in a region and organize workers by trade or related trades. They influence wages by bargaining with employers or through political action by acting as pressure groups to influence government policy (for example, enforcement of minimum wage). They interact with individual employers, employers' associations, and government agencies at different levels for protection of workers or for appropriate policy and social legislation.

Collective Bargaining in the Informal Sector

Collective bargaining is a technique adopted by unions and management to reconcile their conflicting interests in employment conditions (Hoxi in Shister 1951: 148). The phrase is made up of two words: collective and bargaining. It is collective because employees associate together, normally if not invariably, in trade unions to bargain with their employers. In the informal sector, collective action is also on the part of the employers. Most often trade unions as an organized body of workers bargain with employers' associations as organized agents of employers. The process is called bargaining because it involves haggling and/or negotiating in which each side applies pressure on the other. Unions can resort to work to rule and similarly employers can refuse concessions given to workers in the normal time (Clegg 1976: 5–6; Mamoria and Mamoria 1991: 515). The two extreme forms of pressure are strikes and lockouts. There are limits to the pressure that each side can apply on the other in the informal sector because of absence of protection under labor laws, close relationship between employers, and their employees, and then limited strength to withstand significant pressure. As trade unions and employers or their associations are weak in the informal sector, collective bargaining is weak in the sector and their coverage is limited.

Collective bargaining in India had its beginning in the 1920s and gained ground after independence. Its progress was slow in the early years of industrialization (Fonseca 1975: 174), but it is now widespread in several parts of the economy. Studies on collective bargaining in India do not make any reference to the informal sector, as if it does not exist there, but it is not unknown in the informal sector. As collective action on the part of workers is a prerequisite for collective bargaining and as trade unions are weak in the informal sector, it has remained confined to those parts of the country and in sectors that have trade unions in the informal sector. In West Bengal, there are many examples of collective bargaining in the informal sector (Drèze and Mukherjee 1987: 10–22; Rudra 1981). The collective bargaining agreements differ in their scope and coverage. In some industries there are state-wide agreements, while in others there are region-wide agreements.[9] The agreements generally cover more issues than wage rates and the issues covered differ across industrial sectors (Table 8.2).

Table 8.2: Collective Agreements in the Informal Sector: Examples

Employment	*Date of Agreement*	*Issues in Collective Agreements*
Bakery	12/28/95	Wage based on productivity
Cinema	03/12/96	Wage increase, pay scale, VDA, etc.
Rubber	07/03/93	Wage increase, annual increment, HRA, etc.
Power Looms	03/20/97	Wage increase, wage linked to productivity, work load, etc.
Hosiery	07/05/84	Wage, VDA, HRA, implementation of different acts, etc.
Cold Storage	11/29/96	Wage increase, VDA, medical allowance, bonus, HRA, etc.
Goods Transport	08/01/94	Wage increase, annual increment, VDA, medical allowance, bonus, service rule, appointment letter, annual leave, HRA, etc.

Source: Government of West Bengal, Labour in West Bengal, eds: 1993, 1994, 1995 and 1996.

Most conflicts between employers and workers are over payment of wages. The way wages are set and paid influences firms' employment relations. In small firms, the setting of wages is influenced by the state-notified minimum wages or by the collective bargaining agreements between employers' associations and workers' unions. In absence of such external influences, wages are determined through free "individual bargaining" between employers and workers at the individual level. Industries differ in determination of wages: some have notified minimum wages, some have collective agreements, and some have both notified minimum wages and collective agreements. The scope of minimum wages and collective bargaining agreements varies across states, across regions, and over time.[10] Sometimes, there are even agreements for wages lower than notified minimum wages because of the apprehension that payment of minimum wages will make the units unviable (example: "beedi" making, power looms in West Bengal). Unions in such situations use minimum wage notifications to organize workers against employers and to justify demands for higher wages. Sometimes the minimum wage notifications are issued to ensure and extend coverage of collective bargaining agreements.

Small Firms as Contractors of Large Firms

Most large organizations engage contract labor and the majority of the contract firms are small. In India, contract labor is now widespread in almost all sectors. It is more prevalent in activities like construction, loading and unloading, security, canteen maintenance, housekeeping, garden maintenance, and in occupations like gas-cutter, driller, blacksmith, carpenter, and fitter. Increasingly jobs are being off-loaded to contractors with fragmentation of activities (Dash 1996: 234). New technology has created opportunities for engagement of contract workers. Firms that went through major restructuring and introduced new technology engaged large number of contract workers. The main objectives of contracting-out of jobs are reduction of labor costs and overhead costs and increase in labor flexibility. Another advantage is that it allows management to follow different employment policies for the high-skill and low-skill workers. The directly employed high-skilled core workers may be paid high wages and benefits, while the low-skill contract workers may be paid lower wages and benefits. Most contract firms are small and thus outside the coverage of major labor legislations. Employment relations in small contractor firms are different from those in large contractor firms or independent small firms. In large contractor firms, employment relations are no different from those in independent large firms. Usually workers in large contractor firms, who often work in multiple firms, are not considered as contract labor.[11] The legal provisions in relation to regulation of contract labor provide for a system of dual control over contract labor by both the contractors and the principal employers (Box 8.1). Employment relations of contractor firms also differ depending on the types of contracts. In labor contracts where the sole purpose of the transaction is to supply labor, the principal employers have more control over the contract labor than in job contracts. In job contracts, the contractors have greater choices in managing

Box 8.1: Dual Control of the Principal: The Employer and the Contractor

1. The contractors pay wages, but the wage rates and any increase in wages are primarily decided by the principal employers.
2. The Contract Labour Act, 1970, requires that the contractors or the principal employers should not violate the provisions under the Minimum Wages Act, the Equal Remuneration, any wage agreements or awards, or judgments of courts/tribunals.
3. If a contractor fails to pay wages within the prescribed period, then the principal employers are liable to make the payments and deduct the amount from the payments to be made to the contractors (Section 21 of the Act).
4. In wage negotiations between contractors and their workers' unions, principal employers sign only as witnesses, but in reality they have the deciding roles.
5. The linkages of contract workers with principal employers are seen in union demands of wages and benefits at par with the direct workers. Unions often demand for absorption of contractor workers.
6. The Contract Labour Act, 1970, provides for abolition of contract labor in perennial jobs. It does not provide for their absorption in parent firms. However, the legislative intent of policy makers and decisions of some Apex Court argue for their absorption.
7. The social security (PF and ESI) and occupational health and safety legislation (Factories Act, 1948) make the principal employer responsible for implementation of the legal provisions.

Source: Various Acts in Malik 2006.

their employees than the principal employer. As firms differ in implementation of the legal provisions applicable to contract workers, there are variations in their employment relations. The differences are also because some contractor firms have unions, while others do not have unions.[12] All these contribute to variations in employment relations of contract firms, but the main character of employment relations in contract firms is the system of dual control over contractor workers.

In the past, most firms in India engaged large numbers of casual workers; now, contract workers fill most of these jobs. There are many reasons for this shift from the past practices. First, labor legislation in India and the Apex Court's judgments support regularization of casual workers and payment of wages and benefits at par with the regular workers. The Apex Court has observed that concerted effort must be made to regularize casual workers subject to their fulfilling qualifications and availability of work (Supreme Court of India 1992b: 825). Second, the regularization of casual workers has always been a major demand of trade unions. And once they are made permanent, the Industrial Disputes Act, 1947 makes it almost impossible to retrench them. Further, as unions of regular workers generally represent the casual workers, their engagement in union settings increases the possibilities of labor conflicts that also involve regular workers. Third, it is difficult to build high-commitment workplace practices among the core workers when the core has both high-skill and low-skill workers, but it is easier to do so once the low-skill jobs are off-loaded under contractors.

Employment relations in contractor firms have to be studied in relation to the legislative provisions relating to contract labor. The Contract Labour (Regulation & Abolition) Act, 1970 is the main labor legislation concerning contract workers. The Act defines contract labor as workers employed "through intermediaries such as contractors, sub-contractors, gang leaders or other agents who stand between the worker and the principal employer who benefits from his labor" (Monat 1973: 451). It provides for regulation of contract labor and abolition of the practice in certain cases. It applies to every establishment with twenty or more workers and to every contractor who employs twenty or more workers. The Act spells out responsibilities and roles for the principal employers and the contractors in relation to contract workers. There are other Acts that impose responsibilities on the principal employers and the contractors (Box 8.2). In addition, there are legislation that apply to contract workers depending on firm size, but they do not impose any legal responsibilities on the principal employers (the Bonus Act, 1965 and the Gratuity Act, 1972).

Job security of contract workers is always a controversial issue and a source of conflict between management and unions. Conflicts especially arise when there is a change of contractors. The Act does not guarantee continuing of employment of contract workers and a succeeding contractor is not obliged to absorb the workers of the previous contractor (Saran 1987: 11). However, in areas of strong

Box 8.2: Responsibilities of the Principal Employers under the Acts

1. The Contract Labor Act, 1970, specifies the roles and responsibilities of the principal employers and contractors in relation to contractor workers.
2. The Factories Act, 1945, does not make any distinction between a person directly employed and a person engaged through a contractor. Accordingly, a contract labor in a factory is entitled to all privileges and benefits under the Factories Act, including those relating to weekly holidays, compensatory holidays, overtime wages, leave with pay, and so forth.
3. The Employees' State Insurance Act provides that contract labor will be entitled to the benefits under the Act.
4. The Employees Provident Fund and Miscellaneous Provisions Act, 1952, makes the principal employer responsible for enrollment of contractor workers, ensuring payment of contributions and ensuring filling of prescribed returns.
5. Section 12 of the Workmen Compensation Act, 1953, provides that a principal employer is liable to pay the same compensation to a worker employed by a contractor as if the principal employer has directly engaged him.
6. In establishments to which the Payment of Wages Act, 1936, the Minimum Wages Act, 1948, or the enactments on national holidays apply, they also apply for the contractor workers.

Source: The Various Acts in Malik 2006.

union presence, often the new contractors are compelled to engage the workers of old contractor and sometimes there are disputes on working conditions and payment of old dues. Another issue relating to job security is about absorption of contract workers by the principal employers. In India, engagement of contract labor in perennial jobs is prohibited under the Contract Labor Act, 1970, but this provision has remained ineffective because of legal loopholes and lack of faith in its practical application. The Act provides for abolition of contract labor in perennial jobs, but it does not provide for their absorption by principal employer. The provision has been applied in some public-sector units, but it has remained ineffective in the private sector.[13] There have been attempts to remove restrictions on engagement of contract labor. The attempts have failed, but there are indications of change in the perception of policy makers in favor of engagement of contract labor.[14]

Networks of Small Firms

Indian industrial policies have favored segmentation of markets between large and small firms. The large-scale sector, with capital-intensive technology, feeds the higher end of the market and export market, and the small-scale sector produces inferior goods for the lower end of the domestic market. In recent times, however, a more complex picture is emerging in various industries with complex inter-firm relationships and special clustering of small firms (Cook 2000). A typical evolutionary pattern of inter-firm linkages has always existed in the informal arrangements between small enterprises providing mutual support like sharing of implements, exchanging information and other intermittent types of assistance. The recent examples, however, indicate that a more formal arrangement has emerged that includes inter-firm relationships aimed to improve the market participation of small enterprises. While these arrangements indicate horizontal linkages among small firms, there are also vertical linkages with other firms. Evidence indicates development of a multi-layer support network that ranges from government policies to micro-level interventions (Cook 2000).

The industrial district model of flexible specialization described by Piore and Sabel (1984) provides the best example of a network of small firms. It consists of "more or less equal small enterprises in an area or region bound in a complex web of competition and cooperation." It involves cooperation between small firms and sharing of indirect costs in marketing, design, material procurement, and maintenance of machinery. They used their collective capacities to devise innovative products and to get independent access to markets (Piore and Sable 1984: 17; Schmitz and Musyck 1994). One example of this model in India is the garment industry with three types of employers: (*a*) the principal employers, (*b*) the operators, and (*c*) the contractors. The principal employers supply raw materials to the operators; the operators get the work done through contractors and sub-contractors and then send the finished goods to the principal employers, who sell them in the markets (Khanna 1994: 89). Another example of this is the three distinct groups of small textile firms operating in clusters: small spinning units, power looms, and process centers that are closely linked to each other (Das 1998). The industrial district model of flexible specialization is more than an agglomeration of small firms. An agglomeration of small firms can offer few benefits, but the benefits of flexible specialization arise only when networks of suppliers develop, that provide materials, tools, machinery, spare parts, and so on. The spread of flexible specialization depends on the creation of three types of institutions: effective local governments, associations of small firms, and trade unions. These institutions influence employment relations of small firms in clusters.

In developing countries, the lack of institutional framework necessary to promote cooperation and stimulate innovation is a major obstacle in the emergence of the flexible specialization model. In India, the "civil society is weak and necessary political institutions like local government based on a widely shared idea of common good are not well developed" (Holmstrom 1993: 85). There are also problems in development of effective associations of small firms. The study of four European regions by Schmitz and Musyck (1994) indicates that emergence of flexible specialization also needs strong labor unions that can block the low road to competitiveness and promote innovation. In India, unions and employees' associations are weak in small firms. However, in spite of the institutional deficiencies, we find examples of industrial districts in different parts of our country. In these industrial districts, the institutions influence employment relations of small firms in the clusters.

Different Systems of Employment Relations in Small Firms

Employee control in most small firms is simple control. In this system, the personal power and authority of the employer constitutes the primary mechanism of employee control (Edwards 1979). The employer sees everything, knows everything, and decides everything. The employer labors alongside the hired workers and plays the role of chief worker. Family members often work for long hours and provide much of the labor required. In the early days of industrialization, when most businesses were small and run directly by the entrepreneurs, this was the primary system of employee control. Since then, employee control in firms has undergone dramatic changes with changes in firm size and technology use. Big businesses now dominate in many sectors, but an important and substantial segment of production is still carried on by small businesses, where simple control is still the order of the day.

In India, majority of workers work in small firms. Most of them get low wages, have low productivity, and produce low-quality products. Employment relations in most of these firms are free from external influences. However, some firms are subjected to external influences. The influences are of different types like coverage under labor laws, pressures of unions or employers' associations, influence of principal employers for contract firms, and collective influence for uniformity in clusters of small firms. As the extent and scope of the various influences differ across firms, they contribute to variation in their employment relations. I discuss below the different forms of employment relations in small firms:

1. **Small firms without any external influence:** Most small firms in India operate independently and without any external influence. In these firms, entrepreneurial control is informal, sometimes erratic, and subjected to favoritism and arbitrariness. Undoubtedly, workers are often oppressed and exploited by some employers, but they are also enmeshed in a whole network of personal relationships. The personal ties between owners of small businesses and their workers often tend to obscure the real class differences between them and provide the basis for effective employee control. In some small firms like small IT firms, the employer–employee relationship is more like that of partners than the traditional capital–labor relations. Employee control in most small firms is simple control and their employment system is a paternalistic system, where employers and employees directly interact with each other with no formal rules to regulate their behaviors.
2. **Dual control in small contractor firms:** Many small firms operate as contractors of large firms. Workers in these firms are distinguished from direct labor (directly employed by firms) in terms of their employment relationship with the principal

employers and methods of wage payments. Unlike the direct labor, which is on the payroll of an establishment and receives wages directly, contract labor, is neither on the payroll of principal employers nor paid directly. Working conditions of contract workers differ from those of regular workers.[15] Unlike regular workers who are protected under labor laws and enjoy lifetime employment, contract workers in general do not have similar job security. Legally, if a contract worker performs the same or similar job of a regular worker, he/she should get wages and benefits on par with the regular workers, but most often he/she gets lower wages and benefits.

Employee control for the contract workers is a type of dual control with roles for both the contractors and the principal employers. The wages and other benefits of contract firms are higher than those in independent small firms.[16] This is manly because of their legal and physical proximity to the formal-sector firms and legal provisions specific to contract workers. This makes the contract workers different from the other workers in the informal sector and their employee control different from simple control.

3. **Loosely coordinated employment systems in small firms:** Employee control in most small firms is without any external influence, but an increasing number of small firms are now experiencing external influences. The influences are from different sources: labor legislation, trade unions, and employers' associations. We will now discuss them briefly:

   (i) Influence of labor laws: Most labor legislation, in India are for the workers in the formal sector. Some labor laws apply to small firms, but they do not apply to all small firms (Das 1998). For example, the legislations on minimum wage and occupational safety and health apply only to small firms in the notified employments. Labor laws that apply to some small firms restrict employers' arbitrary authority or absolute power in their relationship with their workers. However, as the laws are not very effective in the informal sector, their influences are not very strong.

(ii) Influence of employers' associations: Employer's associations of small firms, if present, influence employee control in member firms. They are formed to protect their members' interests in different forums. Employee management is not the primary purpose behind formation of the associations, but most often they influence firms' employment relations. Some of the associations bargain wages and other conditions of work with the unions (hosiery industry, brick field). Further, even if they are not directly involved they indirectly influence firms to have similar workplace practices.

(iii) Most workers in small firms are without any union, but recent trends show increasing union activity in the informal sector. In addition, there are other forms of workers' organizations such as labor cooperatives and NGOs involved in the informal sector (Aziz 1995). Unions and other labour institutions, if present, influence firms' employer–employee relations.[17]

The labor laws, trade unions, and employers' associations restrict arbitrary and erratic decisions of employers. They promote standardized employment conditions and uniformity in wages and other conditions of work across groups of small firms. They result in more uniformity in wages and other conditions of work across groups of small firms. Employment relations in these groups of small firms are different from other small firms that do not experience external influences. Most often the homogenizing influences are not very strong and as a result the employment system that develops in small firms under external are coordinated, but they are loosely coordinated.

4. **Strongly coordinated (networked) employment systems:** Most often the institutional influences on employment systems of small firms are not very strong. The close proximity of employers to workers in small firms, their personal ties, ineffective enforcement of labor laws, weak trade unions and employers' associations, and high mortality of small firms make the influences weak. This makes their employment relation systems

loosely coordinated. However, the external influences and the pressures for uniformity are stronger when two or more factors work together in concert and then the strongly coordinated system emerges. Looking at the contemporary methods of workplace practices in small firms, we find the strongly coordinated system in the following two types of small firms:

(i) Industrial district clusters: In the industrial districts, collective actions by groups of small firms not only provide common services and bargaining with the local governments and other organizations, they also often lay down guidelines on employee behavior and employee control. In union setting, they bargain wages and other conditions of work with their unions. The institutional influences are from unions, employers associations, their common services, governments, and local bodies. In industrial districts, these influences work in concert and this makes their employment relations strongly coordinated.
(ii) Satellite clusters of small firms: In these clusters, groups of small firms appear as satellites of large firms and operate as their suppliers or contractors. They are best described in the solar system model of flexible specialization (Piore and Sabel 1984). In this model, the owners of small firms bargain with the management of large firms and with their unions. The strongest isomorphic pressure for uniformity is from the management of large firms. This along with other institutional influences makes their employment relations strongly coordinated.

In both the strongly coordinated systems, there are strong institutional influences and network norms and they act in combination. Of the two models, the industrial district clusters are more visible than the satellite cluster model. I have thus presented the four dominant patterns of employment relations in small firms—the simple paternalistic system, the dual control system, the loosely coordinated system, and the strongly coordinated system. Majority of the small firms in India has the simple paternalistic system of employment relations. The next dominant system is the loosely coordinated system, but its share is much lower compared to the simple paternalistic system. The shares of the other two systems are very small as the dual control system is only seen in small contract firms, and the industrial district clusters and the satellite clusters are still not very common.

Summary

Employee control in most small firms is simple control and the employment system is a paternalistic system, where employers control all aspects of workers' work life without any external influences. However, employment relations in some firms are subjected to external influences that limit employers' arbitrary authority. Some of these limitations are legal restrictions imposed by labor laws, some are self-imposed by groups of employers operating in concert, and some are the result of pressures exerted by trade unions. In contractor firms, the principal employers have substantial influence on contractor firms' employer–employee relations. The external influences have led to emergence of a coordinated pattern of employment relations—sometimes loosely coordinated and sometimes strongly coordinated. The external influences are stronger when small firms appear in clusters. With growing concentration of firms in a region, the differences in employer–employee relations become more visible to both employers and their workers. It increases the possibilities of conflict both within and across firms and demands uniformity across firms for their stability. The firms thus come together and develop systems that enhance similarities in employment relations across firms. They develop common guidelines for employees' wages and benefits and help each other collectively in dispute resolution. The external influences have led to growing uniformity across groups of small firms. However, as many small firms still operate without any external influences and the extent of the influences varies across firms, there are now increasing variations in people are being managed at work in the informal sector. This is leading to growing variations in employment relations in the informal sector.

Notes

1. About 91 percent of all workers in India work in the informal sector. The share of informal sector workers is 78 percent in construction, 75 percent in manufacturing, and 98 percent in agriculture (Ghosh and Bharadwaj 1992: 150–154).
2. The changes are somewhat different from the pattern found by Kuznets (1966). According to Kuznets, in a country like India, the percentage of the population dependant on agriculture should decline, and that dependant on industry and service should increase over time. In India, the decline in agriculture has not been accompanied with an increase in manufacturing sector employment.
3. In agriculture, Kohli (1987: 141–142) observes that the wage levels in the unionized blocks are higher than those in non-unionized blocks and minimum wage legislation is more effective in the unionized blocks.
4. For example, most regular workers in the informal sector receive annual bonuses, although they are not covered under the Payment of Bonus Act, 1965. It is a social norm and cultural tradition to pay bonus during festivals. Some contract workers receive gratuity although they are not covered under the Payment of Gratuity Act, 1972. The goods transport workers in West Bengal get house rent allowances even though it is not legally payable (Agreement, 1994).
5. In rural India there exists unofficial minimum wages below which no worker agrees to work; it is seen even in the absence of collective action among the workers (Drèze and Mukherjee 1987: 19).
6. The Trade Union Act, 1928, provides for registration of employees' association but only few are registered under the Act. There were 770 such employers' associations in India registered under the Act in 2000. (Government of India 2003: 141). Most employers' associations are registered under the Societies Registration Act, 1860.
7. In West Bengal, employers' associations in power loom, hosiery, goods-transport, bakery, and cold storage industries regularly negotiate wages and other conditions of work with their trade unions.
8. The number of unions registered in West Bengal during 1985 and 1995 indicate a substantial drop in new registrations, but an increase in the share of informal-sector unions among new registrations.
9. Examples of region-wide agreements in West Bengal: (*a*) small engineering, (*b*) iron foundries, (*c*) brick fields in districts, (*d*) restaurants in Kolkata, and (*e*) cloth markets in Kolkata.
10. In the textile industry in Orissa and refractory units in Bihar there are minimum wages, but in West Bengal, both the industries have collective agreements. In cinema, rubber, and hosiery industries in West Bengal, initially there were notified minimum wages, but are now covered by collective agreements.

11. Section 2 of the Contract Labour (Regulation and Abolition) Act, 1970 provides that "a workman shall be deemed to be employed as contract labor in or in connection with the work of an establishment when he/she is hired by or through a contractor, with or without the knowledge of the principal employer."
12. There are also variations in unionization of contract workers from state to state. While most contract workers in West Bengal have unions, it is not so in Gujarat.
13. West Bengal has issued notification for abolition of contract labor in eleven establishments under the Act. Of these eleven establishments, ten are central public sector units (Source: Labour Commission, West Bengal).
14. The Union Budget 2001–2002 proposed to remove the restrictive provisions under the existing laws to facilitate outsourcing and contract appointments, but it could not succeed.
15. The contract workers are often seen as casual workers. Some managers, when asked whether they have casual workers, replied that their contract workers are like casual workers.
16. At MCPI, for example, the average wage of contract workers is much higher (nearly double) than the statutory minimum wages set by the government, they are covered under the PF, ESI, and Gratuity Act, and are paid overtime wages at double the normal rate like the regular workers.
17. See Chapter 3 for discussions on unions in the informal sector. The Minimum Wage Act, 1948, provides for legal action against an employer if he/she does not pay minimum wages, but the presence of a large pool of surplus labor, poor administrative and financial resources available with enforcement machinery, lack of awareness of minimum wage provisions, and so forth, often limits the minimum wage legislation mainly to the unionized sector (Das 1998).

Chapter 9

Conclusion: Convergences and Divergences

CHANGES IN EMPLOYMENT relations in industrialized countries over the last three decades indicate growing variations in employment relation practices within countries (divergences) and emerging commonalities in employment relation practices across countries (convergences). Katz and Darbishire (2000) conclude this in their study of automobile and telecommunications industries in seven industrialized countries (United States, United Kingdom, Sweden, Germany, Italy, Australia, and Japan). The variations and the commonalities are based on identification of a finite set of employment relation patterns, comparison of the patterns, and their changes over time. The commonalities across countries in work practices that make up the key employment relation patterns are in broad terms; there are some differences across countries in the detailed description of the individual practices. The sources of such differences include country-specific institutions and the nature of unions. Further, countries differ in the relative proportions of the different patterns. This book identifies the different patterns of employment relations in India and their changes in the post-reform period. It examines whether the patterns apparent in India and their changes over time broadly conform to those found in the industrialized countries. This study covers different industries (such as textiles, chemicals, ITES, the small-firms sector) to validate the convergence–divergence hypothesis in the Indian context. Although the sample of industries and firms is not a perfect representative of the population, it does capture the typical employment relation issues. They indicate major changes in the people are managed at work in India.

In India, like in the industrialized countries, there exist a finite set of patterns of employment relations. The key patterns of employment relations are similar to those seen in the industrialized countries. However, there are some differences in the key patterns in the detailed description of the patterns, and in the share of the different patterns. Katz and Darbishire identify the four dominant patterns as low-wage, HRM, Japanese-oriented, and joint-team-based. In the Indian context, the dominant patterns can be identified as the conflict pattern, the low-wage pattern, the joint-team-based pattern, and the HRM pattern. In addition to identifying and documenting the dominant patterns of employment relations, this book also presents how the relative shares of the employment relations patterns have changed over time. Our findings indicate that while the low-wage pattern and conflict patterns dominated in the past, in recent times, the HRM pattern has made its presence felt and the joint-team-based pattern has increased its share. In the pre-liberalization period, employment relation practices in most large firms were characterized by tripartite agreements and a bounded amount of conflict between capital and labor (traditional pattern), while now there has been shift to the HRM and joint-team-based pattern. The increased variations in employment practices are evident both within and across industrial sectors, within union and non-union sectors, within states, and even within the small-scale sector. The changes under way also indicate a number of commonalities across firms and across industries and changes in the processes and structures of labor-management interactions. In brief, the changes in India indicate that they are similar to those seen in the developed countries.

This concluding chapter aggregates the findings of the preceding chapters on employment relation patterns in different firms and different industries. In summarizing the findings, we assume that the overall variation in employment relations in a country can be seen as the aggregate of the variation in employment relations across firms within different industrial sectors and differences in employment relations between the industrial sectors. In each industrial sector, we examine the dominant patterns of employment relations and then find how the shares of the patterns have changed over time. The study finds that the patterns of employment relation systems, shares of each type, and their changes over time vary across industries, across states, and depend on unionization. Important sources of the variations include the global and local influences on firms' employment relations. The study examines how the differences in firms' global linkages (such as foreign ownership or exports) contribute to variations in firms' employment relations. Amid variations in employment relations across firms, there are many commonalities in workplace practices that are widespread and common in all types of firms. Our findings confirm that the commonalities and the variations in employment relations and the way people are being managed at work in India are similar to those in the industrialized countries.

Variations within and across Industrial Sectors

The changes in employment relations in industrialized countries over the last two decades indicate continuing and persistent variations in employment relation systems across firms within the countries. Katz and Darbishire (2000) advance their theory on converging divergences in employment relations based on their study of automobile and telecommunications industries in seven industrialized countries. They find that four dominant patterns of employment systems are emerging in all the seven countries. Our study of textile industry in India (Chapter 4), indicates existence of four dominant patterns of employment relation systems: low-wage, HRM, joint-team-based, and conflict patterns. In the past, employment relations in large textile firms were more or less uniform with centralized tripartite agreements and a bounded amount of conflict between capital and labor. Over time, the low wage, the joint-team-based, the HRM, and the conflict have emerged as the dominant patterns of employment relation systems. The emergence and coexistence of the four dominant patterns of employment relations in the textile industry is a departure from the past practices and indicate increasing variations in employment relation practices within the industry. Further, the changes in small firms in the textile sector through emergence of coordinated paternalistic patterns have added to increased variations in employment relations within the industry.

We now compare and contrast the findings in the textile industry with those in the other industrial sectors like chemical, engineering, and ITES. In industrialized countries, most studies on employment relations are for the automobile and telecommunication industries (both in the engineering sector). Our study, however, focusses on firms in the textile, chemicals, and ITES sectors and includes firms in other industrial sectors. In order to examine the overall variations in employment relation practices, we argue that the overall variations in employment relations in a country can be seen as the aggregate of the variations in employment relations within different industrial sectors and the differences in employment relations across the industrial sectors.[1] First, we compare the findings in the textile industry with those in the ITES sector. The two industries differ widely in terms of their products, skills of employees engaged, technology used, and timing of evolution. The textile industry represents a traditional industry with a history of about a century and caters to both export and domestic markets. In contrast, the ITES industry in India became popular only in the last decade; it uses modern technology and is highly dependent on external markets. We find that in place of the four dominant employment patterns in the textile industry, the ITES sector is relatively homogeneous with little or no difference in employment relations across firms. It exhibits only one dominant employment pattern: the HRM pattern. Thus, though the two industries are radically different, they do share at least one employment pattern—the HRM pattern. Crucially, however, the HRM pattern in the ITES firms is different from the HRM pattern in the textile industry. In the textile industry, the HRM pattern has evolved from the industrial model of work organization, while in the ITES, it has developed from the salaried model.[2]

In developed countries, the studies on the automobile and telecommunication industries show that in spite of similar market forces in an industrial sector, firms differ in their employment practices. There are also inter-industry differences in employment relations. The differences here are in terms of number of the dominant patterns in the sectors (extent of divergence) and nature of the patterns. The findings in the textile industry and in the ITES sectors confirm similar differences in terms of both the number of dominant patterns and the differences in HRM pattern. In Chapters 5 and 6, we have discussed employment relation practices in BOC India and MCPI. Both are capital-intensive firms in chemical industry and subsidiaries of MNCs. While Mitsubishi is a new firm established in year 2000, BOC India, originally established as IOC in 1935, went through dramatic business and employment restructuring in the 1990s. Both the firms have the HRM pattern of employment relations (in some bottling plants, BOC India has the joint-team-based pattern). In chemical industry although the two firms in have the HRM pattern of employment relations, some firms in the industry have the low-wage pattern of employment relations (for example, Nirma). In comparison to the chemical industry with two dominant patterns of employment relations (the HRM and the low-wages pattern), the engineering industry exhibits all the four employment relation patterns seen in the textile industry.[3]

Industry characteristics are less important factors in small firms. In most small firms, employers operate without any external influences, employee control is simple control, and their employment relation systems are the paternalistic systems. However, some small firms are subjected to external influences that restrict employers' absolute authority. The restrictions are sometimes legal restrictions like the minimum wage legislation, sometimes the restrictions are imposed by trade unions or employers' associations, and in contractor firms the restrictions are imposed by the principal employers. Most often, the various restrictions operate independently and sometimes they work in combination. In contract firms, the system of employee control provides control authority for both contractors and principal employers. The system of dual control is reflected in payments of wages and in implementation of legal provisions for contract workers. In brief, the external influences have led to the emergence of a new form of employment relation system in small firms: the coordinated paternalistic system, where employers' absolute authority is constrained by different local institutional norms. Emergence of the coordinated paternalistic system for groups of small firms has increased uniformity in wages and other conditions of work within the groups, but it has increased variations in employment practices in the small firm sector. Increased variations also occur because small firms differ in type, extent, and sources of external influences. In the textile industry, the restrictions are imposed by trade unions or labor laws, but in some small firms industries the restrictions are self-imposed by groups of employers.

The analysis of employment relations for each industrial sector and their changes over time is presented here in two steps. First, we identify the different types of employment relation systems in each industrial sector and then examine how these have changed over time. Table 9.1 presents a summary of the dominant

Table 9.1: Variations in Employment Relations (ER) within and across Industrial Sectors

Industry	*ER Patterns*	*Dominant Patterns*	*Changes*
Textile	Low-wage, conflict pattern, joint-team-based, HRM pattern	Low-wage, joint-team-based	Emerging pattern: low-wage and HRM
ITES	HRM pattern	HRM pattern	New firms, no change
Engineering	Low-wage, conflict pattern, joint-team-based, HRM pattern	Low wage, joint-team-based, HRM	HRM in high-tech firms, low-wage in low-tech firms
Chemical	Low-wage, joint-team-based, HRM pattern	Joint-team-based, HRM	Increasingly HRM pattern

Source: Based on discussions in Chapters 4–7.

patterns of employment relations in four industrial sectors: textile, engineering, ITES, and chemicals industries and how the patterns have changed over time. It shows that some industrial sectors exhibit multiple patterns of employment relations (textile industry), while some industrial sectors exhibit only one dominant pattern of employment relations (ITES). While the variations in employment relations are increasing within the industrial sectors, the HRM pattern is becoming popular in all industrial sectors. In the small-scale sector, a completely new employment relations pattern—the coordinated paternalistic pattern is evolving through networking of small firms or subcontracting networks. The link between large firms and small firms (contractor firms or dedicated suppliers) is also increasing the variations in small firms as some variations in large firms are spilling over to small firms. The net result of all these is increasing variation in employment relations in India.

Variations across States

The convergence argument in the debate on worldwide changes in employment relations speaks about the emerging commonalities in employment relations systems across countries. In industrialized countries, while there is increasing variations in employment practices within the countries, there are emerging commonalities in the nature of the variations across countries. In spite of the differences in country-specific labor market structures and institutions, the countries indicate emerging similarities in the patterns of workplace practices and labor–management interactions. In India, the central government has enacted most important labor laws, but their implementation in most industries rests with the state governments. The states differ in implementation of labor laws, in use of conciliation or adjudication machinery, and in levels of unionization. This has been well documented in industrial relations literature[4] (Venkataratnam 1997). The differences are particularly prominent between West Bengal and Gujarat. While Gujarat is traditionally known as an industry-friendly state, West Bengal is known as a labor-friendly state. They differ in implementation of labor laws, wage setting, unionization, union types, labor conflicts, and capital–labor power balance. This diversity across states in India provides an excellent opportunity for study of geographical and institutional differences in employment relations.

The main source of variations in employment relations across states is the differences in the structure and function of labor institutions. Unionization and union influence vary across states. While most firms in West Bengal have unions and majority have multiple unions, in Gujarat most firms do not have any union or have single union. Most unions in West Bengal are external unions and affiliated to trade union federations, but in Gujarat most unions are organized at the enterprise or unit level and only a few are affiliated to state-level federations.[5] While most contract workers in West Bengal have unions, in Gujarat most often they do not have any union. This study includes examples of firms from the two states to explain the variations in employment relations across states.[6] It appears that although the states have some commonalities in workplace practices, the relative proportions of the different employment relation patterns and the extent to which they appear on a non-union basis differ across states. The conflict pattern and the joint-team-based pattern are common in labor-intensive firms in West Bengal, but it is not so in Gujarat. The low-wage pattern in West Bengal is most often in a union setting (Vikram Spinning), while in Gujarat it is mostly in non-union setting (Aarvee Denim). The HRM pattern in Gujarat appears mostly in non-union firms, while in West Bengal it is also seen in union firms.

The changes under way in employment relation systems across Indian states indicate a number of commonalities. There are some changes in workplace practices that are common in all types of firms and in all states. For example, in all states there has been increased use of contract workers and teamwork, and emphasis on productivity and quality. In all states, most new firms are without any union and increasingly unionized firms are adopting practices common in non-union firms. The HRM pattern is increasing and the conflict pattern is becoming less common in all the states. In new high-tech firms, the industry characteristics are now more important than locations of firms. For example, the ITES firms in all locations have similar employment practices. Overall, the changes are making employment relations in West Bengal similar to those in Gujarat. This indicates convergence in employment relations across the states. The changes across the states indicate that geographical and institutional differences are becoming less important and thus support the validity of the convergence theory in employment relations.

Unions and Variations in Employment Relations

Union influence on firms' employment relations and their outcomes are widely discussed subjects in industrial relations. There is debate about the roles played by the unions, but there is no doubt that unions, if present, influence almost all aspects of employer–employee relations. They alter the behavior of workers and managers and outcomes of their interactions. They raise wages and alter the entire package of compensation including fringe benefits and deferred benefits such as pensions, health insurance, and accident insurance. By adopting pay policies that limit managerial discretion, unions reduce inequality among workers within and across establishments. They provide a voice in determining the rules and conditions of work, and insist on grievance and arbitration procedures for appealing supervisors' decisions. Management in union firms generally operate more "by the book" with less subjectivity and less flexibility than in non-union firms. Union workplaces operate under rules that are more explicit than non-union workplaces. All these make the union sector different from the non-union sector (Freeman and Medoff 1984).

Employment relations of firms in the union sector differ from those in the non-union sector. There are also variations in firms' employment relations within the two sectors. As unions promote standardization of employment conditions, the variations in employment relations are lower in the union sector than in the non-union sector. Firms' employment relations in the union sector vary depending on the level of unionization and management's strategy toward unionization. In India, the variations within the union sector are much more than those seen in industrialized countries. This is mainly because of the differences in union types: internal unions (does not have any outsider as office bearer), external unions, independent unions (not affiliated to any union federation) or affiliated unions.[7] Further, the emergence of multiple unions in various workplaces due to the liberal policies on formation, registration, and recognition of trade unions in India also lead to increased variations in union types. The variation in employment relations is partly due to differences in management strategies toward unions and unionization. In India, there is a spectrum of options available, beginning with "no union" and ending with a cooperative relationship with unions. In some firms, management prefers single union, while in others they recognize multiple unions. Recent changes in the union sector indicate employers' preference for single union and more particularly for internal unions and independent unions.[8] Table 9.2 briefly presents how firms' employment relations vary depending on unionization. Table 9.3 presents examples of firms with different types of unions and their methods of wage determination that influence firms' employment relations. The conflict pattern is most common in multiple union setting, the joint-team-based pattern is common in firms with fewer unions (one or two), and the HRM pattern is common in firms with independent and internal unions.

Table 9.2: Different Types of Firm-level Unions

Union Type	*Central Trade Union/ Political Affiliation*	*Wage Determination*	*Examples*
Multiple external unions	Affiliated to central trade unions and linked to political parties	Industry-wide tripartite agreements	Indian Rayon, Eastern Spinning, Vikram Spinning (Chapter 4)
Single external unions	Mostly affiliated to central trade unions and linked to political parties	Industry-wide/ Plant-level agreements	Reliance Textile, BOC India (Chapters 4 and 5)
Internal unions	Mostly not affiliated to central trade unions	Plant-level agreements	DCM Tyota, Maruti Udyog (Chapter 7)
Workers' committees	Often promoted by management	Committee consulted	MCPI India (Chapter 7)

Source: Based on discussions in Chapters 4, 5, and 7.

Table 9.3: Employment Relations in Union/Non-union Firms

Issues/Types of Firms	*Internal Union Firms*	*External Union Firms*	*High-tech Non-union*	*Low-tech Non-union*
Wage agreement	Unit-level agreement	Tripartite agreement	Individual contract	Minimum wages
Wage dependence on skill/knowledge	Moderate or high	Low	High	Low
Fringe benefits	Lower	Higher	Performance dependent	Statutory benefits
Management strategy	Accommodation	Conflict/cooperation	Accommodation	Union avoidance
Grievance procedure	Standard practice	Detailed and formal	No formal rules	Standard procedure
Functional flexibility	Moderate/high	Low	High	Moderate
Labor law compliance	Moderate	High	High	Moderate
Modern practices	Moderate	Moderate/low	High	Low
Dominant ER pattern	Joint-team-based/HRM	Joint team-based/ conflict	HRM pattern	Low-wage pattern
Examples of firms	MCPI, Hind Leaver Chemicals	Eastern and Vikram Spinning	ITES firms, New BOC plants	Aarvee Denim, Nirma

Source: Based on discussions in Chapters 4–7.

The non-union sector is different from the union sector because of the relative absence of equalizing forces and consequently there is more managerial discretion in the design of firms' employment relation practices than in the union sector. Most small firms in the non-union sector pay low wages, have lower job security, and poor working conditions. There are also some large firms in the non-union sector that operate on the basis of low wages and poor working conditions. In the non-union sector, wages are generally lower than those in similar industries in the union sector. However, some of the best employers in the country—firms offering highest wages and benefits, job security, and desirable working conditions—are large non-union firms. Some of these firms match union contracts to prevent unionization, while others seek to be leaders in the job market for reasons other than threats of unionization. Firms remain non-union because of various reasons, which partly explain the differences in employment relations across non-union firms. The discussions in Box 9.1 indicate various reasons why firms remain non-union. In the non-union sector, the emergence of the HRM pattern as also differences in implementation of HRM practices contribute to increased variation in employment relations in the non-union sector.

Box 9.1: Non-union Firms Differ in Their Employment Relations

1. Most small firms in India do not have any union. There are various reasons for this, more particularly it is difficult to organize workers in small firms. Employment relations control in these firms is simple paternalistic system.
2. Employees in many service-sector firms and in high-tech IT firms are not unionized (Wipro, Infosys, ITES firms). This is partly because employees themselves are not interested in forming unions. Employment relation in these firms is generally the HRM pattern.
3. Most new firms are without any union. Their employment relation is either HRM pattern (Haldia Petrochemical, Torrent, New Gas Plants of BOC India) or low wage pattern (Aarvee Denim).
4. Some firms remain non-union because of management's strong union-avoidance strategy. Their employment relation patterns are the low-wage pattern (Jyothi Weaving, Nirma) or the HRM pattern (MCPI, ITES firms).

Source: Based on discussions in Chapters 4–8.

Now, we examine the changes in employment relations between the union sector and non-union sector. Unions traditionally promote and preserve standardization. However, increased competition and threats of employment loss in the post-reform era have led unions to accept new workplace practices. In the union sector, as management in some firms introduces practices like extensive communication and strong corporate culture, common to the HRM pattern, it increases variations in employment relations in the union sector. In the past, workplace practices of the union sector spilled over to non-union sector. In the post-reform era, the changes are in the opposite direction, some practices of the non-union sector are spilling over to the union sector. As some union firms adopt practices of non-union firms, their employment relations practices become similar to those in the non-union firms. Net result of the changes indicate that employment relations in the union sector are shifting towards those in the non-union sectors.

Emerging Commonalities

Economic policy reform programs initiated in the early 1990s and the changes in economic, technological, social, legal, and political contexts over the last two decades have made the industrial environment highly competitive. The changes have led to changes in employment relations, workplace practices, employment relation patterns, and share of the different patterns. The changes have increased similarities in employment relation practices across the states and between the union and non-union sectors. While geographical locations and union influence are now less important in influencing employment relations, there is now increasing variations in employment relation patterns within and across industrial sectors.[9] Along with the variations in employment relations, there are some similar and widespread changes in workplace practices. The most important of them are indicated next:

1. Employment restructuring and downsizing: Most organizations have reduced employment and changed organizational structures. The shift is toward lean production and

de-layering of organizations. In India, the Industrial Disputes Act, 1947, restricts organizations from laying after retrenching or closing a unit. In spite of such legal restrictions most firms have reduced their workforce during the last two decades. This has been achieved mainly through VRS that typically involve payment of additional compensation with terminal benefits to the workers leaving the organization. The union government has encouraged such schemes by giving income tax exemptions and by introducing them in the public-sector undertakings. The schemes are voluntary in nature, but in reality firms often force their employees to apply for such schemes by putting them under difficult situations like transfer to far away places or allotting inconvenient jobs.

2. Contracting out of jobs: There is now increased use of contract labor in all parts of the world. It is now widespread in all industries in India. Often downsizing of employment has been achieved through contracting out of jobs. Increasingly, firms are adopting strategies that reduce regular employment and increase contract labor. This is particularly seen in non-core activities like security, canteen, transport, maintenance of gardens, and housekeeping. Many of the contract workers work under a labor contract system, where the main task of contractors is to supply labor. Increased use of contract labor has reduced labor costs, overhead costs, and need for capital investments, and has increased labor flexibility. However, unlike previous periods, management is now more involved in managing and controlling contract workers.
3. Separation of regular workers from non-regular workers: The recent trend shows management's attempt to separate regular workers from non-regular workers and protect the interests of regular workers vis-à-vis the non-regular workers. This is seen in their preference for contract workers in place of casual workers. In the past, most firms engaged large number of casual workers; increasingly, contract workers are replacing their jobs. There are many reasons for this shift. First, the labor legislation and court judgments in India favor regularization of casual workers. Second, there are always demands for

absorption of casual workers in permanent employment and payment of wages and benefits on par with regular workers. This is often a source of potential labor conflict. Third, it is difficult to promote high-commitment work practices among the casual and low-skilled workers. By separating the low-skill contract workers from the high-skill core employees, it is now easier for firms to introduce high-commitment work practices among the directly employed regular workers.

4. Increased emphasis on labor flexibility: Firms are increasingly adopting practices to enhance labor flexibility at individual, shop floor, plant, and strategic levels. At the individual level, the emphasis is on increasing workers' ability to perform different jobs through training and skill development. At the shop floor, the thrust is on increasing mobility of workers through multi-skilling, redeployment, and teamwork. At the plant level, the strategy is to gain numerical flexibility that may help to adjust their employment level. At the strategic level, firms adopt strategies like contracting out of jobs that enables them to adjust the workforce working for the firms with changes in demand. It involves control of activities outside the organizations.[10]
5. Performance and skill-based wages: Increasingly, wages are getting linked to individual or group ability, skill and knowledge, performance, productivity, and quality of work. This is particularly seen in high-tech firms that have more skilled and professional workers. Many firms have introduced agreements that link wages to learning new skills and acquisition of multiple skills. Increasingly workers' pay now includes variable components that link their wages to production and productivity. Annual bonus or lump sum payments are being linked to individual, group, and firm performance along with arrangements for profit sharing and stock ownership. In high-tech export-oriented industries, the pay system now resembles the pay systems in the advanced economies.
6. Increasing variations in wages: The total income of a worker is made up of several components and is derived from various sources (wages, rent, dividends, social security, unemployment insurance, welfare, interest), the distribution of different

components of income explains the overall variation of total income. Greater variation is now seen in the different components of wage and in total income. Along with increasing variation in basic wage rates, there is also increasing variation in fringe benefits, which is often more than the variation in wages (Katz and Darbishire 2000: 29). Increasing variations are partly because of the decline of unions and consequent weakening of their equalizing effects on distribution of wages and other financial benefits. Further, incentive schemes and performance based wages contributes to variations in wages as performance vary across individuals and groups.

7. Union avoidance and union substitution: Increasingly firms are adopting union-avoidance and union-substitution strategies. Management strategy toward unions and unionization was always important in shaping firms' employment relations, but it is more so in the post-reform period. Increasingly, new firms are adopting practices that help them to avoid unions. For example, some firms promote workers to administrative and supervisory ranks to take them outside the purview of the Industrial Disputes Act and avoid unionization (Venkataratnam 1993). Increasingly, employers now show preference for a single union in place of multiple unions, internal unions in place of external unions, and independent unions in place of affiliated unions. Employers in some firms promote workers' committees that operate like unions, but oppose formation of external unions. In unionized firms, management is increasingly using union substitution strategy by taking up activities that are traditionally functions of unions.
8. Emphasis on productivity and quality: There is now increased emphasis on improvement of production, productivity, and product quality. This is seen in many collective agreements with trade unions (Das 2000). Most agreements now include clauses on improvement of discipline, increase in workload, incentives, rationalization of manpower, introduction of new technology, and contracting out of jobs. In West Bengal, the industry-wide tripartite agreement in engineering industry provides for a uniform wage structure, but most firms have plant-level agreements on production

and productivity. Overall, employers and unions are now increasingly engaged in joint consultation for productivity and quality improvements.

9. Emphasis on training: There is now increased emphasis on training; it is more so in firms that use relatively higher levels of technology. Training is no longer seen as just a desirable component in HRM, but as an essential contributor to organizational effectiveness (OE). In the high-tech firms and MNCs in India, it is now an integral part of management business strategy. The training programs not only aim to train employees in their specific skills, but also aim to train them in general skills like teamwork, quality improvement, and customer orientation. Many firms have annual plans for training, and some even have long-term plans that aim for individual development.
10. Introduction of high-performance workplace practices: Some firms, particularly the MNCs and reputed capital-intensive firms in India, are increasingly adopting practices that have been successful in developed countries. HRM is now as an exciting new approach to people management, with emphasis on direct communication, employee participation, and flexibility. In India, firms are adopting HRM techniques, but few of them have adopted the full-grown HRM model that involves strategic deployment of a highly committed and capable workforce and uses an integrated array of cultural, structural, and personal techniques. Further, the approach in most firms has so far focused more on managers, supervisors, and white-collar workers than blue-collar workers. However, most firms in India have focused on improving the skill, knowledge, and attitudes of workers. Their focus has shifted from cost containment and conflict management to development of highly skilled, flexible, and productive workforce.

This discussion indicates emerging similarities in the workplace practices and in labor management interactions. The similarities, however, do not indicate universal convergence to a single pattern of employment relations. Clearly, the liberalization of the Indian economy and the consequent increased competition are driving much of the pressures for the similarities. The case studies indicate that global forces and global contexts have now more influence on Indian firms than in the pre-reform period. The global linkages and influences now have more influence on firms' employment relations and that contribute to both similarities and dissimilarities in employment relations.

Global Content and Variations in Employment Practices

Globalization has increased involvement of MNCs in the Indian economy. It is through establishment of their branches, subsidiaries, or joint ventures, or by selling this products in Indian markets or by procuring products from Indian markets. As MNCs with better knowledge of best practices that have been successful in other countries introduce the practices in their Indian firms, it leads to changes in there firms' employment systems. In their attempts to introduce new practices, they are constrained by various factors, such as culture, ownership structures, labor markets, national labor legislation, and the roles of state and trade union organizations. These factors mediate the transfer processes and their outcomes. MNCs differ in their perceived need and ability to adopt global or local practices. This is partly because they differ in foreign or local ownership, share of exports or imports, extent of internal or external competition, and then location within global commodity chains. The differences across MNCs in global linkages lead to differences in their employment relations. Further, the global influences are not only on MNCs, they are also on local firms that try to follow some of the successful practices.

Globalization and the liberalization policies have changed the contexts of employment relations in India. Firms everywhere are now facing influence of globalization and increasing pressure of competition. However, this does not mean that conserving forces of localization have disappeared. The forces of globalization and localization are not uniform across firms. Various external and internal factors influence firms' global linkages and then embeddedness in the local economy. The influences vary depending on factors like firms' foreign or local ownerships, share of export or import, and extent of internal or external competition. Higher foreign ownership or higher exports mean higher global linkages or global content. In contrast, higher sales in the domestic market mean higher local linkages. The examples of firms in Table 9.4

Table 9.4: Firms Differ in Global Content or Local Embeddedness

Examples	*Types of Firms*	*Foreign Ownership*	*Export*	*External Competition*	*Expatriate*	*Global Content Rank*	*Dominant Employment System*
First Ring International	ITES firms	High	High	High	High	1	HRM—mass customized
Mitsubishi Chemical	New MNC	High	Low	High	High	2	HRM—Japanese
BOC India	MNC restructured	Medium	Low	High	Low	3	HRM pattern
Indian Rayon	Indian MNC	Nil	High	High	Nil	4	HRM pattern
Reliance Textile	Indian restructured	Nil	Low	High	Nil	5	Joint-team-based
Eastern Spinning	Indian	Nil	Low	Low	Nil	6	Conflict pattern

Source: Based on discussions in Chapters 4–7.

present how firms' global linkages depend on various factors. The global linkage is highest for the ITES firms, while it is lowest for the traditional industries like old textile units that produce for local markets. The higher the global linkage in a firm, the more likely it is to adopt modern practices in employment relations.

MNCs in India established in the post-reform era have the most advanced practices in employment relations similar to those in their parent country. This is seen in MCPI, subsidiary of Mitsubishi Corporation, as also in the ITES firms that are wholly owned subsidiaries of foreign multinationals. The employment relations in a typical MNC are different from those in local firms. However, some Indian firms also have their employment relation practices similar to those in the MNCs. For example, Wipro, Infosys, and Tata Consultancy Services have employment relations comparable to those in the best firms in developed countries. In fact, they are also MNCs: they are Indian multinationals. Firms with higher global linkages and operating at higher levels of technology generally use the HRM pattern of employment relations. In contrast, firms with low global linkages, low levels of technology, and producing for local markets typically have the conflict or the joint-team-based pattern of employment relations. In summary, the differences in global linkages contribute to differences in employment relations across firms. Further, as the differences in global linkages vary across firms, there is increasing variations in employment relations.

Conclusions

The changes in employment relation practices in industrialized countries indicate growing variations in employment relation practices within the countries (Katz and Darbishire 2000). Our findings on changes in employment relation practices in India also indicate similar growing variations in employment relation practices. This is seen in a number of ways. First, there are increasing variations in employment relation practices within the industrial sectors (textiles, chemicals, and engineering). Second, the increasing variations in employment relation practices are seen both within the capital-intensive sector and labor-intensive sector. Third, increasing variations are occurring both within the union sector and non-union sector. Fourth, within the small-scale sector, the emergence of the coordinated paternalistic pattern has increased the variations in employment relation practices. Fifth, as MNCs have introduced new workplace practices that were not common in local firms, this has contributed to increased variations in employment practices. Finally, there is increasing variations in employment relation practices across different industrial sectors. All these have contributed to overall variations in employment relations in the country. Table 9.5 presents a summary of the changes in employment relations in different sectors and their contributions to the overall variations in employment relations. It shows that the increased variations

Table 9.5: Firms' Employment Relations (ER) and the Overall Variations

Types of Firms	*Employment Relations (ER)*	*Changes: Contribution to Overall Variation*
Capital-intensive firms	ER varies across firms—Joint-team-based and HRM patterns. Some firms introducing best practices.	As some firms introduce new practices, there are overall increasing variations in ER practices.
Labor-intensive firms	ER varies across firms—Low wage, conflict, joint-team-based, and HRM patterns.	Increasing variations in ER practices across firms is leading to divergences in ER practices.
Non-union sector	ER varies across firms—Low wage pattern and HRM pattern.	Non-union sector growing; there is increasing variation in ER practices.
Union sector	ER varies across firms—some firms are adopting practices of non-union sector.	Decline of union sector and union influence is leading to increasing variations in ERs.
MNCs	Mostly HRM pattern. MNCs are adopting and introducing global practices in various forms.	Increased involvement and influence of MNCs increases variations in ER practices.
Informal sector	Most firms have paternalistic pattern; some coordinated paternalistic pattern.	Emergence of coordinated paternalistic system has increased variation in ER in the informal sector.

Source: Based on discussions in Chapters 4–8.

is also due to intra-industry differences in employment relation practices, both in terms of the existence of different patterns and the differences in shares of the patterns (for example, differences between the textile industry and the ITES sector). Further, as the union sector with relatively uniform employment conditions shrinks and union firms adopt practices of non-union firms, they contribute to increasing variations in employment relations. The net result of all these is increasing variations in firms' employment relations in India.

The convergence argument in the converging divergences thesis by Katz and Darbishire (2000) speaks about the emerging commonalities in employment systems across countries. The similarities are in terms of various patterns of workplace practices and changes in the process and structures of labor-management interactions. In the Indian context, we find emerging similarities in employment relations in a number of ways. First, although the states in India traditionally differed in terms of institutional influences more particularly in capital–labor power balance, there are now growing similarities in employment relation practices across the states. This indicates that geographical and political boundaries are now less important than other factors in shaping firms' employment relations. Second, there are growing similarities in firms' workplace practices in all industrial sectors and in all locations. This is evident in the widespread changes like reduction in employment, contracting out of jobs, incentive wages, increases in labor flexibility, emphasis on training, and introduction of HRM practices. Third, as MNCs are introducing practices that have been successful in other countries, this is leading to global convergence in employment relation practices. Fourth as many local firms are also adopting global practices or successful practices of MNCs, they also contribute to global convergences in employment relations. Finally, the changes in employment relation practices in different industrial sectors are similar to those found by Katz and Darbishire for the industrialized countries. In sum, there are growing variations in employment relation practices within India (divergences) and a growing similarity of the practices with other countries (convergences).

Our findings on the variations in employment systems within and across different industrial sectors and within and across different states in India confirm the validity of the converging divergences thesis. The sample firms in the study is not an ideal representative of firms in India, but they are certainly close to the representative sample that can reveal the most important changes in employment relations in the post-reform period. The term "convergence" in the converging divergences thesis does not mean universal convergence of employment relation systems. The meaning is very different from the convergence predicted by Kerr et al. (1964). The convergence is in terms of emergence of similar patterns of employment systems across countries. In the Indian context, the emerging employment patterns are the low-wage pattern, the conflict pattern, the joint-team-based pattern, and the HRM pattern. In addition to the four patterns, some traditional patterns (traditional bureaucratic pattern), though not expanding, still represent a significant proportion of firms in India. Our findings indicate that the emergence of the different patterns and their changes are similar to those seen in industrialized countries. However, the relative proportions of the patterns and the extent to which they operate on a non-union basis in India are different from those seen in the developed countries. The similarities are in terms of broad commonalities with some differences in how the patterns are actually shaped in different countries. For example, in India firms differ in terms of types of unions–internal unions, external unions, or multiple unions. In summary, our study not only confirms the validity of the converging divergence theory for India, it also indicates that the variations in employment relations and their changes in India are similar to those seen in the industrialized countries. They indicate growing variations in managing people at work within countries and growing similarities in managing people at work across countries.

Notes

1. This follows from the decomposition of inequality measures. Inequality (variations) for a population consisting of two groups can be seen as an aggregate of inequality of the two groups and between the groups.
2. The work organization in ITES firms is different from other service sector firms; it is best described as mass customized bureaucracy, which is an HRM pattern.
3. There are different types of engineering firms and they have four different patterns of employment relations. The patterns are: the low-wage pattern

(small fabrication units, small foundries), the conflict pattern (rolling mills), the joint-team-based pattern (steel plants), and the HRM pattern (Ingersol Rand, Alstom Power).

4. In Gujarat, the preference is for adjudication, while in West Bengal it is for conciliation. Gujarat has fifty-six labor courts and industrial tribunals, while West Bengal has only eleven of them.
5. For example, Gujarat Engineering and General Kamadar Union, Gujarat Trade Union Council.
6. The textile units are from both West Bengal (Indian Rayon, Vikram Spinning, Bharti Knitwear) and Gujarat (Reliance Textile, Aarvee Denim). Mitsubishi PTA India, BOC India, Texmaco, Infar India are in West Bengal, while Ingersol Rand, Nirma, Torrent Pharmaceuticals are in Gujarat.
7. Examples: (*a*) Non-union: Nirma, Enfield Electronics, WIPRO IT Limited, Anglo-French Textile, Modi-Xeorx, Pond's India, (*b*) Internal union: DCM Toyota, Eicher, Nova India, Maruti Udyog, Indian Telephone Industries, IOCL, (*c*) External union: ITC Limited, ICI Limited, Asian Paints, Pomlon India, BHEL, BCCL (Mathur 1991: 91–129).
8. Internal unions were not unknown in the past, but there were only a few examples. Bata India, for example, always had a single union. Independent and internal unions are now popular in the fertilizer, pharmaceuticals, chemical, petroleum refinery, power generation, electronics, and consumer products industries (Ramswamy 2000: 58–59).
9. The study does not include public-sector firms. Many public-sector firms are increasingly adopting practices that have been successful in the private sector, and the sector no longer represents a homogeneous group in terms of their employment practices. The changes are also leading to increasing variations in employment relation practices within the public sector. Employment relations in the profit-making public sector units are different from those in the sick public-sector units. Profit-making public sector units are introducing private sector managerial practices including HRM practices, while sick public sector units are performing poorly and having adversarial employment relations.
10. A study covering 300 collective bargaining agreements in the Indian private sector found that half of them included provisions for greater numerical flexibility and closer cooperation in labor-management relations (Venkataratnam 1997). Although the legislation has not changed, firm-level strategies now emphasize numerical flexibility more than anything else. Overall, there is a shift from "maintaining labor peace" to "enhancement of firm-level competitiveness through flexibility."

Bibliography

Amadeo, Edward J., Ricardo Paese Barros, Jose Marico Camrago, and Rosane Mendonca. 1995. "Brazil." In Gustavo Marquez, ed., *Reforming the Labor Market in a Liberalized Economy*. Washington D.C.: Inter American Development Bank, pp. 35–71.

Amante, Maragtas S. V. 1993. "Tensions in Industrial Democracy and Human Resource Management: A Case Study of Japanese Enterprises in the Philippines." *International Journal of Human Resource Management,* Vol. 4, No. 3, pp. 129–158.

——. 1995. "Employment and Wage Practices of Japanese Firms in the Philippines: Convergence with Filipino-Chinese and Western-Owned Firms." *International Journal of Human Resource Management*, Vol. 6, No. 3, pp. 642–655.

Anant, T. C. A. and Omkar Goswami. 1995. "Getting Everything Wrong: India's Policies Regarding Sick Firms." In Dilip Mookjerjee, ed., *Indian Industry: Policies and Performance*. Oxford: Oxford University Press, pp. 236–288.

Appelbaum, Eileen and Rosemary Batt. 1994. *The New American Workplace: Transforming Work Systems in the United States*. Ithaca, New York: ILR Press (An imprint of Cornell University Press).

Ascher, Kate. 1987. *The Politics of Privatization—Contracting Out Public Services*. London: Macmillan.

Aziz, Abdul. 1995. "Organizing the Unorganized Labor: Some Issues." *Indian Journal of Labor Economics*, Vol. 38, No. 4, pp. 701–708.

Bae, Kiu-Sik. 2000. "Work Organizations and the Restructuring of the Telecommunications in British Telecom and Korea Telecom" of Warwick

Business School: Industrial Relations and Organization Behavior, Ph.D. thesis. Available online at www.kli.re.kr

Bamber, Greg J. and Russel D. Lansbury. 1998. *International and Comparative Employment Relations*. London: Sage Publications.

Banerjee, Deoprasad. 2001. *Reorganization of Manpower at the Enterprise Level with Special Reference to BOC India Limited*. Kolkata: Indian Institute of Social Welfare and Business Management.

Bangert, David and Jozsef Poor. 1993. "Foreign Involvement in the Hungarian Economy: Its Impact on Human Resource Management." *International Journal of Human Resource Management*, Vol. 4, No. 4, pp. 817–840.

Batt, Rosemary. 2000. "Strategic Segmentation in Frontline Services: Matching Customers, Employees, and Human Resource Systems." Working Paper 00–06, Center for Advanced Human Resource Studies. Ithaca: Cornell University.

Benson, John. 1996. "Management Strategy and Labor Flexibility in Japanese Manufacturing Enterprises." *Human Resource Management Journal*, Vol. 6, No. 2, pp. 42–55.

Bhattacherjee, Debashish. 2000. "Globalizing Economy and Localizing Labor." *Economic and Political Weekly*, October 14, Vol. 35, No. 42, pp. 3758–3764.

——. 2001. "The Evolution of Indian Industrial Relations: A Comparative Perspective." *Industrial Relations Journal*, Vol. 32, No. 3, pp. 244–263.

Bhowmik, Sharit Kumar. 1992. "Tea Plantations in West Bengal." In Sarath E. A. Davala, ed., *Employment and Unionization in Indian Industry*. New Delhi: Friedrich Ebert Stiftung, pp. 11–39.

Bird, Allan, Sully Taylor, and Schon Beechler. 1998. "A Typology of International Human Resource Management in Japanese Multinational Corporations: Organizational Implications." *Human Resource Management*, Vol. 37, No. 2, pp. 159–172.

Black, John, Anne-Marie Greene, and Peter Anckers. 1997. "Size and Effectiveness: A Case Study of Small Unions." *Industrial Relations Journal*, Vol. 28, No. 2, pp. 136–148.

Bloom, Mathhew C. and George T. Milkovich. 1999. "A SHRM Perspective on International Compensation and Reward Systems." Research in Personnel and Human Resources Management, Working Paper, 98-11, CAHRS, Ithaca: Cornell University.

BOC India. 2001. *Ten-Year Financial Data, Annual Report 2000*. Kolkata: BOC India.

——. 2002. *Ten-Year Financial Data, Annual Report 2001*. Kolkata: BOC India.

——. 2007. *Ten-Year Financial Data, Annual Report 2006*. Kolkata: BOC India.

Brewster, Chris. 1999. "Different Paradigms in Strategic HRM—Questions raised by Comparative research." In Patrick M. Wright, Lee Dyer, John W.

Boudreau, George Milkovich, eds, *Strategic Human Resources Management in the Twenty-First Century*. Stamford, CT: JAI Press, pp. 213–238.

Briscoe, D. R. 1995. *International Human Resource Management*. Englewood Cliffs, NJ: Prentice-Hall.

Buchanan, R. T. 1992. "Measuring Mergers and Concentration in UK Unions 1910–1988." *Industrial Relations Journal*, Vol. 23, No. 4, pp. 305–314.

Budhwar, Pawan S. and Naresh Khatri. 2001. "A Comparative Study of HR Practices in Britain and India." *International Journal of Human Resource Management*, Vol. 13, No. 5, pp. 800–826.

Burawoy, Michael. 1979. *Manufacturing Consent: Changes in the Labor Process under Monopoly Capitalism*. Chicago: University of Chicago Press.

Business India. 1993. "Corporate Reports: IOL-The Big Comeback." *Business India*, March 29–April 11, pp. 74–76.

Caligiuri, P. and L. Stroh. 1995. "Multinational Corporation Management Strategies and International Human Resources Practices: Bringing IHRM to the Bottom Line." *International Journal of Human Resource Management*, September, Vol. 6, No. 3, pp. 494–504.

Cappelli, Peter, Bassi Laurie, Harry Katz, Konke David, Paul Osterman, and Michael Useem. 1997. *Change at Work*. New York: Oxford University Press.

Card, David. 2001. "The Effect of Unions on Wage Inequality in the U.S. Labor Market." *Industrial and Labor Relations Review*, Vol. 54, No. 2, pp. 296–315.

Chalmers, Norma. 1989. *Industrial Relations in Japan: The Peripheral Workforce*. London: Routledge.

Chandra, Pankaj. 1999. "Competing through Capabilities—Strategies for Global Competitiveness of Indian Textile Industry." *Economic and Political Weekly*, February 27–March 5, Vol. 34, No. 9, pp. M17–M24.

Chari, Sharad. 2000. "The Agrarian Origins of the Knitwear Industrial Cluster in Tirppur, India." *World Development*, Vol. 28, No. 3, pp. 579–599.

Chatterji, Rakhahari. 1980. *Unions, Politics, and the State: A Study of Indian Labor Politics*. Madras: South Asian Publishers Pvt. Ltd.

Clark, John and Mary Davis. 1991. *A Simple Guide to Structural Adjustment*. Oxford: Oxfam.

Clegg, Hugh. 1976. *Trade Unionism-Under Collective Bargaining*. Oxford: Basil Blackwell.

Cole, Robert E. 1971. *Japanese Blue Collar*. Berkeley: University of California Press.

Cook, Paul. 2000. "Support Mechanisms for Inter Firm Linkages among SMEs: Impact and Assessment." Presented in the Asian Development Bank and the Organization for Economic Cooperation and Development Workshop on Small- and Medium-Sized Enterprise Financing in Asia, July 3–4, 2000.

Covarrubias, Alex V. 2002. *Diverging Convergences in the Transformation of Employment Relations Systems in the Auto Industry: A Cross-National*

Comparative Study of Two Ford Plants (Mexico, Brazil). Ithaca: School of Industrial and labor Relations, Cornell University.

Cummings, Thomas G. 1980. *Systems Theory for Organization Development*. New York: Wiley.

Das, Subesh K. 1998. "Wage Policy Issues in the Informal Sector." *Indian Journal of Labour Economics*, Vol. 41, No. 4, pp. 893–902.

——. 2000. "Collective Bargaining and Productivity: Experiences from West Bengal." *Productivity*, April-June, Vol. 41, No. 1, National Productivity Council, New Delhi.

——. 2004. "Collective Bargaining for Improvement of Organisational Productivity, Product Quality, and Labor Flexibility." *Indian Journal of Labor Economics*, Vol. 47, No. 4, pp. 1143–1158.

——. 2008. "Trade Unions in India: Union Membership and Union Density." *Indian Journal of Labour Economics*, Vol. 51, No. 4, pp. 969–982.

Das, Subesh K. and P. Panayiotopoulos. 1996. "Flexible Specialisation—New Paradigm for Industrialisation for Developing Countries." *Economic and Political Weekly*, Vol. XXXI, No. 52, pp. L57–L61.

Dash, M. R. 1996. "Maharastra." In C. S. Venkataratnam, ed., *Industrial Relations in Indian States*. New Delhi: Global Business Press, pp. 312–334.

Datt, Gaurav. 1999. "Has Poverty Declined since Economic Reforms?—Statistical Data Analysis." *Economic and Political Weekly*, December 11–17, Vol. 34, No. 50, pp. 3516–3518.

Davala, Sarath E. A. 1992. *Employment and Unionization in Indian Industry*. New Delhi: Friedrich Ebert Stiftung.

DeCieri, Helen and Peter J. Dowling. 1997. "Strategic International Human Resource Management: An Asia-Pacific Perspective." *Management International Review*, Vol. 37, Special Issue, pp. 21–42.

——. 1999. "Strategic Human Resource Management in Multinational Enterprises: Theoretical and Empirical Developments." In Patrick M. Wright, Lee Dyer, John W. Boudreau, George Milkovich, eds, *Strategic Human Resources Management in the Twenty-First Century*. Stamford, CT: JAI Press, pp. 305–327.

Dev, Mahendra S. and C. Ravi. 2007. "Poverty and Inequality: All-India and States, 1983-2005." *Economic and Political Weekly*, February 10–16, Vol. 42, No. 6, pp. 509–521.

DiNardo, John, Nicole Fortin, and Thomas Lemieux. 1996. "Labor Market Institutions and the Distribution of Wages, 1973–1992: A Semi-Parametric Approach." *Econometrica*, September, Vol. 64, pp. 1001–1044.

Doeringer, Peter B. and Michael J. Piore. 1971. *Internal Labor Markets and Manpower Analysis*. Lexington: Health Lexington Books.

Domberger, Simon. 1998. *The Contracting Organization—A Strategic Guide to Outsourcing*. Oxford: Oxford University Press.

Dore, Ronald P. 1973. *British Factory-Japanese Factory: The Origin of National Diversity in Industrial Relations*. Berkeley: University of California Press.

Dowling, Peter J. 1989. "Hot Issues Overseas." *Personnel Administrator*, Vol. 34, No. 1, pp. 66–72.

Dunlop, John. 1958. *Industrial Relations Systems*. New York: Holt, Rinehart, and Winston.

Drèze, Jean and Anindita Mukherjee. 1987. "Labor Contracts in Rural India: Theories and Evidence." Discussion Paper No. 9.7, The Development Research Program. London School of Economics, February.

Ebbinghaus, Bernhard and Visser, Jelle. 2001. *The Societies of Europe–Trade Unions in Western Europe since 1945*. Mannheim Center for European Social Research. London: Macmillan/Palgrave.

Edwards, Richard C. 1979. *Contested Terrain: The Transformation of Workplace in the Twentieth Century*. New York: The Free Press.

Egger, Philippe. 1997. "Contract Labor and Employment: Some Proposals for Further Consideration." *Contract Labor Looking at Issues—Nine Country Cases*. Geneva: ILO.

Emmerij, Louis. 1974. "A New Look at Some Strategies for Increasing Productive Employment in Africa." *International Labour Review*, September, Vol. 110, No. 3, pp. 199–218.

Endo, Koshi. 1998. "'Japanization' of a Performance Appraisal System: A Historical Comparison of the American and Japanese Systems." *Social Science Japan Journal*, Vol. 1, No. 2, pp. 247–262.

Erickson, Christopher L. and Sarosh Kuruvilla. 1998. "Industrial Relations System Transformation." *Industrial and Labor Relations Review*, Vol. 52, No. 1, pp. 3–21.

Farnham, David. 2000. *Employee Relations in Context*. London: Chartered Institute of Personnel and Development.

Fei, John C. H., Gustav Rainis, and Shirley W. Y. Kuo. 1978. "Growth and the Family Distribution of Income by Factor Components," *Quarterly Journal of Economics*, Vol. 92, No. 1, pp. 17–53.

Fiveson, Keith. 2001. "The Indian Call Center Advantage: Competitive Options in a Tough Economy." *E-Submit Online International Journal*, Norwalk, August, Vol. 20, No. 2. Available online at www.tmcnet.com, CustomerInter@ction Solutions

Florida, Richard and Martin Kenney. 1991. "Transplanted Organizations: The Transfer of Japanese Industrial Organization to the United States." *American Sociological Review*, Vol. 56, No. 3, pp. 381–398.

Fonseca, A. J. 1975. *Wage Issues in a Developing Economy—The Indian Experience*. Bombay: Oxford University Press.

Fox, Alan and Allan Flanders. 1969. "The Reform of Collective Bargaining: From Donovan to Durkheim." *British Journal of Industrial Relations*, June Vol. 7, No. 2, pp. 151–180.

Freeman, Richard. 1993. "How Much Has De-Unionization Contributed to the Rise in Male Earnings Inequality?" In S. Danziger and P. Gottschalk, eds, *Uneven Tides: Rising Inequality in America*. New York: Russell Sage Foundation.

Freeman, Richard and James Medoff. 1984. *What Do Unions Do?* New York: Basic Books, Inc, Publishers.

Frenkel, Stephen J., Tam May, Marek Korczynski, and Karen Shire. 1998. "Beyond Bureaucracy? Work Organization in Call Centers." *International Journal of Human Resource Management*, December, Vol. 9, No. 6, pp. 957–979.

——. 1999. *On the Front Line-Organization of Work in the Information Economy*. Ithaca: Cornell University-ILR Press.

Friedman, Milton and Rose D. Friedman. 1962. *Capitalism and Freedom*. Chicago: University of Chicago Press.

Frost, Ann C. 2000. "Explaining Variation in Workplace Restructuring: The Role of Local Union Capabilities." *Industrial and Labor Relations Review*, Vol. 53, No. 4, p. 559.

Furnham, Adrian. 1992. *Personality at Work: The Role of the Individual Differences at the Work Place.* London: Routledge.

Ghosh, Jayati and Krishna Bharadwaj. 1992 "Poverty and Employment in India." In Henry Bernstein, Ben Crow, and Hazel Johnsonson, eds, *Rural Livelihoods—Crisis and Responses*. Oxford: Oxford University Press, pp. 150–154.

Gindling, T. H. and Katherine Terrell. 1995. "The Nature of Minimum Wages and Their Effectiveness as a Wage Floor in Costa-Rica, 1976–1991." *World Development*, Vol. 23, No. 8, pp. 1439–1458.

Goldberg, Victor P. 1980. "Bridges over Contested Terrain: Exploring the Radical Account of the Employment Relationship." *Journal of Economic Behavior and Organization*, Vol. 1, No. 3, pp. 249–274.

Government of India. 2000. *Economic Survey, 1999–2000*. New Delhi: Ministry of Finance, Economic Division.

——. 2002. *Annual Report: 30*. Ministry of Textile.

——. 2003. *Indian Labor Statistics, 2002–03*. Shimla: Labor Bureau, Ministry of Labor.

——. 2008. *Annual Report 2007–08*. New Delhi: Ministry of Textile.

Government of West Bengal. 2006. *Labor in West Bengal, 2005*. Kolkata: Department of Labor.

Gupta, S. P. 1995. "Recent Economic Reforms and its Impact on Poor." *Economic and Political Weekly*, Vol. 30, No. 22, pp. 1295–1313.

Guptan, Sunil Unni. 1992. "Power Sector in Andhra Pradesh." In Sarath E. A. Davala, ed., *Employment and Unionization in Indian Industry*. New Delhi: Friedrich Ebert Stiftung.

Hart, Keith. 1973. "Informal Income Opportunities and Urban Employment in Ghana." *Journal of Modern African Studies*, March, Vol. 11, No. 1, pp. 61–89.

Hart, P. E. and E. H. Phelps Brown. 1957. "The Size of Trade Unions: A Study in the Law of Aggregation." *Economic Journal*, March, Vol. 67, pp. 1–15.

Hiers, Wesley and Sarosh Kuruvilla. 2000. *Globalization and Industrial Relations in India: A Study of Industries and Firms*. Bangkok: ILO, Regional Office for Asia and the Pacific.

Himanshu. 2007. "Recent Trends in Poverty and Inequality: Some Preliminary Results," *Economic and Political Weekly*, February 10–16, Vol. 42, No. 6, pp. 497–508.

Hirsch, Barry T. and David A. Macpherson. 2000. *Union Membership and Earnings Data Book: Compilations from the Current Population Survey*. Washington D.C.: The Bureau of National Affairs, Inc.

Hobsbawm, Eric. 1996. "The Age of Extremes: A History of the World, 1914–1991." In *The Crisis Years*. New York: Vintage Books, pp. 403–432.

Holmstrom, Mark. 1993. "Flexible Specialization in India." *Economic and Political Weekly*, August 28, Vol. 28, No. 35, pp. M82–M86.

Houseman, Susan and Machiko Osawa. 1995. "Employment in Japan." *Monthly Labor Review*, October, Vol. 118, No. 10, pp. 10–18.

Hoxie, Robert F. 1920. *Trade Unionism in the United States*. New York: Appleton and Company.

Hyman, Richard. 1975. *Industrial Relations: A Marxist Introductions*. London: Macmillan.

ILO. 1993. *World Labor Report 1993*. Geneva: ILO.

———. 1997. *Contract Labour Looking at Issues: Nine Country Cases*. Geneva: International Labour Organization.

———. 1998. *Industrial Relations, Democracy and Social Stability*. World Labor Report 1997–1998. Geneva: ILO.

ILO-SAAT. 1996. *Economic Reforms and Labor Policies, 1996*. New Delhi: UN Development Program, ILO and South Asia Multidisciplinary Team.

Jagannathan, N. Vijay. 1987. *Informal Markets in Developing Countries*. Oxford: Oxford University Press.

Johri, C. K. 1992. *Industrialism and Employment Systems in India*. New Delhi: Oxford University Press.

Joshi, Vijay and I. M. D. Little. 1998. *India's Economic Reforms: 1991–2001*. New Delhi: Oxford University Press.

Kaizen Institute. 2010. "Gemba Kaizen—A Commonsense Low Cost Approach to Management." Available online at http://nz.kaizen.com

Kapalinsky, Raphael and Anne Posthuma. 1994. *Easternisation: The Spread of Japanese Management Techniques to Developing Countries*. London: Frank Cass.

Kapur, Devesh. 2002. "The Causes and Consequences of India's IT Boom." *India Review*, Vol. 1, No. 1, pp. 91–110.

Kashima, Yoshihisa and Victor J. Callan. 1994. "The Japanese Workgroup." In H. C. Traiandis, M. Dunnette, and L. Hough, eds, *Handbook of Industrial*

Organization and Psychology, Vol. 4. Palo Alto: Consulting Psychologist Press, pp. 610–646.

Katz, Harry C. and Owen Darbishire. 2000. *Converging Divergences: Worldwide Changes in Employment System*. Ithaca: Cornell University Press.

Katz, Harry C. and Thomas Kochan. 2000. *An Introduction to Collective Bargaining and Industrial Relations*. New York: McGraw-Hill Inc.

Kerr, C. 1983. *The Future of Industrial Societies*. Cambridge, MA: Harvard University Press.

Kerr, Clark, John T. Dunlop, Frederick Harbison, and Charles Myers. 1964. *Industrialism and Industrial Man*. New York: Oxford University Press.

Khanna, Sri Ram. 1994. "Profile of India's Textile and Apparel Industries." *Textile Outlook International*, July, No. 54, p. 69.

Kochan, Thomas A. 1999. "Beyond Myopia: Human Resources and Changing Social Contract." In Patrick M. Wright, Lee Dyer, John W. Boudreau, George Milkovich, eds, *Strategic Human Resources Management in the Twenty-First Century*. Stamford, CT: JAI Press, pp. 199–212.

Kochan, Thomas A., Harry C. Katz, and Robert B. McKersie. 1986. *The Transformation of American Industrial Relations*. New York: Basic Books.

Kochan, Thomas A. and Russel D. Lansbury. 1997. "Changing Employment Relations and Governance–International Auto Industry." *Journal of Management and Governance*, Vol. 1, No. 1, pp. 85–102.

Kohli, A. 1987. *The State and Poverty in India—The Politics of Reform*. Cambridge: Cambridge University Press.

Korpi, W. 1983. *The Democratic Class Struggle*. London: Routledge & Kegan.

Kuruvilla, Sarosh. 1996. "Linkages between Industrialization Strategy and Industrial Relations/Human Resource Policies: Singapore, Malaysia, The Philippines, and India." *Industrial and Labor Relations Review*, Vol. 49, No. 4, pp. 635–647.

Kuruvilla, Sarosh, Subesh K. Das, Kwon Hyunji, and Kwon Soonwon. 2002. "Trade Union Growths and Decline in Asia." *British Journal of Industrial Relations*, Vol. 40, No. 3, pp. 431–463.

Kuruvilla, Sarosh and Wesley Hiers. 1997. *Globalization and Employment Relations in India*. Ithaca: Cornell University.

———. 2000. *Globalization and Industrial Relations in India: A Study of Industries and Firms*. Bangkok: ILO, Regional Office for Asia and the Pacific.

Kumar, Nagesh. 1994. *Multinational Enterprises and Industrial Organization: The Case of India*. New Delhi: Sage Publications.

Kuznets, Simon. 1966. *Modern Economic Growth: Rate, Structure and Spread*. New Haven: Yale University Press.

Lee, Wonduck and Joohee Lee. 2001. "Will the Model of Uncoordinated Decentralization Persist? Changes in Korean Industrial Relations after the Financial Crisis." Paper Presented at the Conference on the "Changing Nature of Structure of Collective Bargaining: Is Coordinated Decentralization the Answer?" ILR-Cornell University, October 5–7, 2001.

Leicht, Kevin T., Michael Wallace, and Don Sherman Grant. 1993. "Union Presence, Class, and Individual Earnings Inequality." *Work and Occupations*, November, Vol. 20, No. 4, pp. 429–451.

Locke, M. Richard. 1992. "The Decline of the National Union in Italy: Lessons for Comparative Industrial Relations Theory." *Industrial Relations Journal*, December, Vol. 27, pp. 289–303.

——. 1995. *Rethinking the Italian Economy*. Ithaca: Cornell University Press.

Locke, M. Richard, Thomas Kochan and Michael Piore, eds. 1995. *Employment Relations in a Changing World Economy*. Cambridge: MIT Press.

Majumdar, Sumit K. and Pradeep Chibber. 1998. "Are Liberal Foreign Investments Policies Good for India?" *Economic and Political Weekly*, February 7–13, Vol. 33, No. 6, pp. 267–270.

Malik, P. L. 2006. *Handbook of Labour and Industrial Law*. Lucknow: Eastern Book Company.

Mamkoottam, Kuriakose. 2000. "Industrial Relations in a Globalizing India." In Debi S. Saini and Sami A. Khan, eds, *Human Resource Management—Perspective for the New Era*. New Delhi: Response Books, pp. 230–249.

Mamoria, C. B. and S. Mamoria. 1991. *Dynamics of Industrial Relations in India*. Delhi: Himalaya Publishing House.

Marglin, Stephen A. 1974. "What Do Bosses Do? The Origin of Hierarchy in Capitalist Production." *Review of Radical Political Economics*, Vol. 60, No. 2, pp. 60–112.

Mark, Young S. 1992. "A Framework for Successful Adoption and Performance of Japan." In *The Academy of Management Review*, Mississippi State: Academy of Management, October, Vol. 17, No. 4, pp. 677–700.

Mathur, Ajit N. 1991. *Industrial Restructuring and Union Power*. New Delhi: ILO-ARTEP.

MCC PTA India. 2001. "MCPI News—A House Magazine of MCC PTA India." Haldia: MCC PTA India.

Meyer, Alfred G. 1970. "Theories of Convergence." In Chalmers A. Johnson, ed., *Change in Communist Systems*. Stanford: Stanford University Press.

Monat, Epstein. 1973. "Labor Contracting and Its Regulation." *International Labor Review*, May, Vol. 107, No. 5, pp. 451–470.

Mookherjee, Dilip. 1995. *Indian Economy—Policies and Performance*. New Delhi: Oxford University Press.

Mookherjee, Surya. 1996. "Gujrat." In C. S. Venkataratnam, ed., *Industrial Relations in Indian States*. New Delhi: Global Business Press, pp. 146–169.

Moore, Mick and Ladi Hamalai. 1993. "Economic Liberalization, Political Pluralism and Business Associations in Developing Countries." *World Development*, Vol. 21, No. 12, pp. 1895–1912.

Morishima, Motohiro. 1995. "Embedding HRM in a Social Context." *British Journal of Industrial Relations*, Vol. 33, No. 4, pp. 617–640.

Morris, Jonathan, Barry Wilkinson and Max Munday. 2000. "Farewell to HRM? Personnel Practices in Japanese Manufacturing Plants in the UK."

International Journal of Human Resource Management, December, Vol. 11, No. 6, pp. 1047–1060.

Nakamura, Takafuse. 1988. *Labor in Japan: Q and A*. Tokyo: Ministry of Labor.

NASSCOM. 2002. "NASSCOM-McKinsey Report 2002." New Delhi: NASSCOM.

NASSCOM Foundation. 2008. "Indian IT/ITES Industry: Impacting Economy and Society, Catalysing Change 2007–08." New Delhi: Lipi Associates.

NCEUS (National Commission for the Enterprises in the Unorganized Sector). 2009. *The Challenge of Employment in India: An Informal Economy Perspective*. New Delhi: NCEUS.

Oliver, Nick and Barry Wilkinson. 1992. *The Japanization of British Industry*. Oxford: Blackwell.

Ornatowski, Gregory. 1998. "The End of Japanese-Style Human Resource Management?" *Sloan Management Review*, Vo. 39, No. 3, pp. 73–84.

Osterman, Paul. 1987. "Choice of Employment Systems in Internal Labor Markets." *Industrial Relations*, Vol. 26, No. 1 (Winter), pp. 46–67.

Papola, T. S. 1992. "Informal Sector: Concept and Policy." In M. K. Rao, ed., *Growth of Urban Informal Sector and Economic Development*. Delhi: Kanishka Publishers and Distributors, pp. 31–56.

Parthasarathy, G. 1996. "Unorganized Sector and Structural Adjustment." *Economic and Political Weekly*, July 13, Vol. 31, No. 28, pp. 1859–1869.

Patel, B. B. 1997. "Contract Labor in India in Manufacturing, Construction and Forestry." *ILO: Contract Labor Looking at Issues: Nine Country Cases*. Geneva: International Labor Organization, No. 106/107, Labour Education 1997/1–2, pp. 38–44.

Patil, B. R. 1993. *Collective Bargaining: Perspectives and Practices*. Madras, India: Universities Press.

——. 1998. "A Contemporary Industrial Relations Scenario in India: With Reference to Karnataka", *Indian Journal of Industrial Relations*, vol. 33, No. 2, p. 331.

Phillips, Edward J. 1992. "India: The Next Manufacturing Frontier." *Manufacturing Systems*, July, Vol. 10, No. 7, pp. 712–721.

Pil, Frits K. and John P. MacDuffie. 1996. "The Adoption of High Involvement Work Practices." *Industrial Relations*, Vol. 35, No. 3, pp. 432–55.

——. 1999. "Transferring Competitive Advantage across Borders: A Study of Japanese Transplants in North America." In Jeffery Liker, W. Mark Fruin, and Paul S. Adler, eds, *Remade in America: Transplanting and Transforming Japanese Production Systems*. New York: Oxford University Press, pp. 39–74.

Piore, Michael J. and Charles F. Sabel. 1984. *The Second Industrial Divide–Possibilities for Prosperity*. New York: Basic Books.

Pot, Ferri. 2000. *Employment Relations and National Culture: Continuity and Change in the Age of Globalization.* Northampton: Edward Elgar.

Purcell, John. 1999. "High Commitment Management and the Link with Contingent Workers: Implication for Strategic Human Resource Management." In M. Wright Patrick, Lee Dyer, John W. Boudreau, George Milkovich, eds, *Strategic Human Resources Management in the Twenty-First Century.* Stamford, CT: JAI Press, pp. 239–257.

Pyatt, Graham, Chau-nan Chen, and John J. 1980. "The Distribution of Income by Factor Components." *Quarterly Journal of Economics*, Vol. 95, No. 3, pp. 451–473.

Raghuvanshi, Uma. 1993. *Origin and Growth of Trade Union Movement–Society, Social Security, and Politics.* New Delhi: Radha Publications.

Ramswamy, E. A. 2000. *Managing Human Resources—A Contemporary Text.* New Delhi: Oxford University Press.

Rasiah, Raja. 1988. "Production in Transition within the Semi-conductor Industry and Impact on Penang." *Journal of Malaysian Studies*, Vol. 6, No. 2, pp. 85–111.

Rosenzweig, Philip M. and Nitin Nohria. 1994. "Influences on Human Resource Management Practices in Multinational Corporations." *Journal of International Business Studies*, Vol. 25, No. 2 (Second Quarter), pp. 229–246.

Roy, B. 1993. "Left Trade Unions and New Economic Policies." *Economic and Political Weekly*, Vol. 28, No. 51, pp. 2777–2779.

Roy, Tirthankar. 1998. "Economic Reforms and Textile Industry in India." *Economic and Political Weekly*, August 8–14, Vol. 33, No. 32, pp. 2173–2182.

Rudolph, Lloyd I. and Susanne Hoeber Rudolph. 1987. *In Pursuit of Lakshmi: The Political Economy of Indian States.* Bombay: Orient Longmans.

Rudra, A. 1981. "Extra-Economic Constraints on Agricultural Labor: Result of an Intensive Survey of Some Villages Near Shantiniketan, West Bengal." *Asian Employment Working Paper*, ARTEP, ILO, Bangkok.

Sankaran, T. S., R. K. A. Subramanya, and S. K. Wadhawn. 1994. *Development of Social Security Programs in Developing Countries.* New Delhi: Har Anand Publications.

Sano, Yoko. 1995. *Human Resource Management in Japan.* Tokyo: Keio University Press, Inc.

Saran, G. 1987. *Commentaries on Contract Labor (Regulation and Abolition) Act 1970.* Lucknow: Eastern Book Company.

Schmitz, Hubert and Bernard Musyck. 1994. "Industrial Districts in Europe: Policy Lessons for Developing Countries?" *World Development*, Vol. 22, No. 6, pp. 889–910.

Schuler, Randall S., Peter J. Dowling, and Helen De Cieri. 1993. "An Integrative Framework of Strategic International Human Resource Management." *Journal of Management*, December, Vol. 19, No. 2, pp. 419–459.

Sen, Abhijit. 1996. "Economic Reforms, Employment, and Poverty–Trends and Options." *Economic and Political Weekly*, Special Number, September, Vol. 31, No. 35/37, pp. 2459–2477.

Sen, Ratna. 1992. "Jute Industry, Engineering Industry." In, Sarath E. A. Davala, ed., *Employment and Unionization in Indian Industry*. New Delhi: Friedrich Ebert Stiftung, pp. 41–62.

Senju, Shizou. 1992. *TQC and TPM*. Tokyo: Asian Productivity Organization. (Originally published in 1987 by the Japan Institute for Plant Maintenance, Tokyo. Distributed in the US by Quality Resources, White Plains, NY 10601.)

Sheth, N. R. 1993 "Our Trade Unions: An Overview." *Economic and Political Weekly*, Vol. 28, No. 6, pp. 231–236.

Shimada, Haruo. 1983. "Japanese Industrial Relations: A New General Model?" In Taishiro Shirai, ed., *Contemporary Industrial Relations in Japan*. Madison: University of Wisconsin Press, pp. 3–25.

Shister, Joseph. 1951. *Readings in Labour Economics and Industrial Relations*. Chicago: J. B. Lippincott Company.

Shorrocks, Anthony F. 1982. "Inequality Decomposition by Factor Components," *Econometrica*, Vol. 50, No. 1, pp. 193–211.

Shorter, Edward and Charles Tilly. 1974. *Strikes in France, 1830–1968*. Cambridge: Cambridge University Press.

Shrouti, Arvind and Nandkumar. 1994. *New Economic Policy and Changing Management Strategies: Impact on Workers and Trade Unions*. Delhi: Freidrich Ebert Foundation.

Singh, Nirvikar. 2002. "Information Technology and India's Economic Development." Paper presented in the Conference on Indian Economy, Cornell University, April 2002.

Sinha, Jai B. P. 2004. *Multinationals in India: Managing the Interface of Cultures*. London: Sage Publications.

Smith, Wendy. 1983. "The Relevance of the Japanese Model of Industrial Relations for the Analysis of Management–Labor Relations." In IIRA Sixth Congress: Validity of the Japanese Model of Industrial Relations. Vol. 5, Geneva: IIRA.

Sorge, Arndt and Wolfgang Streeck. 1988. "Industrial Relations and Technological Change: The Case of Extended Perspective." In Richard Hyman and Wolfgang Streeck, eds, *New Technology and Industrial Relations*. Oxford: Basil Blackwell, pp. 19–47.

Sparrow, Paul and Jean M. Hiltrop. 1994. *European Human Resource Management in Transition*. Englewood Cliffs: Prentice-Hall.

Srivastava, Sadhana. 2003. "What is the True Level of FDI Flows to India?" *Economic and Political Weekly*, Vol. 38, No. 7, pp. 608–610.

Storey, John. 1992. *Developments in the Management of Human Resources*. Oxford: Blackwell.

Strauss, George. 2001. "HRM in the USA: Correcting Some British Impressions." *International Journal of Human Resource Management*, September, Vol. 12, pp. 873–897.

Streeck, Wolfgang. 1984. *Industrial Relations in West Germany: A Case Study of the Car Industry*. London: Heinemann.

Supreme Court of India. 1992a. *State of Haryana & Ors. vs. Piara Singh & Ors.* 1992(4), SCC 118; SCC (L & S) 825.

——. 1992b. "Workmen Vs. Management of Reptakos Brett & Co. Ltd., All India Report," p. 504.

Taira, Koji. 1992. "The End of Convergence Theories: Japanization of U.S. Human Resource Management and Industrial Relations." In A. R. Negandhi and M. G. Serapio, eds, *Research in International Business and International Relations*, Vol. 5. Greenwich, CT: JAI Press, pp. 241–258.

Tapscott, Don. 1995. *Digital Economy—Promise and Peril in the Age of Networked Intelligence.* New York: McGraw-Hill.

Tewari, Meenu. 1998. "Intersectoral Linkages and the Role of the State in Shaping the Conditions of Industrial Accumulation: A Study of Ludhiana's Manufacturing Industry." *World Development*, Vol. 26, No. 8, pp. 1387–1411.

Thurley, Keith. 1983. "How Transferable is the Japanese Industrial Relations System? Some Implications of a Study of Industrial Relations and Personnel Policies of Japanese Firms in Western Europe." In IIRA Sixth Congress: Viability of Japanese Model of Industrial Relations, Vol. 5: Geneva: IIRA.

Torrington, Derek. 1994. *International Human Resource Management—Think Globally Act Locally*. New York: Prentice-Hall.

Tzeng, Rueyling and Brian Uzzi. 2000. "Business Globalization and Local Embeddedness: The Case of Foreign Investment in Taiwan." In *Embeddedness and Corporate Change in a Global Economy*. New York: Peter Lang Publishing, Inc., pp. 211–237.

Vaidya, Shanta and A. K. Arora. 1992. "Ports and Docks." In Davala Sarath, ed., *Employment and Unionisation in Indian Industry*. New Delhi: Friedrich Ebert Stiftung, pp. 85–112.

Venkataratnam, C. S. 1993. "Impact of New Economic Policies on the Role of Trade Unions." *Indian Journal of Industrial Relations*, Vol. 29, No. 1, pp. 56–77.

——. 1994. "Changing Role of Trade Unions in a Period of Transition." In C. S. Venkataratnam, Gerd Botterweck, and Pravin Sinha eds, *Labor Unions in a Period of Transition*. New Delhi: Friedrich Ebart Stiftung, pp. 3–44.

——. 1996. *Industrial Relations in Indian States, Industrial Relations Research Association*. New Delhi: Friedrich Ebert Foundation and Global Business Press.

Venkataratnam, C. S. 1997. "Overview: Globalization and Labor Management Relations in South Asia." Paper presented at Regional Industrial Relations Conference Organized by the South Asia Multidisciplinary Advisory Team, ILO, and the Indian Industrial Relations Research Association, New Delhi, December.

Venkataratnam, C. S. and Anil Verma. 1997. *Challenge of Change: Industrial Relations in Indian Industry*. New Delhi: Global Business Press.

Verme, Samar. 2002. "Export Competitiveness of Indian Textile and Garment Industry." Working Paper No. 94, Indian Council for Research on International Economic Relations, New Delhi.

Visser, Jelle. 2006. "Union Membership Statistics in 24 Countries." *Monthly Labour Review*, January, Vol. 129, No. 1, pp. 38–49.

Vrijendra. 1995. "Organizing the Unorganized Workers in Small Scale Units: Problems and Prospects." *Indian Journal of Labor Economics*, Vol. 38, No. 1, pp 709–716.

Wasti, Syeda Arzu. 1998. "Cultural Barriers in the Transferability of Japanese and American Human Resources Practices to Developing Countries: The Turkish Case." *International Journal of Human Resource Management*, Vol. 9, No. 4, pp. 608–631.

Watanabe, Susumu. 1976. "Minimum Wages in Developing Countries: Myth and Reality." *International Labor Review*, May–June, Vol. 113, No. 3, pp. 343–358.

Willamson, Oliver E., Michael L. Wachter, and Harris, Jeffrey. 1975. "Understanding the Employment Relations: The Analysis of Idiosyncratic Exchange." *Bell Journal of Economics*, Vol. 6, pp. 250–278.

World Bank. 1995. *World Development Report, 1995: Workers in an Integrating World.* Oxford: Oxford University Press.

——. 1996. *World Development Report, 1996*. Oxford: Oxford University Press.

Wright, Patrick M., Lee Dyer, and George T. Milkovich. 1999. *Strategic Human Resource Management in the Twenty First Century*. Stamford, CT: JAI Press.

Wright, Patrick M. and Scott A. Snell. 1998. "Toward a Unifying Framework for Exploring Fit and Flexibility in Strategic Human Resource Management." *Academy of Management Review*, October, Vol. 23, No. 4, pp. 756–772.

Index

About the Author

Subesh Das is presently working as the Principal Secretary to the Government of West Bengal. He joined the Indian Administrative Service in 1982 and worked in different positions for the Government of West Bengal. During 1995–1996, he received a fellowship under the Colombo Plan for training in the United Kingdom and earned a master's degree in Economics in Social Development at the Centre of Development Studies, University of Swansea, UK. He worked as Labor Commissioner, West Bengal, in two phases: 1992–1995 and 1996–1999. As Labor Commissioner he was engaged in matters relating to conciliation of industrial disputes, enforcement of labor laws and collective bargaining agreements, labor welfare, and labor rights in West Bengal. After working in the government for seventeen years, Mr Das joined the Ph.D. program in the School of Industrial and Labor Relations, Cornell University, United States. He has published articles in journals and edited volumes.